ANIMOSITY FARM

ANIMOSITY FARM

Diary of a Farmer's Wife

GINNY LANE

authorHOUSE®

AuthorHouse™ UK Ltd.
1663 Liberty Drive
Bloomington, IN 47403 USA
www.authorhouse.co.uk
Phone: 0800.197.4150

Published by AuthorHouse   09/03/2014

ISBN: 978-1-4918-9093-6 (sc)

FOREWORD

Apart from some name changes to protect the guilty, everything you are about to read—every single word—is true.

By the end of it, therefore, I'm sure you'll agree with me that it is an account by a remarkable woman. She is also my sister. The downside is, as I read these diaries, my heart breaks to be reminded of the many ordeals Virginia has had to face, usually at the hands of thoughtless, selfish or, worst, vindictive and, yes, evil people.

It is not easy for a brother to read and relive these events. It's been even more difficult to witness many of the events first-hand. I will always be humbled by my sister's sheer inner strength. She has survived the events herein against the odds. Most people would have crumbled and, even today, I sleep uneasily when I think of dear Virginia and her husband, who continue to be abandoned by the very people we rely on to show some duty of care and protect us from harm—the police, the local council, the elected MP. The list goes on, but it will unfold before you through these diaries.

The intention was to write daily about events from the point Chatsworth Estates decided to evict Virginia and Alan from their marital home, which was also their living—land they had farmed together for over ten years, and a farm that had been in the family for nearly forty—to the point when they were happily settled in a new home. Sadly, one of the lessons reinforced through these pages is that society often revels in creating victims and, once you have been identified as such—weak, vulnerable, helpless, ripe for the picking—Heaven help you as the force of the bullies who lurk in all sections of society is unleashed upon you.

Hope and pray you never yourself experience this because you will lose faith in everything you hold dear, everything our grandparents and great grandparents fought for over two World Wars. Many of you probably have little faith in our elected officials anyway, let alone the unelected officials who inhabit our council offices, but when you lose faith in your police—when you realise the failings in local police divisions can be endemic—it becomes truly frightening because who then can you turn to? This is the position Virginia and Alan find themselves in.

As for big business and big money, well that's another story, isn't it? Our expectations might be much lower but, at the outset of this story, it is sad to see the once great Chatsworth Estates resort to low tricks to maximise their profits. If it had all ended there, it would have been a tale in itself and one the Chatsworth Estate won't want told. But as others have jumped upon these two victims, such is the human condition, the story has continued and will fill further volumes.

Just remember, and you have my word on this, everything happened as described. Some sections might appear mundane. Often, Virginia's love of animals and the natural world shines through—these are the source of much of her great strength. At other points, you will be shocked by man's inhumanity to man.

I suggested to my sister that she starts this volume with an attempt on her life. Far-fetched? Actually, it was witnessed by the police and illustrates the extent of the vindictiveness my sister has faced in the most recent few years of her life.

Rob Lane

Had I known on that fateful morning in April 2007 what lay ahead, what I would trigger, I maybe would have hidden away as normal. I have kept away from Alan's family for my own safety and to avoid trouble for many years. As the tractor sped towards me at high speed, my life flashed before me. It took me back to over twenty years ago when Alan's father had driven at me with a tractor as I backed a young horse. The horse went berserk, rearing and bucking. Alan's father left me semi-conscious in the field and drove off as if nothing had happened. My horse, having landed on a stone wall, ran lame and frantically towards the safety of her mother, my dear old horse, Lady.

Here I was again in the path of yet another tractor and had a five foot wide muck fork staring at me. The driver was different but not so far removed. The driver on this occasion was Alan's brother-in-law. He had turned up on the farm this morning, in an attempt to take a tractor from Alan. This is the tractor that we use to feed our animals daily. We could not lose our only means of feeding our stock. I stood on the gate as the tractor sped towards me. I raised my hand, urging the driver to stop. There were numerous animals in the field and removing the gate would have spelt disaster and carnage, had the animals escaped onto the A619 at this busy time. The driver put his foot down on the accelerator, as his face distorted with hatred and greed. The gate had become part of the hedging, as it had been there so long. The tractor lunged towards the gate; the spikes of the muck fork, by the grace of God, passed by my limbs as I was thrown 12 feet or more into the air. I landed with a thud by the side of the road, lying stunned as lorries thundered past, inches from my head.

Alan's cold and callous sister stood above me screaming at him. I lay confused and wracked with pain. This was the last thing my already pained body needed right now! With the history of this family's violence towards me, luckily I had already called the police. The brother-in-law had no idea of this and was unaware as he sped towards me that on the other side of the hedge were police officers! They witnessed the whole incident and arrested him on the spot. I ask them not to bother but they stressed that having witnessed such an attack they had no option.

As I was taken to the hospital worse was yet to come. I felt sick and shocked as I was bundled into the back of the ambulance. No not pain but the words of the paramedic that will haunt me forever. The man seemed caring and compassionate and I felt in safe hands until he turned to me and asked, "Is that your son outside the ambulance, love?"

The man they felt sure was my son was actually my husband who, just as a matter of interest, is 16 years my senior. Well, forget the suspected spinal injury and twisted bruised limbs because nothing could compare to the pain this paramedic had just caused me!

This tractor incident is what I believed set off the chain of events that have led to Alan's father allowing Chatsworth Estates to take back the farm we have lived in all our married life. This was behind our backs and we had absolutely no idea! Hell hath no fury like a father-in-law scorned.

MARCH 17TH 2009

Here I am at 46 years old having just found out I am about to lose my home and my animal sanctuary. Hysterics are the first thing to set in. Fear is the second—fear of the task ahead, fear of dealing with the establishment and fear of what I am going to do with my rescue animals. We have many animals on the farm including several old cows that Alan rescued when his dairy business folded. Included in the cow collection is old Crunchy, who now only has one eye. We have dear old Daisy, who is a sweet little old lady and a super old mum. Daisy is aged now but every summer she blossoms like a beautiful young cow. We have two cows called Lovebird. One is black and one is white. And we have my namesake, Virginia, and of course she is a stunning cow! If you ever get called a cow you must never take offence. Cows are the most wonderful, graceful and dignified animals you could meet.

We have many cats (around forty at this moment in time) that have been rescued from various predicaments that animals find themselves in. I cannot list all the cats but you will no doubt get to know one or two of them through my diaries.

We have three Great Danes and a Jack Russell and we have several rescue horses and ponies. Summer was a pony that was destined for slaughter when she was part exchanged by a farmer for an old tractor. She was purchased from the farmer before he sold her on for meat. I was told what an ugly pony we had coming into the rescue. She was actually adorable and simply had a large cyst on her neck. She is a sweet little mare but very timid. Although having just rubbed her own mane off entirely, due to allergic reaction to midges, she looks a little odd. However when her mane is to its full golden glory she takes on a look of Pegasus, as she gallops across the fields and over fences.

We have Bella who was purchased by someone as an eventer but she was not up to the job. She came here to do lighter work. The owners were told by professional people that the horse was worthless. The horse was due to be put to sleep as a right off! It was a worrying time as I heard about a dealer who had offered to take the horse from the woman for £500 as a favour! I tried to tell the owner that the horse still held good value. I know the dealer and had she got her hands on this lovely mare, she would have sold her the following week for £5000. For the safety of the horse the owner gifted her over to me, knowing that she would be safe for the rest of her life.

Velvet is a tiny little pony who came via a rescue that did not want her. The poor little pony had been part of the fixtures and fittings of a house sale. The purchaser of the house was panicking as he knew nothing about horses. It is as well he sent her to the sanctuary. When the spring came it was evident she suffered seriously from sweet itch. This is a terrible condition that needs strict management. The problem arises from the midges that bite the ponies. Some ponies are allergic to the bites and this is what causes sweet itch. The pony will scratch until they bleed, if they have this condition. As soon as the midges appear, Velvet has to be rugged up with a special rug that stops the midges biting. This continues through the whole summer.

Velvet, bless her, had been kept in a field with no company for 12 years. When we picked her up she looked happy enough. However, when we put her in with our horses, it was apparent that she was suffering from severe anxiety due to having been alone for so long. She saw the other ponies and latched immediately on to Dancer, another old pony. If you knew Dancer you would understand the funny side here. Dancer is a real loner type and likes her space. This is not to say she wants to be alone as horses and ponies do prefer to be in herds; safety to them is in numbers. Dancer likes to be with the group but on the outskirts, so that the group is there for her if she needs them.

Velvet stuck to Dancer's bottom like glue while Dancer just looked back at her wondering what the hell she was doing there. Velvet would not let Dancer's bottom out of her sight. This was where the evidence became apparent that Velvet was mentally scared by the years she spent alone in the field.

If by chance we had to take Dancer away to be ridden, Velvet would go berserk and scream with the emotional pain of the separation. It is hard to witness this poor pony expecting to be left alone and bereft again. Over the years with us she has calmed down considerably and has become a proper herd member. Yet still the emotional scars return when her friends are taken out of the field. Hence when ponies are fetched from the meadows, Velvet will amble along behind them unhindered. When I teach children in the fields, Velvet joins us freely and the kids love it. Velvet need never be alone again.

I'm not a go getter. I'm not one of life's adventurers. I am simply a home bird who enjoys baking and being around my family and my animals. I enjoy going to sleep in my own bed and waking up there. I enjoy settling down for "Coronation Street". Yet here I am about to embark on the biggest, most unwelcome adventure of my life.

I have got such a headache today and I'm not sure why. It could be that I am trying to come off my painkillers but I did not realise I was that addicted. Or it could be the fact that I am about to lose my home! Don't worry, this has been coming for the last ten years. I have the father-in-law from hell and he will not rest until me and my husband are ruined—homeless and without a penny between us.

The home I live in is a rambling seven bedroom farm house on a hundred acre farm. It is owned by Chatsworth House Estates and they want it back! Since the kindly old Duke died in 2005, the ethos behind the Estate's management has changed dramatically. The loss of my home is just one of many changes that have taken place.

I am fortunate as I have a very positive personality and I know God is on my side. I have known for a long time that this is not where God wants me to be. I have prayed every day to him that we may keep the farm. I knew in my heart He did not want me to keep it. Therefore I accept that although we have many tough months ahead, the long term outlook is really good. We just have to hold on to our faith and keep going. I accept that there is little I can do to prevent us losing our home. This does not mean I will take it lying down!

I am so lucky in that I have some good family and friends around me at this time. They really care so much about me and Alan and the plight we are in. They are as sad as we are. Our good friends have enjoyed farm life with us at every opportunity. Then you get the other side of the coin, people who thrive on others' misfortunes, such as my neighbours, unpleasant neighbours whose only desire appears to be that I lose my favourite horse, Jaffa. They need to take note, those wicked people who thrive on the misfortune of others, that the only chance of me losing my horses is if I should die!

Jaffa has been with me for many years now and my neighbour knows Jaffa means the world to me. Jaffa will take me anywhere at anytime. She is even trained to pull up alongside the gate when I return home from a ride. Jaffa knows I need the gate to climb off from her as I cannot dismount properly due to my physical problems. Jaffa is one of my best friends and riding through the woods on her is the best therapy I could ever have. She is so amazing; she even told one of my other horses off twice for being rough with me!

I feel so sad for those who want to do us harm and I pray everyday for them. I pray they may someday have as happy a life as me and my husband. Because despite my terrible in-laws and the dastardly Duke, despite the fact that I now have to pack my seven bedroom house into little boxes, I have the most wonderful husband a woman could ever be blessed with. I am so happy just to be tending to my animals in the sanctuary every day. The sanctuary will carry on as normal, I hope. I will try to turn no needy animal away. My needs in this life are very simple and this is why I am so happy. My needs are so simple, I can access them daily.

Our only major concerns are our farm animals and our many rescue animals, along with the logistics of moving our family of animals to another home. We also have so many possessions to move and I cannot see us able to fit them in to our proposed mobile home. Well, yesterday I visited the depths of despair and tried to kill myself by overdosing on chocolate and cake. I survived and this is a sign that I must soldier on.

I have been through so much worse than this in my life so I know I am tough enough to beat it. I went to hell seven years ago and managed to return. I am not going to hell this time and hope I will never go there again. I am not sure I could do the return journey this time. It was the loss of my beloved mum that took me there. She was my best friend, my life force, my rock, she was every breath I breathed, and then she was gone. I recovered, although it took a very long time. Hence I know I can do this; it won't be easy but I can do it. I will do it.

I am looking around my spacious kitchen. It's a real tip with a settee full of Great Danes and baskets full of cats. The sides are cluttered with my many cooking utensils and ingredients. The table is covered in paper and magazines and all our office work. A small Jack Russell and a little black and white cat are asleep in the middle of the table. How on earth am I going to cope in a mobile home? I say mobile home, as our plan B (should we lose our home) is to turn up on the farm where Alan toiled for most of his adult life and set up camp—alongside the father-in-law's farmhouse! The old man got us into this mess so for once in his life he will face consequences for his despicable actions. I cannot tell anyone of plan B as he cannot know of our plans.

Forewarned is forearmed and we don't want that!

MARCH 18TH

A beautiful day full of sunshine. Although our world has caved in, we are trying to keep going and stay normal. It's very hard and difficult to do. How can you be normal when you are about to lose the home you love, the home that houses all the precious animals that will have nowhere else to go?

Alan is constantly on the phone and trying to find out what our rights are. As usual we have none, despite us having lived here for the whole of our married life.

Alan and I have lived in the shadow of his bitter old father all our married lives—he ranted he would see his son on the streets if Alan married me. Alan has been constantly blackmailed by his father over our home. It did not really matter at one time as Alan actually had his own home on Syda Farm, the farm which he had run all his working life. However, when the business faltered his father made sure Alan's house at Syda was the first asset to be sold. All part of his master plan, to see us on the streets! You may read this and think I am exaggerating, but this is the truth. I have never met with such animosity as that which comes from my husband's father! As Alan has traced back the beginnings of the loss of Rufford House Farm, it converges with the sale of that alternative home at Syda. The house was sold to pay off the bank; the buildings were sold to stop Alan from farming on Syda ever again.

Alan and I are very blessed really as we both require very little in material possessions to keep us happy. Our lives are full of nature and animals and we both laugh so much each day. Alan is a wonderful man and a wonderful husband. This is what makes it all so sad; he does not deserve the treatment he has suffered at the hands of his father. But for Chatsworth House Estates to apparently take advantage of this situation is cruel and underhand. The old Duke of Devonshire would never have behaved in this abominable way. The old Duke was a true gentleman, God rest his soul. All the years of his good, kind and caring work are being rapidly undone.

For the record, we paid our rent when we realised a payment had not gone from Syda's farm accounts yet our landlord chose to seize the moment, hand monies back and then take the farm on grounds of unpaid rent! And this is how gentlemen behave? Little people against big people, moneyed people against ordinary people. A travesty but they will no doubt triumph. Let's just hope the Duke and his cowardly land agents have plenty of Horlicks to help them sleep at night.

Alan has worked hard all his life and was even kept out of school many days to work the farm. He is now aged 62 years and is still having to work and fight. I long for the day the fighting is over and we can settle down.

MARCH 19TH

Another beautiful day at the farm. I am trying to soak up as much of Rufford as I can. This is just in case we do lose it all. I will be sad of course. Mind you, the saddest thing is the way the landlord has neglected the farm. The drainage has been terrible for years and the mud has been very difficult to live with. The window frames inside the house have rotted. The house is so damp, all the wallpaper peels off in certain rooms. The light sockets were outlawed years ago and the electrics are very dangerous. I guess they will soon repair everything now, for the new, no doubt rich inhabitants of the house.

Mind you, personally speaking, if I had money and a choice of where to live I would not choose Rufford House Farm. Don't get me wrong, I love the place but I have to turn a blind eye to realities of life here! I have to ignore the main road and the variety of vehicles roaring past our farm at over 100 miles per hour. I have to ignore that every time I cross the road it could be my last time, such is the danger. I have to pretend not to notice the drug users as they park up in the lay-by next to the house. I get fed up with going out of my house to find someone peeing outside my gate. We even had a "lady", some woman, pull over to change her baby's nappy. She cleaned the baby's bottom really well and left all the soiled wipes and the nappy in the tree outside our gate.

Yukk. Anyway, let someone else have it all! Oh, and they can have the people who pull into my gateway to throw up. They can have the couple who pulled up as I sat in my garden. The passenger threw something inside the gate where I was sitting enjoying a cuppa with a friend. I went over to see what it was and picked it up. It was cat sick in a pile of tissues. I strolled over and threw it back inside the car. Needless to say, they left hastily. Well, I will be leaving all that behind and that won't be a bad thing.

Alan has visited our landlord's agents on numerous occasions over the last couple of years. They were totally aware that Alan was desperate to take over the tenancy. Len Barstarg, representing the landlord, promised my husband they would "look favourably on him" if he did this, that and the other, to improve the house and land. Alan did this, that and the other (including dry stone walling and chopping extensive hedging down), in between major back and knee surgery he was undergoing. All along, it transpires, they were planning to take the property from us. They lied and manipulated Alan to get some fine work out of him and not have to pay a penny. That's the rich and powerful for you. Barstarg has since stated that he could not inform us due to data protection!! Funny how they have kept my neighbours and other sundry people linked to the Estate informed. No need for data protection, there, then!

When Len Barstarg last visited us, he made it plain that all the work my husband had carried out on the farm was irrelevant. It was the house they were interested in. I can't believe the ruthlessness that rotten Barstarg. He has been stringing my husband along. This is how representatives of a world-renowned Estate behave! Oh, and they no longer want animals in the buildings. They seemed horrified that chickens and ducks are free on the farm! Farming stands little chance really if that is the case.

Well, they will have been disappointed about the house no doubt. I tried hard to make it look good but sadly the shock to my Hoover was too great and it died. Again! But I did tidy up, I promise!

MARCH 20TH

Phone calls all day again. Getting in touch with our solicitor is a nightmare. I am so sick of watching Alan waiting in for the return calls that just do not come! Well at least the solicitor's bills are reliable. Anyway, we are seeing our MP tonight. Maybe she will give us some hope.

<u>There are many things that I could easily leave behind with Rufford House Farm:</u>

- Strange neighbours
- Mud
- The main Road
- The noise of the traffic
- The emergency services up and down all day tending to fatalities on the road.

I forgot the stinking lay-by that is actually a public toilet! People also gather there to do drugs, etc. So there are a lot of plusses to leaving this farm behind. But I am concerned for my animals, as they need the space.

I remember many beautiful sunny afternoons (particularly weekends) when I would be putting my ponies in the fields adjacent to the lay-by. Cars would be parked with lots of youths sitting inside. The windows were always open and I took little notice of them. I was always aware of a strange smell. You know the smell when you have a cabbage in the fridge for a day or two or even three (ok, I admit it, a month). You open the fridge and the kitchen suddenly smells disgusting. It was that sort of smell; I could never understand why that smell was on the lay-by.

One weekend, putting the ponies away, I had a thirteen year old family friend with me. As I closed the gate behind the ponies he exclaimed, "Eh, they're doing drugs, I can smell 'em!" This opened up a whole new world to me. A child that could recognise the smell of drugs in a split second. Oh, what a sheltered life I have led.

<u>Things I will miss about Rufford</u>:

- The beautiful rambling fields that are home to our many horses and cows
- The lovely people that come to buy eggs
- The lovely trees dotted around the fields
- The Swallows who come here every April and reside with us until the autumn, while raising their young
- The bats that swoop and flap around the yard at dusk.

That's not bad really is it? I mean really the house is big and cold as our landlord has never done any work on the property. The roofs leak in many of the rooms and how we have managed to survive the terrible wiring that we have here I do not know. Plugs on appliances have melted away inside the sockets, such is the safety of our electrics provided by our esteemed Landlord on the Chatsworth Estate.

MARCH 21ST

Tough day today. Had a table top sale for the sanctuary. I could not get my heart into it. My brain seemed unable to function properly and I was fuzzy all day. Luckily it's Saturday and that means Alan will cook me fish and chips for tea. Home made chips will make me feel a lot better. So many times throughout the day I wanted to burst into tears. I am either fine or a complete wreck at the moment. There is no 'in-between' anymore. I look at the animals and worry so much about them. They are my family and I don't want to let them down.

My good friend Mavis is constantly praying for our future. She is an adorable lady and gives me so much support. She introduced me to St Martin who looks after all the animals. Each time I have a poorly or depressed animal, I report them to her and she will pray her little socks off. It usually works well, although they don't always live. Animals, just like people, have their right time to shuffle off their mortal coils. However, the prayers help them to go quietly and peacefully, with dignity intact. You can't ask for much more than that.

Since I was introduced to St Martin I too pray to him on a regular basis. If ever I have a poorly animal I will call upon St Martin to make them well. If he cannot make them well he will always make them comfortable. This is a very comforting thought for me, as I tend the animals. I feel sure he listens and I know he guards my animals daily. If ever I am late home for my chickens, instead of panicking like I used to, I ask St Martin to protect them from predators till my return. He has never let me down yet.

Each night before I go to sleep I ask him to take care of my animals and keep them safe. I sleep much better for having him around. If I have an animal that I know will not recover from illness due to old age, then I will pray to St Martin for a swift and painless passing.

MARCH 22ND

Took my wonderful horse to Linacre Woods and revelled in every moment. The wind was raging today but it was still lovely. The woods are an amazing place to ride. It is thick with trees and little streams run through the woods. Wildlife is abundant as the squirrels jump from tree to tree. The birds flutter around taking fruit and buds from the hedgerows. The winding path through the woods crunches under the horses hooves. I love the sound of clomping hooves; it is a more beautiful sound than any band or orchestra could play; more beautiful than any song that could be sung. Since I was a small child, the sound of hooves on the ground has been so special to me. As the mud begins to squelch beneath Jaffa's hooves, I asked her to gallop like only Jaffa can. Dog walkers and hikers beware; nothing will stand in the way of Jaffa's run through the woods. Such bliss. Tired and blowing, I pull hard to slow her on the corners; you never know what is around them. The ground hardens and we trot then walk again. Both tired and weary, we make our way slowly home, taking in wonderful, natural sights and sounds as we go.

MARCH 23RD

Hope on the horizon, again! We keep clinging onto hope. Alan's dad has woken up to what he has now done. Three generations of the Shirts were scheduled to live on this farm and not even one generation has finished. Alan's father has taken this farm away from his son and his descendants. The old man is going to see the Chatsworth agents tomorrow. I am breathing again but for how long? Could this be the one time in his life that the old man does not get his own way and feels forced to backtrack in the name of common decency?

I look at my Alan and cry inside myself for the lovely man he is. He deserves none of this and not only is my heart broken for our animals but it is broken for Alan too. He is the kindest and most genuine man on this earth. He is one of a rare and dying breed. He has been called a liar and a thief by his father. His father in turn has convinced others that Alan is a liar and a thief. Oh good grief, this could not be further from the truth. He could not tell a lie if his life depended on it!

Only this week, he informed me of yet another farmer that has shunned him at market. This is actually a sheep farmer who is keeping his livestock at Syda Farm. Alan actually arranged all this and Alan and his father should have shared the income. This was carried out the first year, as Alan organised it. However, it became evident after the first grazing that the old man liaised with the sheep farmer and the sheep farmer has not even contacted Alan or paid him any rent since. It has all gone to his father and the sheep farmer now ignores Alan at market. We don't know what will have been said about us but obviously it will not be good. Alan's father can charm the birds out of the trees; oh, if only people knew the reality that is this malicious, bitter old man!

John Richards, another neighbouring farmer, took the mowing of the land at Syda. He too asked Alan if it was ok when he first went on to mow the land. Then, having dealt with the old man, he has not even contacted Alan since. I don't understand such shallow behaviour myself. The sad thing is, John Richards knows the score deep down, they all do! For their own gain, they are prepared to overlook the injustices, such, it would appear, is human nature. Maybe they should be thinking a little further ahead?

Alan dutifully went to Chatsworth House Estates and had to receive the blame for the state of the farm. One minute we are told it's nothing to do with us but then it's everything to do with us. The sad thing is the place looks like a farm, so how ironic is that? A farm with cow muck and chicken poop, that's terrible isn't it? Perhaps I ought to invent a "Chicken Poop a Scoop," to prevent many farms from looking like farms. I will get onto it first thing!

The Prodigal Son has his feet firmly under the table in waiting. This is Alan's brother, the man who has stolen the family business three times now! It got to the point that his poor, dear mother would have nothing to do with him. Now, he scents more money and has sidled up to his weak, old, vulnerable father, pushing forward the campaign to make me and Alan homeless!

Anyway, for all the old man's last minute, feeble attempt at preventing the repossession, the landlord is now intent on having the farm back and that is that. I have to confess, I went in to complete shock and was hysterical. The dogs were very upset to see me this way. Annie, the eldest of my Great Danes, gave me one of her smelly toys to help make everything ok. I must admit, Annie and the toy did help. While Alan and I reeled in shock, the Prodigal Son was busy stalking around the farm counting animals, primarily horses, to report back to his father. We would not have even known he had trespassed, except for our squeaky gate. It alerted us, but only as the spineless creature left the farm. I had to watch Alan be degraded once again at the hands of his family. He approached the Prodigal Son to ask him what he was doing. He was so rude to Alan, simply because we have horses on the land. His dad thinks we are making a load of money on livery. Ha, I wish. These are my rescue horses or my own babies. No profit, no monetary gain, but these are not people to understand that some people might find fulfilment in things other than money.

We went out and enjoyed a meal at the Donkey Derby. I rationalise that nobody has died so I should not feel too distressed. It is when you lose a loved one that all is bleak. I have Alan and he has me and that's forever. I simply cannot stop worrying about the future of all our family of animals. We have rescue cats and horses and old cows that my husband rescued from certain death at the farm sale when his business finished. They were too old to sell and we brought them to Rufford and have tried hard to give them a good life rearing calves. At times, it's been very hard but, when it's gone well, it has been bliss to watch the old cows with their offspring or adoptive children. Cows are wonderful animals and never cease to amaze me. We have had one or two cows that have lost their calves at birth or shortly after. We have either dashed to market to buy a calf or sourced one locally. When you present the bereaved cow with a replacement, they home in on that replacement and that becomes their calf. It's as if they never lost one!

We had one that we presented with two replacement calves. Do you know, she only homed in on one as that is the number she gave birth to? Eventually, she did take to the second one but it was many weeks later. Once they have bonded, it is a very strong bond. I often think it would be so wonderful for humans to be able to take their bond to another child when one is lost. It would be wonderful to replace a stillborn baby with another live baby to heal a bereaved mother. Oh, if only!

MARCH 25TH

It's 4am and, after hours of tossing and turning, we are both having a cup of tea. The dogs are still fast asleep without a care. We chatted and then, around 7am, went back to bed.

8.30am. Up again to face yet another day of uncertainty. I do not seem able to get going at all and my motivation has totally gone. I am floating around in a void with no control over my destiny. I had to rush around at the last to make our appointment at the Law Centre. I must say, I was very impressed with the man we saw. We felt a little ray of hope was presented to us. If justice prevails, we will be safe.

Alan took me out for breakfast and we enjoyed that very much. I then had to go to the dentist. I am very nervous as I hate the dentist (it's not personal but a phobia). My last visit to the dentist involved a half bottle of vodka and I still could not cope. The dentist seemed upset when I clamped my teeth on his finger. Surely this is one of the hazards of earning a substantial living putting your fingers in people's mouths?

Came home and went to bed with no motivation left at all. I suddenly feel so useless and worthless. I am apparently responsible for all Alan's problems and the mess we are in; that's the gospel according to the old man. We have spent all our married lives under that big cloud. I hope it will soon finally all be over and we will be free. I trust in God and know that, whichever path we go down, we will be ok. Despite my faith, I still feel so depressed tonight and I am struggling not to give up completely. I know I have been through so much worse in my life but, somehow, I am beginning to feel I cannot cope with this. I am feeling sorry for myself. We are just a couple of people who would not wish harm on anyone, yet there seems to be so many out there wanting to do us harm. The dastardly Duke is out to maximise his profits, but what kind of father and brother plot together to see a son homeless and on the streets?

MARCH 26TH

Woke in the early hours feeling depressed and panicky. My legs feel really weak, even though I am laid down in bed. I recall some of the terrible events over the years that have been life-changing and life-draining. Events that have been beyond my control. Here I am again, with no control over tomorrow. I became rather panicky at the thought of losing Alan. I worry about the stress upon him. Although he keeps it hidden, I can tell by the way he is talking that he is taking it all hard. Alan is hurting, and it's kept inside; this is not a good place to keep it. I am 46 years old and have no security at all. I am only just coming to realise how serious it is. Although we have always had the threat of losing Rufford House Farm, I never really thought the old man would go this far. I did not think for one moment that that DD (that dastardly Duke) would use a family feud in such an underhand way. The old Duke would never have stooped so low.

The land agents knew Alan and his dad were not talking and therefore Alan could not act when their solicitors presented the first papers towards possession of our home—we wouldn't even be privy to the on-going shenanigans, so how could we act to save our home and the animals' sanctuary? So they just dealt with a very nasty old man who had a vendetta against his son and his son's wife, and that suited their purpose fine. No need for a bit of common humanity. Dastardly, beyond belief.

I am totally opposite to Alan. My heart is firmly carried on my arm for all to see. It is there for people to see at its happiest and its saddest. All can see it and if they so wish they can give it a good old bash, which many cruel people often do. I will never bury my feelings, as this is a dangerous thing to do. Alan on the other hand will keep his feelings of hurt and anguish deep down inside; this is not a good place for them to be. I worry that keeping his feelings inside will damage his health.

Alan has been told by his father that he let it go this far with Rufford House Farm to "gee him up". This refers to Alan's refusal to accept peanuts to walk away from his life's work—Syda Farm is now 'disputed land' because Alan is determined to have his rightful share. We have recently had it confirmed by an old family friend that, on our wedding day, Alan's father vowed that he would see us on the streets. She also informed us that the old man planned from the start of the farm sale in 2006 to sell Alan's house and all the buildings, so that he had no work and nowhere to live. Well, he is certainly well on his way to achieving those ambitions for his son. I vow we will not be defeated by such evil actions.

MARCH 28TH

Having just managed to walk down the stairs, here I am again, starting my day with a cup of tea. For the first time in a while, we had slept well last night. I personally feel the shock has subsided and I am now in more of an accepting mode. Indeed, I have actually started sorting stuff ready for our new life. My fibromyalgia is at its worst right now. Although I rarely speak of this condition, it does make life very hard. Each morning, it takes me over an hour to break through the pain barrier, to get dressed. Stress is a major component in the severity of the attacks. So here I am, stressed up to the eyeballs with pain soaring through every muscle in my tired aching body.

During this ordeal, I am learning so much about my husband. I already knew that his father engineered the end of Alan's first marriage and tries hard to finish his second. I already knew that Alan and his first wife, starting married life in a caravan, built a beautiful house for themselves on the family farm. They had been given this wonderful opportunity by Alan's mother and father. Alan and his wife took a tractor and trailer many miles for many weeks in order to collect the stonework for their new house. Alan and his wife designed the house. I was already aware that once they had finished the house (which took much toil and sweat in between Alan running the farm), it was taken from them by Alan's father.

I already knew that Alan and his wife then had to stay in the original farmhouse that his parents now vacated. What I was unaware of was that it had actually been promised them for their wedding present. I feel sadness over this travesty, yet it is so typical of his father. The old man took the house from him with the words, "It's far too good for you!"

I didn't know Penny, Alan's first wife, but I always say to Alan that I fully understand why his marriage did not work. I fully understand why Penny had to leave. I love Alan dearly and can never imagine having the desire to leave him for another man (I wouldn't have the time or energy, anyhow). I can never imagine myself knowingly causing him such pain. I love him so much and feel so protective towards his feelings and his heart. But, as a young married couple living under the gloomy cloud of his father, Penny and Alan did not stand a chance. It's a tragic love story really and my heart aches the more I learn about it!

We are currently sitting in limbo waiting to find out our fate. It's hard but, I have to confess, I have now prepared myself for the worst. Those around us, friends and advisors, think it is simply a matter of moving up to the other farm—the very farm that has engulfed Alan's life with no recompense! However, it's not that simple? Bear in mind that we are dealing with a mad man and his greedy offspring. Bear in mind that I have received serious threats from most of this greedy family just for breathing!

The hate-hate dynamics I receive from Alan's family span 20 long years. It began when I worked for Alan on the farm. I was working my butt off for the farm and always tried hard to please. I was milking the cows for weeks while Alan was making hay. I was very tired and after many months of extremely hard work, I was suddenly offered a great opportunity. My brother, Rob, a teacher, had organised a school trip to Wales. It was a trekking holiday for his teenage pupils. I could not believe it when Rob said I could go along free and help the youngsters with their riding skills. This was an opportunity of a lifetime.

I could not believe that I had the chance to ride all day every day for a week in beautiful Wales. Could I get the time off? I asked Alan first of all. Alan thought I had worked so hard that I deserved the holiday and his mum said the same. However, when I approached the old man, his response was a resounding, "No Way!"

The holiday was less than a week away and Alan's father was adamant I was not to be given the time off. Alan and his mum thought I really should go and decided that a vote of two to one was good enough and I must go. Alan's mum kindly paid me some wages so I had money to spend. Due to the old man's behaviour, she had to smuggle me some money from her catalogue takings. Right up to the last moment, Alan's father said I could not go.

With Alan and his mum giving their blessing, and the old man proving to be intractable, I packed my bags and headed off to Wales. Next morning the old man's first question to his wife and son: "Where is Ginny this morning?"

"You know she has gone to Wales, dad," Alan replied. And with that his father turned on his heels and went into the house in a temper. When I returned, he demoted me and dropped my wages by £20 per week (I was only being paid £80 in the first place). He never ever forgave me for taking my once in a lifetime holiday without his blessing and this is why he has held a grudge against me ever since, because no one must ever, ever challenge the old man's authority!

Still bearing his hateful grudge weeks later, the old man was working in the fields at Rufford, while I was riding a young horse. I could suddenly hear the tractor getting dangerously close and my horse was agitated. I looked round and saw the old man steering the tractor purposefully in our direction. I heard the engine revving loudly. The tractor hurtled towards me. Alan's father smirked knowingly, as my horse became rigid with fear. Suddenly, the horse reared and fell onto a wall and I was thrown to the ground with great force. The old man turned the tractor close to my head as I lay in shock on the ground. I reported this to no one. I should have called the police but it was Alan's dad so how could I? It took me many months to recover from this ordeal. I would ride along the roads happily until I saw what I would imagine was Alan's dad driving towards me. I would panic and look for walls that I could jump my horse over to get out of his way.

Within that same year, I was approached by another mad family member desperate that Alan should not have a relationship with anyone. After all, it impinges on the amount of hours he can work. The four hours a week he was let out to spend with me (occasionally but not always with 'pocket money') amounted to a lot of lost labour. I walked across the yard at Rufford to see my horse, Lady. At this stage it housed Alan's niece and her husband, the latter who ran across the yard with foam coming from his mouth. He threatened me—I should not come onto the property, despite my horse being kept there with Alan's permission. He held up a large wooden fence stake and thrust it at me. His eyes were staring wildly and spit flew from his sagging jowls. Such is the hatred Alan's father has built against me with his bitterness. I stood my ground as I had every right to be here. I had come to see my beautiful horse, Lady, and I was not going to leave without seeing her. He backed down. With his head hung low, he turned towards the house. Still shaking from the shock of another attack, I made my way to see my dear horse.

The next event was quite recently. A party of three came to the farm to remove Alan's tractor. Amongst the number were Alan's sister and her husband. I asked them to leave. I had always stayed out of their way to avoid trouble and now they had come to my home. At this stage, I knew from past history and verbal threats that I was in danger. I called the police and to this day thank God I did! Within minutes of the police arriving, all hell had broken loose. As I climbed on a gate to stop Alan's brother-in-law from taking the tractor, he put his foot down and came straight at me. The tractor had several sharp prongs on it that, by the grace of God, did not kill me as it hit the gate that I was perched upon. I was thrown 12 feet in the air and landed inches away from the main road. Another inch and I would have been killed by the speeding lorries that thundered past.

The police had witnessed the whole episode from behind a hedge. My attacker was totally unaware that police officers were there. He got such a shock when he was grabbed by the police and handcuffed. I asked them not to bother arresting him but they said, having witnessed such a violent act, they had no choice. He was thrown into the back of the police car, as was the old man.

As I lay on the ground, semi-conscious, Alan's sister, Linda, stood over me, shouting abuse at Alan. She was shouting like a banshee out of control (a pose she often strikes, as for her there's nothing to it, and it is a highly apt simile). John was rightly taken to a prison cell in Buxton. I called later but the police advised against charges, due to his age and an otherwise clean record. He is just a sad old man poking his nose into something that should not concern him. Alan's father is now too old to be physically dangerous, but with a daughter and son-in-law like that pair, the venom can still be unleashed. I have vowed silently to myself that, should they ever even so much as look at me the wrong way, I will dial 999.

MARCH 29TH

The weekend has been fairly pleasant although I am feeling very unsettled and my emotions are up and down. I no longer look upon Rufford as my home. It's not home at the moment; it's just a base. Usually, I go to bed and feel really cosy, especially since Alan and I bought a lovely new duvet. It's so thick and warm and oh so cosy. But right now it's lost its cosy feel and I just sleep to forget.

I still have to keep going with the rescue as animals still need help regularly. Upon receiving a frantic call about a stray cat about to give birth, I prepared a warm and safe environment for her. Upon meeting the finder of the stray at the gate, I took the cat carrier from her by torchlight. The box felt unusually heavy. I peered inside and saw a big ginger cat. The size of the cat told me this had to be a boy. His jowls were huge and his colour (being solid ginger) told me instantly that this was no pregnant female. This was in fact a beautiful, neutered male, who had also fortunately been microchipped. A phone call to the microchip company led me within minutes to his frantic owner. The cat and his owner were reunited by nightfall.

MARCH 30TH

I woke up dreading today! TT(tuberculosis testing) on the cows had to be carried out and it is always a life threatening nightmare. However, it's even worse today as all the animals need to be tested in order to sell stock and move stock. As we are being forced to move, it needs to be done. By the end of it, all of us, including the vet, had our usual bruises and injuries to nurse.

TT testing involves trapping the cows and heifers in a 'crush'. This is a large crate that keeps them still and hopefully secure. Cows panic so much when trapped and can do themselves serious injury. More than a few farmers have been killed when carrying out this task. These are animals that are used to being free in the fields. They will go to any length to get away from the handlers. They will and do jump five foot gates from a standstill, or even barbed wire fences, which, as you can imagine, does serious injury. We even had one poor beast today that jumped from a window. She was fine but I was left with a sprained wrist trying to stop her.

Elaine and Charlotte came to see Wilma (a beautiful home bred horse I have) and Charlotte had a lesson on her. Wilma was very good and they are going to have her on loan. This will be the first time in my life I have put a horse on loan with a view to purchase. Elaine and her family are so lovely but I will be heartbroken. Wilma is Lady's grandchild. Lady was my first ever horse and so dear to me. I have a serious problem in life when it comes to letting go! It looks like I am now being forced to let things go. Maybe this is why God has set out the problems we have right now. It could be His way of forcing me into letting go of the past.

Phoned RABI (Royal Agricultural Benevolent Fund), an organisation that helps farmers when having problems. I also spoke to Farm Crisis Network; it feels like we have little support. Still, it's comforting to know that Alan's father is safely tucked up in his own home.

April 1ˢᵀ

Lovely sunny day, but who cares. I have neither the energy nor the inclination to do anything outside. John, from the group RABI, came to see us, but I am not sure if they can be of any help to us. I left the room for a while but when I returned I noticed that Alan's face showed signs of shock. He had just been told by his solicitor that the old man did not care to fight Chatsworth to retain tenancy of Rufford House Farm. Maybe he will care to do so next week, who knows? Well, I think he is in for a bit of a shock when we finally lose our home (Plan B, remember?). I think this spells out the start of a war.

I knew it would be bad when that born again Christian, Alan's brother, the Prodigal Son, came down and counted the horses. The old man has always hated my horses and made it plain they are not allowed on the farm. I look around and see nothing but impossible challenges. That's just in the house before I even think about outside. I am just wandering around, trying to figure out how people can behave in such a way to their fellow men (let alone blood relatives). I do not just mean the old man and his Prodigal Son, but the agents and trustees at Chatsworth, too.

The Chatsworth House Estate does a lot of good work for charity. Does charity not begin at home? If you are going to do good, charitable work, surely nasty behaviour with your tenants counteracts such work. I guess the charity stuff is just good PR. I do not get it. I would not mind if Alan was not such a good, kind man. He is actually rather like the late, great Duke and would be better placed to run Chatsworth Estates in the spirit of that much missed, much loved gentleman.

I am afraid I got very upset today and lashed out at Alan. I told him I would be better off not being alive! It's just the thought of all the physical work ahead. My body is unable to cope with heavy physical tasks. I just cannot cope with all the lifting and moving that lies ahead. Help! Even just moving one box of belongings will cause severe pain in my back and limbs, such is the nature of fibromyalgia. How will I be able to move the entire contents of our home and farm?

APRIL 4TH

I am just about coping! That is of course till I see my neighbour hovering around trying to pump my friend, Dot, for information. She is like a vulture waiting for her kill. Someone who thrives on other people's misery is beyond belief for me. Do we have to resign ourselves to this being a natural part of human nature? I hope not.

I upset Dot as she felt I did not trust her to keep details private. Another friend had to be restrained from going round to give a piece of her mind. Bless her; it was like clinging on to a highly strung Rottweiler. Anyway, after this incident we had a lovely afternoon with the ponies.

Dot is clearly not a loyal friend and I have suspected this for a while. She seems to relish the situation I am in, despite the fact she must be aware of my vulnerability. Last week (the week that we found we had lost the farm) the woman next door approached Dot and her son for the first time ever (so transparent) asking them if they would go for a ride with her. This is a woman who has not ridden her horse for six months and certainly not ridden the horse away from home for well over a year. I could see through her and I would have hoped Dot could have seen the same. It's sad really that my neighbour has no friends of her own. She clearly scented Dot's weaknesses—that lack of loyalty and desire to gossip— and was determined to get her on side to hear all about my business. Well, she has at least inspired a good business idea for when I finally settle—I will call it "rent a friend". The point is though, it is absolutely true that, when your chips are down, you discover your true friends.

Alan did a car boot for our rescue. He is such a good soul (mind you he was doing the car boot with a pretty blonde so that will have helped spur him on). The sale made a welcome little forty quid so that should buy some decent food for the animals. Many of the cats are so fussy when it comes to food. Only the best will do for some of them. Tommy Tucker is a prime example. He is a dear old boy and loves only the finest food. And the little darling has to be stroked while he eats or he won't even eat the best stuff. I only found this out by accident one day when I walked in to see why he had not eaten his breakfast. As I went in and spoke to him, he ambled over to his bowl and started eating. I turned away and he stopped eating. I love bringing him pleasure in this way and he's just so sweet.

I so wish we could find a good home for Tommy. I hate it when the older cats get stuck in our sanctuary. He is only here because his owner died. He is a lovely old chap and he drools when you give him a fuss. I had dinner prepared in the slow cooker so, when we finished, late, we just crashed and ate tea. We were both so shattered at the end of the day.

APRIL 5TH

I waited around for Dot and her son but they decided to garden first. Unfortunately, they failed to inform me of the change of plan! I must confess, having seen Dot's disloyal behaviour, I was more than happy to go out on my own with my lovely horse. Animals can never let you down like people so often do. I decided to go off and have a good old ride through Linacre Woods. Wow! It was great; Jaffa, my beautiful horse, can cure any woes, anytime. It's true what they say about animals and their healing properties, as my horses always get me through dark days.

Years ago when my darling nephew passed over with leukaemia, my beautiful horse got me through. I wanted to die and yet each day I struggled out of the bed to ride my horse. I swear to this day she kept me alive! I still think of my dear nephew and all the joy he brought to our lives. Children should not die before their parents. It's not right. It is the saddest, most traumatic loss any human can go through, the loss of a beloved child.

APRIL 6TH

Yet another day travelling to the solicitor in Belper. The news was no better. We still look set to lose our farm and our days in our home appear to be numbered. However, I was not in any shock today and was well prepared. I cried most of the way to the solicitors. I was just very sad and emotional. Holly, my little dog, kept washing my tears away. I just kept reliving memories of my beautiful farm. All the green fields on the journey reminded me what a lovely life I was about to lose. Memories of all the good times I have had at the farm were going around in my head. All the beautiful loved ones I have lost in my life came into my thoughts too. My mind was just working so hard all the way to Belper. As the memories overloaded my brain, the tears fell freely. I was grieving at my impending loss.

The solicitor was as pleasant as ever. Who wouldn't be for £230 an hour? I couldn't half be pleasant with folk if I had that much cash at the end of it. It's great that they have a cuppa waiting (even if it is made in a cup and not a warmed teapot!). I just wish they would invest in a proper teapot so they could really make a proper cup of tea for clients. I think it would make a huge difference; it would to me anyway.

What I was surprised to hear was that Chatsworth House Estates have committed a fraud—allegedly. I knew what they were doing was wrong in terms of basic human decency and immoral but to hear that it is also illegal—allegedly!!! However, we need the evidence to prove it (we do have some). Worse still, we need at least £30,000 to take them on. Then, if we lose, which the solicitor said is possible, we get their costs as well.

The fraud comes about because the land agents accepted a cheque for rent, only to send it back a week later. They then claim the rent was not paid. Cad like behaviour, which you would not expect from such a highly regarded business.

I asked our solicitor if I could send a letter to the 'Dowager Duchess' but he said I could not. This might upset Chatsworth House Estates and make them even more determined to get the house back. Well, that's fine by me. Rest assured, when this is over and they have nothing to hold over me (like the roof of my home), I will go public. I do not believe anyone should get away with such injustice. It won't help us but they will be exposed in my diary.

The old Duke is being so let down in all of this. He and his wife 'built' Chatsworth with a kind heart. He cared for his tenants and would never have behaved in such an ungentlemanly manner.

APRIL 7ᵀᴴ

Such a struggle today. I keep thinking how terrible I am to be so weak. I feel positively ill and almost grieving. Not like grief in its most terrible form (something I know all about), but a different grief. I feel so sad and low yet I am aware that I have been through so much worse. I fear the tasks ahead. I know the move is not a bad thing and I am certain good will come. I am so afraid of losing important things. Not big things but little things. An example would be a special broach I was given by my mum as a birthday present. She went to so much trouble to purchase this beautiful handmade broach for me. I have always treasured it and worn it with pride. It is a mare with a foal by her side. They are both running. I worry that I will mislay it and other smaller items that are so important to me.

I am not a materialistic person at all, yet I have items that carry memories of all I have loved. I have items that are my history; they are memories and trigger more memories of special times in my life. That is all and I am so frightened. I am a sentimental fool and that has always been what I consider a bit of a downfall.

I fear the heavy work and the lifting. Silly, I know, but I am so worried about not having the stamina. My normal days are hard to get through but this!

I felt so weak today, unable to focus on the present moment. I am tired like I have never known. I feel too tired to live.

April 9th

Alan has to get the first of many animals to the market. Unfortunately, I woke up unable to move my back and my ankle. I was so upset at feeling so useless to Alan. We managed to get the girls loaded and then I had to feed around the animals as best I could. Lynne, an artist friend, came and helped me; she was great and made me laugh. We gave everyone hay, food and water and then went in for a cuppa. We started to pack things and organise the move. I knelt at my bookcase and sorted my book collection. I sorted it into half to sell and half to keep. I missed Alan while he was gone all day. I don't think I would have managed had my dear friend not been here. Alan came home and brought in some doughnuts; these made everything alright.

Dot came and was clearly agitated. I sensed immediately it was because I had not cleaned her horse out (although he normally lives out, and we have no arrangement that I muck him out or indeed take any form of responsibility; I have simply performed these tasks from time to time out of friendship and my love of horses). She was really mean about it and never gave me the chance to say I could not manage physically. I decided to take her rudeness on the chins.

FRIDAY APRIL 10ᵀᴴ

Good start to the day and I managed to muck out for her horse, as I usually do. However, Dot came and delivered a dramatic lecture about my neglect of her horse the day before. It was uncalled for and sadly I took it very much to heart. While I am walking so close to the edge, the last thing I need is for someone I thought was a friend to push me over the precipice. Poor Alan did not know what to do with me as I was inconsolable. It wasn't just Dot's attitude to me; it was the fact that no matter how much I do for people, it can never, ever be enough. This is how everyone ends up with me, sooner or later! So much is expected and taken for granted and when I don't deliver . . . . bam! I'm suddenly treated with animosity. I have really had enough and would like to move to a remote island and keep away from the rat race. I am very depressed tonight and wonder how I will overcome this setback.

I realise now that Dot, as I suspected, was never really a friend. She is just an extremely mercenary individual with no heart and no soul. I will just have to bide my time and tell her that she will not be moving with us after all. I want her out of my life. She just uses people. As she has become so cosy with next door, I am certain she will be able to move her horse there.

I went to bed, not wanting to get up again. I missed Shirley's visit (she's one of my animal welfare contacts); she had brought another cat for me. He is a cruelty/neglect case but he is safe now. A lovely cat that has been completely shaven. This is due to severe neglect and matting of the coat. He looks rather sweet but, boy, does he stink. Having just been neutered, the smell of tomcat urine is rather pungent. He hisses a lot but seems rather friendly on the whole.

I am really low tonight so I am happily aware that the only way is up. We had always aimed to return to Syda Farm one day so I must, as Rob, my brother says, make the best of this adventure. Alan has always kept hold of his Syda Farm number plates, such has been his desire to return home.

SATURDAY 11ᵀᴴ

Trying to pull myself together and regain my usual happy heart. Have to do a car boot for the sanctuary today so I have to keep going. I really don't want to but it's better than being around the farm with Dot and her son coming up. I felt like a complete wreck going off to the car boot. Met Emma on route and we had a bit of a laugh. Emma and I have so much in common and share a passionate love of animals. We spent the morning laughing about our animals and their antics. We made £40 for the sanctuary. Exhausted when I got home, still rather depressed. I am going to see if the doctor can help me this week. I know I will just sit and blubber when I see him.

Picked Rob up at the train station and we came home and had a lovely tea. Alan made us chips, accompanied by pie and other leftovers. Lit a fire and settled down for the evening.

Easter Sunday

Did the usual feeding round and then ate Easter eggs. Rob and I spent the whole day clearing stuff. I am beginning to calm down about the tasks. I guess so long as I have my precious bits and bobs, all's not so bad. My horse book collection has to be halved. I will hopefully sell some on eBay and maybe put a list in the saddle shops. I have an extensive collection of around 200 books. I have always been so proud of my book collection but it's time to let go of many things. From a Feng Shui point of view, my life is totally bad so let's see what a good old de-cluttering will do . . . .

It was a long but satisfying day. After evening feeds I managed to cook a lovely dinner. My Yorkshires were lovely thanks to my new recipe—cup of flour, cup of eggs, cup of milk—perfick!

EASTER TUESDAY

I am eating for ten people at the moment, which can only mean one thing—stress. Oh well, I will finish all my chocolates and then try and regain control. Sad day today as Alan loaded our dear Pearl into the cattle wagon. Her two lovely calves went with her to market. She was a lovely cow that Alan bought at market when he first went solo in his business. She was so beautiful but so timid. When she first arrived, you could not keep her in a shed. She would go into the sheds fairly well but would jump out over the door within minutes. She seemed to suffer from some sort of claustrophobia. You could not get near her to touch her. She gave us a calf within a day of arriving on the farm. Our beautiful Red Boy; Pearl gave birth in the safety of a bramble bush. Well, she thought it was a good idea. Boy, she loved that calf; she was one of the best mums I ever did see.

It broke her heart and ours when our little Red Boy died at eight months old. When we found him dead he was raw from her tongue, as Pearl had licked him really hard as she tried to wake him. I longed for her next calf to be born to help heal her. Only weeks later, Red gave birth to a stillborn calf. We were distraught. And do you know what the worst thing was? Like many animals, she would come down for feed and then go back to her dead baby. I find it heart breaking and very difficult to witness. We removed the little body while she ate. The little calf would have been totally blind, had he lived; his eyes were completely white.

Alan had been to a local farmer to fetch two babies for Pearl. As one of the new calves in the trailer called, she swung round and really thought we had brought her baby to life. She chased over to the trailer and appeared so pleased to see her baby had "not died" after all. She adopted the little calf immediately. However, she was not daft and knew she had only given birth to one calf. It took a lot longer for her to accept the second calf. It was touch and go but we got there in the end.

It was sad to see them all go to market today, as Pearl was scheduled to have many years with us, until we lost our home. Alan said she walked in the sale ring as proud as Punch. She strode around the ring with her two babies. I do so wish we didn't have to say goodbye. I will never forget our lovely Pearl. She destroyed so many shed doors and could jump like a professional. If she had been a horse, she would have been worth thousands with her jumping skills.

THURSDAY 16TH APRIL

We looked after Alan's granddaughter for the day, which was very pleasant. We went to Sheffield to see a solicitor for a second opinion about our situation. Her view was the same as our own solicitor; Chatsworth House Estate is committing fraud and behaving in a despicable manner. However, they have deep pockets and, with us being ordinary folk, with little money we cannot risk a very costly court battle. It is too much of a risk. Nevertheless, I am determined to use my diaries to make this public, even though we appear to have lost our farm. Does justice only exist for those with money? Why does our system allow the wealthy to trample on the poor? My diaries are an honest, day by day account of events leading to the loss of our home—perhaps they will try to stop these being published, too.

Friday 17th April

I look at my horses and ponies and I cry. I have been spoilt with all this space and I cannot bear the thought of change. It has always frightened me to undergo any changes in life. While I can see it will benefit us in the long run, it is not easy. I am always happy to just mosey along and let life happen. Now I am being forced into action. It will be for the best so I am trying to be really positive about the future. I thank God every time my positive nature is restored.

Anyway, I have already been to see my potential new home—a static caravan. We had been offered this home for a small price as a favour. However, upon inspection, it was clear that it wasn't worth much. I must admit, it was a bit of a shock. It smelt stale. As I removed my shoes to go inside, my feet started to freeze straight away. I suddenly thought, "Oh dear!"

21ST APRIL

Business as usual and, after receiving a phone call from Peak Vets regarding two cats requiring help, beds were made up. The two cats had been taken to the vets to be put to sleep. Their only crime was the owner developing asthma. Two beautiful cats, one big ginger fellow and his little wife, a gorgeous tortoiseshell. Both long haired, so they should be homed quickly. On arrival, the two cats were put into their little home. They are beautiful cats and have very sweet natures. They settled in really quickly.

WEEKEND 25-27TH APRIL

Gosh, time is flying at a tremendous rate and September is only around the corner. Although there is no formal agreement yet with the landlord, we have kind of accepted our fate. We are literally in God's hands. Rob pointed out to me today that the Duke of Devonshire is somewhere near the top of the rich list at the moment. Well he might be but it doesn't stop him throwing a farmer, his wife and all their animals out on the street. An old fellow called for some free range eggs on Friday. I told him about what the landlord is doing to us and he called them an unmentionable name. He was angry within seconds. He rightly pointed out that, since the new Duke was in charge, they were only interested in making money, allegedly. Every person we speak to seems to have the same view of Chatsworth House Estate at the moment. People who live around here have seen what is happening and how things have changed since the grand old Duke died.

The weekend has been so perfect and the weather delightful. The horses and the cows are shedding their old winter coats and look amazing. It's so lovely just to be around our beautiful farm.

We have decided to ask our solicitor not to deal with our landlord for us anymore. He is charging £230 per hour; we can do it ourselves for nothing. We were going to Chatsworth for a meeting before the solicitor said not to; we have a letter for the Dowager Duchess, but the solicitor said not to send it. So we are no longer able to follow our hearts and have to pay to be told to desist.

We have accepted that we are losing the farm. At times I can find myself getting rather excited about our new venture. Mind you, it will be a case of moving next to the father—in-law from Hell! Oh well, I suppose he has only made two serious attempts to injure me. I think he is getting a bit old now to be considered a danger. However, he has his bulldog of a prodigal son and his money-motivated daughter to fight for him now. I think that woman has money running through her veins. She is like a money vampire, constantly needing more of the stuff in order to stay alive.

WEDNESDAY 29TH MAY

We went to see Alan's ex-solicitor, from his days running Syda Farm, with whom he still keeps in touch. We suddenly realised we have no wills in place, should the worst scenario occur; that is, me and Alan popping our clogs together. I mean, it would be lovely in theory (not yet of course) but it seems daunting to think that Alan's siblings would be laughing all the way to the bank.

It was more complex that we thought. We learnt a bit, one bit being that if Alan and I do go together, it's rather complicated. As I am the younger of the two then whatever happens at the end, if it happens to both of us at the same time, I will be considered the second to pass over. This would mean that everything will go to my siblings and Alan's children would get nothing. Not a good scenario for Alan. Well, at the moment all we have to leave is livestock, books, a little jewellery, tools and horse tack, etc. There may be a little cash when the time comes, who knows?

May Bank
Holiday weekend

I am showing severe signs of mobile home obsession! They seem to be popping up everywhere. One of our dear rescue horses moved house this weekend. Dot's son, who has adopted our horse, Henry, wanted to take him nearer to his home. I was sad about this as I expected him to be with us on the farm forever. I have to say I did not want him to go but, considering our circumstances, it would have been churlish not to allow the move.

He was his usual naughty self and as Dot's son took him towards the lorry, Henry put his head in the air and dragged Joe back towards the field. It was horrendous as he dragged Joe through the undergrowth. Henry, with all his bulk and strength, was totally unaware of the relatively small human hanging from his head. We attempted it once more; off Henry went up the road with Joe hanging precariously from his head collar. As the horse raced up the A619, all the traffic ground to a halt. Joe was exposed to all the stationary drivers as a mere human. He dangled from the halter like a little rag doll. When Henry decided to call a halt to the humiliation of the poor chap, they both ambled calmly back to the farm. After all his fun, Henry made his way up the ramp with what looked like a small grin on his face.

The journey to Cambridge was not pleasant and it took an hour just to get through Chesterfield town centre. Once on the open road, Henry and everyone else relaxed. Carol, a little local lady with few friends, had come along for the ride. Four hours and lots of frayed nerves later, we arrived at Henry's new home in Cambridge.

It was a home from home. The yard was totally dishevelled, as a farm should be. Dogs and chickens were scattered round the yard, apparently enjoying every waking moment. There was even a little collie with a tumour on its mouth. Though receiving no treatment, except of course tender loving care, this dog was enjoying life to the max. Henry came out of the lorry unscathed and he stood proudly in the little farm yard. Once taken to his field, he settled down in no time.

I got an even more pleasant surprise when we were taken into the house for a cup of tea. The house was on a par with my own in the untidy and disorganised stakes. I think maybe I have one or two more cats on my work surfaces at home. I felt at home immediately and revelled in the idea that maybe I am not so abnormal after all. And anyway, when the wise choice is to be outdoors with nature and the animals, we can't be expected to keep house as well.

We checked on Henry before we left and found him attempting to jump out of the field. We waited until he had been given companion ponies and then we said our goodbyes. We set off on the long journey home, arriving back just in time for "Casualty" and a delicious dinner cooked by hubby. Headache came on and I made my way steadily to bed.

Back to the mobile home obsession! On the little farm, they had a couple of mobile homes where people were actually living (no planning permission or anything). It was a lovely set up and made me very optimistic. I kept attracting mobile homes like a radar on the journey home and found myself rubber necking just to get a glimpse of them. The upshot is, they look really cosy, so I can't wait (maybe that's a slight exaggeration—but it pays to be positive when faced with adversity).

Bank Holiday Sunday

Up bright and early to lovely sunshine, although there was a very strong wind. Alan called me from bed with a cup of tea and the news that one of our young heifers was about to calve. Emma had arrived to feed the cats so the birth was something she was going to share with us.

Phoned the vets to see how my little cat, Scoop, was managing. Alan had taken her to the vets yesterday while I was in Cambridge. She has a really bad cold and has not responded to a treatment of antibiotics given to her last week. It was the vet's wife who answered the phone and I asked her how my little cat was today. Her reply took me somewhat by surprise as she explained that nothing more could be done for her. She had not responded to treatment and also has a heart complaint. Nothing can be done for her now, I was informed.

With tears in my eyes and a heart so heavy I felt sick, I drove to see my little Scoop. What would I tell her daughter, Dotty, who lives with us? How could I have missed the signs of a bad heart? Everything made sense in my mind. It seemed to explain why sometimes she would sleep curled up on my pillow, next to my head, and sometimes she would sleep downstairs. How could I have missed such obvious signs? Then I worried I had done something to cause her a bad heart; it's always me, I always blame myself if one of my animals gets sick or dies. I knew I could not possibly go out to dinner tonight, as planned.

As I walked in the doors of the surgery, the vet's wife looked at me with sympathy. "Wait for the vet," she said, before changing her mind. "Actually, you had better go through now, the cat's not at all well."

I could not get through the doors quickly enough and, as I scanned the room full of animals, I eventually located my Scoop. I held her little face in my hand and kissed her. I was sure she had improved from yesterday, I was sure she looked a little better. I told Scoop that we would seek a second opinion! As I soothed my little cat, the vet's wife walked in. "Your daughter's on the phone," she announced, to my surprise. I have no daughter and asked who it was. The vet's wife looked at me perplexed and then exclaimed that she had got my cat mixed up with another woman's!

Scoop had no heart condition and was not going to die.

I was overwhelmed with relief but looked round to see a ginger cat stretched out in a cage. His notes were the ones the vet's wife had read when I called. *If no improvements by morning, recommend euthanasia.* My happiness spelt out sadness for some other cat lover so the moment was bitter sweet.

Arriving home I found Alan and Emma holding a vigil in the field, as our heifer was about to calve. As we all sat in anticipation, the calf was delivered quickly and without our intervention. Well actually, Alan did give a bit of a pull at the last. The heifer finished her job and walked away without as much as a backward glance. As we looked down, we saw that the beautiful little heifer calf was dead. The mother had obviously been aware that she was delivering a lifeless calf. In disappointment and with sadness, we all walked away . . . .

MAY 4TH

The heifer that produced the dead calf was taken to a nearby farm where Alan's son works, as we have no milking facilities. She needed to be made comfortable by being milked. Sadly, she still produced milk, even though her calf had been stillborn. We went to see her and she did look good. The farmer seems to look after the animals really well, and our cow was laying down in a lovely, deep bed of fresh straw.

On the whole this week was delightful weather wise. I managed a night out with my sister and her family. I managed to make a real effort and go out feeling very smart. It was lucky for me that nobody was aware I had fallen behind with my washing and was thus wearing a pair of Alan's Y fronts! Well, nobody's perfect.

Alan took Betsy, my horse lorry, for her yearly MOT. I could not go this year as I find it too stressful. You can fail a car MOT and drive happily home. Well, maybe not happily but you can drive home. However, if the lorry fails on certain things, they condemn it and take it off the road there and then, leaving you stranded many, many miles from home. It wouldn't be too bad if it was local but we have to go all the way to Sheffield, which is over twenty miles away. Anyway, it was just as stressful waiting at home as Alan called to say that the battery was flat. Somehow, he managed to get it going and took it through the MOT. He was not allowed to drive it away as it had no diesel cap. Poor Alan had to walk to the nearest garage and attempt to get a cap. The lorry is thirty years old so they don't make these caps any more. I think for next year's MOT, I will take a holiday abroad while Alan deals with it. Eventually they found a cap that did the job, just, and they let Alan drive home. It had failed and has to go back tomorrow with a cap and a couple of minor jobs done. That means one thing—I have to take it back myself as Alan is at a sale!

WEDNESDAY 6TH MAY

Off to Sheffield for the MOT, no problem. Followed Alan's instructions to the letter. Everything went fine, at least until I reached the final directions which would get me to the MOT station. Pulled up at roundabout, as per instructions, but realised it was not a roundabout, more a "teardrop—shaped—about". That was it for me and of course panic set in. I called Alan on my mobile phone and pleaded for help. I needed him to confirm the shape of the roundabout; was it supposed to be shaped like a teardrop? Why I was in such a panic I will never know. As I shrieked down the phone for help, Alan tried to pacify me. Cars horns hooted behind me. I sat behaving in a most unhinged manner, even by my standards. Eventually, I set off and accepted that I was not going to make it to the MOT. However, as I careered around the lanes looking for a way home, I stumbled upon a sign post, 'MOT station'. Feeling very proud, I pulled into the testing bay, passed my test and took off home with my certificate (before anyone could change their minds!).

Anyway, I made it and was delighted. Alan had gone to his sale in Nantwich and did not return home until 10pm. Bit of a late finish. He arrived home with the Land Rover limping into the yard. Our Land Rover is proving to be a bit of a nightmare. The turbo did not sound good at all. The sad thing is, this Land Rover replaced our reliable old one that was stolen from our yard many months before. Our old one is proving difficult to replace. Alan managed to get it into the garage, when the engine flickered one last time; the vehicle collapsed, exhausted. It is a miracle that Alan got her home at all. He left the stock he had bought in the trailer over night. I was taken out to see them by torchlight and they were lovely. After providing them with water and hay, we left them warm and content.

THURSDAY 7TH MAY

Took my beloved Great Dane, Annie, to the vet as she has been unwell lately. Carol told me about a £30 MOT for older animals. I know Annie is getting on a bit but I want to do all I can to keep her that bit longer. Annie was our first born when we married eleven years ago. Everyone marvelled at my beautiful dog and then proceeded to tell me how short a life span the breed had. It has stayed with me always that we would not have long together. Well, here we are, eleven years later, popping down to the vets for a check up.

She was so pleased to be out and about and strode into the pet store with a jaunt in her step. It was wonderful to see her looking lively and engaged. She was so brave and had a blood test in no time at all. Then we went off in the recovered but still dodgy Land Rover, ticking off our list of bits and bobs. Annie really seemed to enjoy being out in the Land Rover. We will do it more often, as she always loved going out for a drive.

FRIDAY MAY 8TH

I had an appointment at the hospital about my knee. That is the knee that Alan's brother-in-law injured when he drove at me with the tractor. This act of violence has left me with several problems and one of those is a very bad knee joint. The sad thing is that the brother-in-law and his fellow thugs will be pleased that they have left me injured. He will be less happy about the caution he received as a result of his attack.

The hospital has decided that I am to have an operation on my knee. I have had several weeks of physiotherapy, which has just made my knee worse. I think I upset the physiotherapist by telling her my knee had deteriorated further. She was outwardly shocked and decided that if that was the case I could go back to my doctor. I don't think she'd had a failure before. Or maybe nobody dared to tell her the truth!

Saturday 9th May

Alan needed a hand to get the herd across the main road for the fresh grazing. Should be simple enough, as the road is blocked half way across by road works. This means we only have half a road to cross. We also had a few friends round and thought it would be so easy with all hands on deck.

I, being the most experienced after Alan, adopted the role of chief nut shaker. This involves the complicated task of shaking the cow nuts in a bucket in front of the herd. The idea is that they follow the nuts and go wherever we want them too. Well, with all my experience safely tucked under my belt, one of the cows pinched the nuts off me. I dropped the bucket and all hell was let loose. Carol's sister, Lynne, who has very little experience with driving cattle, clapped her hands vigorously to encourage the cows back to the field. What she did not realise was that clapping hands behind the cows would send them away from us.

The cattle ran at tremendous speed down the main road towards Chesterfield. I decided in a moment of madness to do a fast sprint, to head the cows off at the pass! I managed it, much to my surprise, and turned them back up towards the farm. At this point, I noticed next door's gate was open and willed the herd not to notice. They did notice and off we went up the neighbour's lane. The neighbour was totally unaware I had spotted him dodge behind a tractor to avoid me and the rest of the cows. However, the cows don't like being snubbed in this way and headed straight for him, to expose him cowering behind a tractor. He looked rather embarrassed but I hadn't time to worry. Luckily, I managed to turn them round and head at great speed back down the path and up to our farm. Carol shook her nuts with great vigour and the cows ended up in the field where they should have been half an hour earlier. With my head hung low from embarrassment, we made our way into the house for a well earned cup of tea.

Sunday 10th May

Woke up unable to move a muscle. Racked my brains to think what I had done to cause this. Then I remembered the minute mile I had performed yesterday. I paid the price for that throughout the rest of the day. Every cloud has a silver lining and we ended up having dinner at Kelly's house. We had such a lovely evening with her family. Our little god-daughter, Lexee, is a joy to behold. I enjoyed helping bath her and putting her to bed. I have never seen a child smile so much and so beautifully; she is amazing.

MONDAY 11ᵀᴴ MAY

I enquired about Annie's test results, which left me rather shocked to say the least. The liver count was 1200 more than it should have been. The vet booked Annie in for a scan the next day. He said it could be a spleen tumour. I felt very sad and shocked not only at the results but that my beautiful dog was going downhill rapidly. Cancer, the dreaded word, and yet in my heart I was aware Annie had always been a lumpy dog. Driving home, we decided Annie was not going to have the scan. What would be the point of being told what's going wrong inside my dog? They would only want to open her up and mess around inside. No chance! My Annie is not going to be put through any operations, not at her delicate stage in life. I just want her with me for as long as possible. Until the day I die would be great.

Planted our potatoes up the field; it's a good feeling that our allotment is underway. Didn't think we would do it this year but we are trying to carry on as normal. Actually, I am a little worried as I seem to have my head well and truly buried in the sand.

TUESDAY MAY 12TH

I took my darling Annie to see my own vet today. Annie loved going out in the Land Rover again. I took her for a walk as we were early for the vet. I could not keep up with her as she trotted down the road. She seemed to have a new lease of life. She even managed to do a poo, which was a bit inconvenient. Luckily, I had a wee sample for the vet and had placed a plastic bag over it. It was only a thin bag so it was a bit risky and very warm to the hand. This of course left the wee sample exposed and numerous little seeds from the trees floated on the top of it.

Saw Elisa, the vet; I respect her as much as I do Ian, the senior at this practice. The first thing she did was take Annie's temperature. Result? Very high. She prescribed antibiotics immediately. Do you know, by nightfall Annie was getting better already? The high street vets had not even taken her temperature. I was sad that Annie had been ill for a further week as a result of their oversight.

As the week went on, Annie just got better and better and back to her old self. Remind me never to change my vet routine again. So much for tumours—my Annie simply had a virus!

Tomorrow morning, I have to take my lovely Tommy Tucker to the vet for a dental. He has been dribbling a lot lately; much of the dribble has a bit of red in it. He should be a lot better with a few bad teeth out.

MAY 14ᵀᴴ

Up bright and early as Alan is off to market in Derby. I decided to go with him and spend a couple of hours with Rob. I have to say it was a brilliant idea and I had a lovely time. Rob took me on a beautiful walk, which was the walk he used to do with his lovely dog, Cassie.

Cassie was Rob's first dog and he adored her. Sadly, she took very ill with cancer and died. She died ever so peacefully but Rob was so upset. It made him question whether he could love another dog. The loss was just so sad and unfair as he only had her a year. He loved her so much and Cassie adored him. It was a beautiful relationship that brought me personally great warmth and joy. It was lovely to know Rob was being looked after by his faithful friend. I do hope one day he will give another rescue dog such a wonderful home. I am certain he will, in time. The bond that they shared was beautiful to the end. I remember her last day with us. Rob came over and sat with Cassie, caressing her tired, thin body. She barely had energy to breath and yet, as we sat with her, she twice raised her head to see that her master was still with her. It was poignant to say the least and, moments after her last glance to Rob, she slipped peacefully away.

Rob showed me where Cassie had all her fun. He showed me where she lost her coat one night. Next day she found it again and was ever so excited about it. She ran around and around displaying pleasure at finding her coat. Whoever could say dogs are not intelligent and sentient beings? Whoever says this has not had the joy of caring for a dog. If you truly care for animals, particularly dogs, you will know they are very aware and feel very strong emotions on all the issues a human does, except politics of course. It was clear by her behaviour that she was thrilled to find the lost coat.

We had such a wonderful time remembering Cassie. The morning culminated in meeting Alan for a pub lunch. Alan had enjoyed a fruitful day at the market. We picked up Tommy Tucker on the way home—it was good to have him back.

FRIDAY 15TH

Wet, wet, wet and yet more wet. Not ideal weather for delivering two horses to a new home. Oh well, best foot forward and off I went to fetch the chosen two from the field. Wilma came like a little lamb and walked hastily up the long steep field. I could feel my chest tightening and was finding it difficult to breath. Not unusual and not a problem as I would simply finish the task and take a couple of puffs from my inhaler. Placed Wilma in the ménage and popped off to fetch Ed. Glanced at my watch and realised I had plenty of time. Ed came up to me like the gent he is and I threw the ropes over his neck. Well that was it, having never experienced the long rope head collar, he took flight with me clinging on for dear life. Well, that was the start of an hour-long nightmare. The whole group of horses went crazy and started galloping in a frenzy. I called for help and Alan brought buckets of food up to me. All hell was unleashed yet again and, sadly, I forgot the golden rule of keeping calm.

Alan suggested ringing the awaiting horse adopters to explain I could not catch the horse. I felt this was not a good sales pitch so I declined. Eventually, after removing all the horses one by one, I managed to catch Ed. No longer one of my favourite horses! We left the farm only an hour late and the rest of the mission went well. The girls met us at the bottom of the lane and the horses were delivered as promised. The rain was still pouring, as I turned and left my beautiful babies to their new life. Still panting for breath, I hurried for my inhaler as soon as we reached home.

17TH & 18TH MAY

Alan's birthday on Sunday, so when I got home we had a relaxing afternoon. I had made lots of scones and a nice cake for any visitors. We had several guests through the afternoon and it was all really pleasant. Scones and cream went down a treat. Alan's son and his family came and my sister and niece, amongst others. It was lovely and Alan enjoyed himself.

MAY 18TH

Alan off to market early morning to sell some more of his stock. However, he 'inadvertently' ended up buying two young calves. Mind you, they are a cute little pair. A little brown and white and a black and white. Alan put them both in a stable in the horse yard. Oh, he is a naughty boy; that's space for my horses.

Rob came over in the evening to celebrate Alan's birthday and bring him some presents. We had Rob's favourite tea, pasta jumble.

MAY 19TH

Jack Wood came for the day to help Alan. Have I told you who Jack is yet? It's a long story. I answered an advert in Irving's (our local tack shop), from a young girl who wanted to ride horses for someone. I was lucky really as she turned out to be a good rider. Most good riders have horses of their own. Anyway, she is a good little rider so this means that I can finish work on Angel. Angel is one of my young horses and was a beautiful accident. I looked after a stallion for a friend and well, you know, things happen. Eleven months later, Angel appeared and I considered her a real gift from God, hence the name Angel. She has the most amazing blood lines and is actually related to one of the Queen's horses.

We are blessed as we always seem to receive help when it is most needed. It somehow just turns up at the right time. Jack appeared just at the right time to help Alan set up the allotment and plant all the seedlings. It is very unusual to have a teenager that actually genuinely wants to help.

Sally and Missy, two rescue cats, went out for a play. I left the pen doors open as normal for their return. Missy was home by tea time. Sally, however, was not to be seen. I was in and out all night and suddenly saw her by the cattery. That little sod, Justin the cat, was sat guarding so she could not go into the cattery. I felt sure she would be in the cattery by morning. Nipped to the cattery first thing, but no Sally at this stage; I was unaware that this was the start of a mini-adventure!

23RD MAY

Kelly rang first thing, inviting me to go to a garden centre with her and Lexee. Went off and had a lovely time. Kelly is a very dear friend and we had a super time. The garden centre was massive and there were many other shops. I bought a yoghurt maker and can't wait to use it.

Put Alan's new heifers from Nantwich in with the herd and they settled really well. They are a couple of beauties. Alan certainly knows his animals.

Up the field with the girls and ponies, and as usual had a super time. There is little can compare with an afternoon up the field with my ponies. The weather was out of this world and it was like being in Heaven. I know that sounds a bit dramatic but that's how it can be at Rufford and this is what we are soon to lose. Mind you, when it's at its best, it feels like heaven but the opposite side of the coin is that it can also be hell. This is when the wind and rain lash down on me as I try to get about my daily chores, my feet steeped in mud that is the result of the poor drainage.

Sunday 24th May

I was a little disappointed today as I rode up on Jaffa to see my Ed and Wilma. Luckily, I arrived in time to find Wilma with a very badly placed numnah (this goes under the saddle and should keep the horse comfortable); the girls were fine and allowed me to adjust it before they went off. If a numnah is put on incorrectly then it can cause serious injury or, at the very least, discomfort to the horse. They asked me to join them on a hack, which I happily did. I was glad to have gone as my eyes were opened up a little. I felt sad for Wilma; she had just moved to a strange place and was then expected to go out on the roads with a complete novice in the saddle, who just sat as a passenger. I was very proud of Wilma, how she coped, but it left me uneasy. I went home a little unsettled and concerned for my horse. Although I had placed her with very kind people, I felt uneasy at the lack of experience I witnessed.

TUESDAY 26TH MAY

Over to Emma's for tea. Emma really spoils me and Alan when we go to her house; she always cooks us a delightful vegetarian meal and conjures up a lovely pudding. We really went to see her new rescue chickens. Emma is so proud of them and she is set to spoil them rotten. We were served the most delightful curry and a beautiful, home baked pudding.

MAY 27ᵀᴴ

Bill's birthday today. Bill is my sister's partner and he is an amazing cook, so off we went to their house for tea. Oh boy, what a meal as ever. Massive shepherd's pie that needed two people to lift it out of the oven. Bill always makes enough to feed 10 times the number of guests present. Well of course by the end of it I was stuffed to the hilt and felt really rough. It was worth it though but I will never eat so much again . . . .

Monday 1st June

Having received a phone call from Jo regarding fetching Wilma back, we set off early Monday to bring my baby home. I told Sara that, in light of Ed being 17, I would fetch him back if she would like. She decided she would like to have another week getting to know him. I felt very sad for Wilma who had gone to this holding on the back of many promises and none had been honoured, not one. The more ponies I loan out the more I become disillusioned. The only thing Wilma received from these people was to be frightened to death taking novices hacking on the roads. She had been taken on the roads without due care and caution. The riders just sat and let her get on with it as they knew no better. Thank goodness I went up by chance on the previous Saturday and witnessed what was going on with my own eyes. Had I not managed to witness the scenario, I would have had no choice but to accept their tales of Wilma's shortcomings. However, now I was happily aware that the only shortcomings belonged to the novice riders themselves. Don't get me wrong—lovely ladies, but they just didn't fulfil their promises to me. I am just so glad to have my baby home.

JUNE 2ND

Had a trip down to Derby to see Rob as it's his birthday tomorrow but I will be in hospital. I look forward to visiting Rob. We always have a lovely time and share the same joy of pizzas and "Coronation Street." Rob often saves me bits of telly he thinks I will enjoy; he's not got it wrong yet.

Holly, my sweet Jack Russell, had a bath and put her party dress on; oh, she did look pretty. Well, as I would be having a rest tomorrow, I thought I would tackle Rob's garden. I went at it like a possessed Alan Titchmarsh. I pulled up all the weeds in his garden and gave scant regard to the repercussions on my health!

We ate loads of pizza and watched "Coronation Street". Bliss! Sat a while and had some birthday cake and left for home.

June 3ʳᵈ

A busy morning preparing for my hospital visit. Made sure all animals were fed and watered and cleaned. Alan nipped me to Holmewood to see Carol as she had bought me some sweets and magazines. I must admit I am looking forward to relaxing. Having an operation provides an excuse to relax which is something I don't often do. Got to my hospital bed and, as I was nil by mouth, I had to suffer watching everyone eat dinner. That was like a form of torture. Had a little read then fell asleep. Later, the nurses wheeled me to the theatre and the next thing I knew I was back in the ward but had missed tea! Life can be a bitch at times. A nurse managed to find me a cheese sandwich.

I relaxed after a cup of tea and waited for Alan to come and see me. When he came the nurse said I could go home. I was so pleased, as much as I enjoy a little stay in hospital. My dogs went mad when I walked in the door. Home sweet home.

JUNE 8TH

I have been in agony since my operation. However, it's not my knee that is the problem, it's my back. Can't even use my arms, the pain is so intense. I was under an illusion that I had been thrown around on the operation table until I suddenly remembered the gardening I did at Rob's. I will never garden again as long as I live.

Trying to utilise spare time by packing and clearing stuff. Overdid it today and ended up unable to move by tea time. Not my knee of course but my wretched back. Oh, the joys of fybromyalgia. I think it's going to be weeks before my back recovers from my burst of gardening. I am annoyed with myself as I could have done without the extra pain on top of my operation. I will be more cautious in future.

Alan, bless his heart, has been looking after all my animals since my operation. I never worry when he is doing them as he is great and does a better job than I do. Luckily, he spotted a sick chicken and separated her from the flock. She looked very sickly and was placed in a comfortable warm bed, to see if she would rally. Late at night, I fetched her into the house and wrapped her in a blanket. I felt sure she was going to die within minutes. I left her cosy and peaceful as I went to bed. In the morning, I would get the surprise of my life, finding her perched on the side of the basket. I could not believe it.

Alan's dad is in hospital and we are actually discussing jumping into the farm house if anything should happen to him. Well, it is Alan's home after all and we are being rendered homeless by his father and nobody gives a damn. I feel awful with such plans but it has become clear that, to the rest of Alan's family, we are nothing. They are more than happy for us to be on the streets so as far as we are concerned we are now fighting for ourselves and will think nothing of how they feel about our actions. They are made of stone and I am sure they will denigrate us to the farming community even further. Do you know what? We don't care anymore!

I dreamt last night that we returned to Syda. All Alan's relatives were there and Alan and I were planning a takeover bid. His father was full of life and totally unaware of our plans. I woke after the dream and my nerves were in tatters. It does not do me any good at all and I feel like this step will push me over the edge. It needs to be done and the sooner the better.

June 11th

We have a Magpie on the farm that is causing havoc. It's bad enough that we have lost numerous fresh laid eggs to this bird. Yesterday, he upped the anti and trashed a little swallow nest and all its adorable contents. Alan wants to shoot it. I struggled with this idea until he started on the swallow nests. We reached a compromise, after lengthy debate. Alan and Jack constructed a trap made with a pair of braces and a cage. I do hope we catch him and then we can transport him away from our farm.

My chicken is getting better by the day, thanks to TLC and some antibiotics from the vet. With sustained and rapid progress, he will soon be returned to the flock. I have never seen a chicken so determined to live.

Well, God is sometimes so good to me. As I struggled through the day with the most painful of headaches, I ploughed on with a bit of packing and sorting. I suddenly stumbled upon an Easter Egg Tin. I rattled it and it had some contents. My brain reasoned that whatever was in it would be mouldy by now. I opened the tin gingerly and peered inside; I saw a large chunk of Easter egg. I was very upset that it had been left there to go off as it was Cadburys to boot. As I lifted the chocolate out of the tin, I realised that it was as fresh as the day I bought it. Well, that was a nice little interlude from cleaning and a break from my day of dieting. Oh, bliss.

My wonderful Uncle Paul is coming tonight and is due to arrive early evening. He has promised us fish and chips for tea. As things transpired, he was really late and looked so dehydrated when he arrived. I was cross as he had been travelling for nearly seven hours and had not had a drink. Anyway, chips for supper at 10.30.

12ᵀᴴ JUNE

Great start to the day! Post was early; it came just as I was about to go for a walk with my dear Uncle Paul and the girls. Anyway, I grabbed the mail and made the huge mistake of reading it. One was an unpleasant letter from our solicitor, who has already been paid £13,000 and yet still feels able to send Alan a letter giving him a good ticking off for writing personally to the land agents. Not only was Alan ticked off but another letter was enclosed from the land agents, stating their distress at Alan's missive. It's as if they are so special, Alan must not consider contacting them. Well as far as I am concerned, they are and never will be as special as my Alan. I was furious; this is the second time Alan has been "ticked off" by our solicitor and it will sure be the last if I have any say in the matter.

I must admit I was very upset and on top of this my little chicken gave up the fight for life. I had left her in the sunshine and as I looked out the window I saw her suffer a massive heart attack. I ran to her and she died as I held her in my arms. I was choked up and ready for a good old sob. Could not indulge; I had to get in uncle's car and go to have the stitches taken out of my knee. Uncle chatted to me as the tears rolled down my cheeks. I'm not sure if uncle noticed but, if he did, then he pretended not to.

I feel very depressed tonight. It's just that my head has been pulled out of the sand again and it's scary! I climbed the stairs to bed with such a heavy heart and weary limbs. I felt very low and stifled the tears as, thankfully, I fell quickly to sleep.

JUNE 13TH

The time is 5.30 am and I am wide awake. I raid a box of Viennese Whirls and down a hot chocolate. I wondered why we are being put through the things we are experiencing. Especially Alan; farming has been his life and all he knows. He is such a gentle person and is beginning to look tired and weary of all this nastiness. It also concerns me that I have eaten the whole box of Viennese Whirls. Can I really let my uncle know I have such a lack of willpower? I decided to put the empty box in the dog bed and let him make his own conclusion.

JUNE 14TH

I went to Hasland Gala with Rob and our uncle. I knew I should not have gone but life is too short to rest. It was a fabulous, sunny day. Holly got her first ever prize in the dog show, 'best terrier'. She came fourth, although obviously she is best ever to me. She did me proud as she pranced around the ring. Came back so tired I could have slept forever. Gosh, that would solve a few problems, wouldn't it?

Well, so much for being too tired to live! Alan checked on our heifer and she was starting to calve. Oh no, not tonight! Somehow managed to drag myself up the field three times. It's a boy; I knew that straight away as its head was too big to come out. Our heifer was brilliant and made so little fuss; I was humbled. Alan went to fetch the ratchet. Out came the little boy and Carol, the heifer, was a proud mum. She licked and nuzzled the calf and even sucked his ear like it was a delicious lollipop.

Off to bed shattered and unable to do another thing (oh, except eat a beautiful piece of chocolate cake). Off I went to bed and fell into a deep sleep.

June 15th

Woke up remembering I had left the remains of the chocolate cake on the kitchen side. I rushed down hoping that the dogs would not have spotted it. Alan was already down there wondering where all the cake crumbs had come from. Really, I know I have a terrible reputation regarding cakes and biscuits, but this time it was not me!

Alan had to hand-milk Carol as the calf had not drunk any milk. I held her on the end of the halter. She was so good, bless her. As Alan milked, I was filled with sadness. This was a heifer we were going to keep and unfortunately she had become too much quality for her own good. Not only did she look beautiful but she had produced so much milk, we had to find someone to take her from us. My heart broke as I thought the days of separating babies from mums had gone. Alan had no choice for she would have become ill from having too much milk. She has gone to a lovely farm up the road. Within an hour, they milked her to relieve her discomfort and brought the colostrums back down for the calf. From feeling very sad I was elated that she has gone to such caring people. We are getting regular updates and the new owners adore her. Colostrums refer to the first milk that the calf must ingest within eight hours; this ensures the calf receives the vital antibodies necessary for survival.

June 16th

Lovely morning. I walked the dogs in brilliant sunshine. Decided that I would take Rob and uncle to town for a coffee. The postman pulled up as we were leaving. I wish he hadn't. Opened a letter from the Prodigal Son, you know the one who stole the family business three times—now he parades around under the guise of a born again Christian (lol). He is also known as 'four weddings and a funeral'. He's had that many wives, we've lost count. Anyway you can see the contents of the letter for yourself.

Unfortunately, I am easily intimidated by such things. I slowly calmed down when I realised that everyone else around me thought it was a hilarious letter.

> Dear Alan
>
> As an indication of the potentially catastrophic consequences of what is proposed within this letter, I shall use Dad's initials throughout this letter.
>
> It would appear that the point has now been reached where a negotiated settlement appears impossible. I suggested to SES that before he moves to force closure you should be made aware of his intentions. Albeit reluctantly, SES is now

ready to act, in order he can move on with his business.

The first issue is that a lack of agreement remains over the residue monies from the sale of the farmhouse. You probably know that there are only two ways that a closure can be brought about.

a. Negotiated settlement
b. A decision taken by the courts

In February 2009, an offer was made included all the stock and dead stock withdrawn by you from the farm sale on August 30th 2006. In addition there was to be a single cash payment of £25,000. It is SES understanding that £15,000 has already been passed to your solicitor. As there was no response by the deadline the offer has now been withdrawn. As SES feels he has made every effort to reach an agreement and can provide the necessary evidence he alone should be the recipient of the remaining monies.

The second issue is that since he found you had attached your name to the deeds of the land at Syda SES has asked that this be removed. There has been no movement in this issue either. Unless this is done immediately, he will, as a partner in the partnership you will not currently allow to be wound up, apply to the courts in an effort to retrieve the value of the stock and machinery. He maintains that both were taken without permission or knowledge. Again this action will be taken reluctantly but will be taken by SES.

As a brother, I feel the need to express my own, albeit non-professional opinion on these issues for what they are worth.

Although the exact number of animals withdrawn form the farm sale has been requested on several occasions, this has not been forthcoming. The animal movement sheet suggests a total of 42 animals were actually disposed between 1st September 2006 and 18th September 2007, or an attempt was made to do so. In addition to these, the ownership of 29 animals was transferred to the name of A E and V A Shirt. It is suggested that the value of these animals could be set at an average of £425, a realistic value of livestock therefore being perhaps £30,000; taking into account age breeding and pedigree.

I feel that as you either sold or transferred the ownership from SES and Sons to V A and A E Shirt without informing SES, may be construed as a fraudulent act. That you sold 9 animals two days after the sale and kept all the proceeds can only add further cadence to this belief.

I urge you to consider closely the above and be in no doubt over two things. The decision made by SES to press for court actions has not been taken lightly; you are, after all, his son. But neither are they empty threats. He feels the time has come to bring closure on what was never going to be a pleasant task. He has tried to do it through negotiation but this has failed. Please seek the counsel of your solicitor at the earliest opportunity to avoid either of these actions taking on a life of its own and causing additional stress to the parties involved.

<u>This is the funny bit</u>

Whatever you may think of my agenda within all this, let me assure you I am acting out of a sense of wellbeing for my father. I have tried to remain impartial throughout but I have to agree with him on the simple fact it is time a line be drawn underneath what has been almost three years.

Your brother
<u>Geoff</u>

Cows at Syda

Hope and Mimi resting

Gin's home made Stollen

Crunchy, my favourite old cow

17TH JUNE

My missing cat, Sally, has been spotted and worryingly this is on the other side of the road. I made a mercy dash to Matlock, to fetch a cat trap. I have to trap her before she has an accident crossing the road. Anita, my friend, provided me with a trap and a cup of coffee. Uncle and I decided to go to the saddle shop but I took him the wrong way. Not to worry, we had a lovely drive through some unspoilt countryside. I found myself feeling rather up and down. I am very vulnerable as I feel totally out of control of my own destiny. I hate change of any sort and try to avoid it at all cost. It seems I am so often forced into change, whether I like it or not. I thought back to my childhood, losing my dad. Why did I have to lose my dear father when I was only nine years old? Sometimes life just seems unfair. I try not to moan but I just feel scared at what will happen next. My family was singled out to suffer tragedy when we were all so young. My mum became a widow when just forty. I know that terrible things can and do happen. But over the years events have taken place that, ordinarily, I would have said, "That would never happen to us." I looked around the countryside at the pretty farms. I felt sad that I was soon about to lose my beautiful farm through no fault of my own.

Alan has a farmer calling today about purchasing some mowing grass. We are trying to get as much money in as we can in order to be prepared for the move. I asked God to give me a sign; if the grass is sold when I get home, our future is good. If not, I am doomed. Guess what? The grass was sold and life is looking good.

I waved my dear uncle off on his journey back to London. I hate it when he goes; I hate it so much that I'm not sure he should even visit. Is that not the craziest thing? I just wish he could come and live at the farm with us; he makes a nice cup of tea and lots of them!

I placed the cat trap across the road for Sally. I was in and out all night and she was always sitting beside it. Her little eyes were shining in the dark. I went across with Rob to put a cover over it, as it was raining. Sally kept running up the field, away from us, when we went over. By the early hours, she was not in the trap so I had to go to bed.

18TH JUNE

What a vision! I saw Alan walking across the yard carrying a cat trap. I could tell by how he struggled that the cat was in it! Oh, I was so pleased to see Sally and we hastily reunited her with her sister. Sally just wanted love, food and a warm bed. Never have I seen a cat so happy to be home. It is the strangest thing that she could not get herself home. I know she was a feral kitten yet she was brought up from a kitten as a domestic pet. I can only assume that the feral gene had kicked in during stress and remained in action until we caught her.

Alan sold my lovely Rover car to the scrap man. It was such a lovely car and, as I cleaned it out, Annie and Meg decided to go in and have a sleep. I had to fetch Annie in at midnight. The car was our mobile kennel when it was on the road. We had some amazing fun in it. The two dogs used to guard it like it was a house. If anyone approached it, they would go mad and the car would bounce off the floor. People used to laugh when they saw it. I always felt so safe when I was out in the Rover with my guards. Mind you, I also knew that, should we have an accident, nobody would be able to help me! Well today the car was gone, but not the many many memories of the very special lady who bought the car originally. That was my darling mum.

When I inherited the car, I did not know how to cope with it. I wanted to keep it in pristine condition, yet I seem to be unable to do this with my lifestyle. So I made my mind up that I would enjoy this car and drive it into the ground (with the help of my dogs, of course). I knew that mum would look down from Heaven and enjoy me enjoying myself with her car. The morning the car was going, I went out to it secretly. I kissed the car goodbye and thanked it for the fun we had shared.

I sent out several press releases to the tabloids. Someone must be interested in what is going on here. Now I just have to sit back and wait. I have also phoned several MEPs, but they don't seem to be too much help (so much for their espousal of human rights). Today we received confirmation from Chatsworth House Estate that we have until September to vacate the home we have lived in together since we married. It is a massive contract.

As yet, I refuse to sign it. We keep being told we have no rights so why should we have to sign anything? Why, to sign away the few rights we do have, I suppose. They must think we're idiots.

We discovered tonight that Alan has lost a small black case that contains the majority of his evidence against his father. We are both frantic as we can only assume it has gone to the charity shops. Some of this evidence spans thirty years so you can imagine how upset we are. Alan normally photocopies everything, but not this time! God help us. We have taken a lot of boxes to local charity shops so it will be impossible to trace the missing black case.

28TH JUNE

Well the time had to come; I went into mum's bedroom and started the much dreaded task of sorting her stuff. I don't speak much to anyone about the loss of my mum, my best friend. I only speak to close family and friends, so those reading this diary will be unaware of my loss. Just to let you know that she was the most precious person in my life and it took a long time to come to terms with her going. So stepping into mum's shrine was difficult and something I was intending to do another day, a long way off. Of course, that day would probably never have come so maybe this is why God is turning my life upside down. Only good can really come of it.

I walked into her bedroom and sobbed; the memories of her sitting up in bed with her cup of tea came flooding back. I read all the poems I had written to her, realising my words must have made her feel adored. I cried but managed a hearty laugh when I read words Alan had written in her birthday card:

Roses are red
Violets are blue
Just my luck
To get a mother in law like you

I laughed at the thought of her reading it. She had a great sense of humour and a funny little laugh. I still miss her every waking moment and I know I always will.

We dragged mum's bed to the front door and loaded it into the cattle wagon. When we moved mum up to Rufford House, we moved her in the cattle wagon. Well, not mum actually but all her furniture and belongings. What a wonderful time that was. She was at bingo while we arranged all her furniture into her little south wing.

Went to Derby to deliver the bed to Rob, for which we were well rewarded. You guessed it, pizza. We sat in his garden and tucked in as the cool night air embraced us. Home late as usual. I closed the door on mum's bedroom again, replacing the barrier to my other world. I will have to try and keep doing bits in there; otherwise it will become a place of fear again. Fear sounds an awful word to use about my mum's room. But my feelings are of fear, fear of opening the wounds again, fear of the pain and the sadness and, most of all, fear of my loss fully manifest again.

JUNE 30TH

We went to Tesco at Clowne to replace our sanctuary poster. Each time it is put up, it gets removed by someone on the same day. It reduces the amount of cat food donated, as this leaves only a poster for a nearby dog rescue.

Katie, my sister, and her family came up for a cream tea of sorts. It was only spray cream so it was not as authentic as it should have been. We munched away in the front garden. A lovely evening in the sunshine.

July 1st

Woke at 5am and came down for a cup of tea. A load on my mind and time is running out for us at the farm. I walked up the field with Holly, as the rest of the girls slept. Bailey, the rescue Siamese, walked up with us, as did Hoppy, one of my first rescue cats. Dear little kitten found in a cardboard box. The box had been thrown into the middle of the road. He walked with a limp, which is how he got his name. We all watched the Sun rise over the farm. Yes, I did shed tears at this beautiful sight and I soaked it up into my heart to take with me wherever I end up. I took a picture as well! Velvet the pony joined us too. She came to us as her new owner did not know about horses at all. Why did he buy her, I hear you ask? She came free with a house purchase!

I took Alan a cup of tea in bed and then I fell into a really deep sleep. Woops! Woke later with a headache and went with Alan to check on the new calves. Black Girl and her little boy were there, but Carol's little boy had gone and joined next door's herd. Carol's little boy just follows anything that is black and white. We went in the Land Rover to fetch him back. He was really hungry and stuck to Black Girl like glue. He's been really good since but we have to keep checking.

As we are trying to clear the house, we are trying to do a few car boots. We managed to get over to Barlborough and set out a really good stall. It was also a desperate attempt to sell off our back log of duck eggs. Well, the only thing we did not know is that folk in Barlborough don't actually spend any money. It was the hardest job we have ever done. Managed to make a meagre £7. Oh well, afterwards we headed for a carvery; this kind of made up for our wasted efforts but also, of course, swallowed up our meagre earnings.

Alan spent the evening looking for his little black case. I joined him and we both came to the same conclusion—it was not in the house. I went outside as the Sun set and sobbed. Could we have any more go wrong? "Please God," I asked, "no more, please."

I went into the house as I choked back the tears; we sat on the bed and hung our heads in despair. Suddenly it came to me! I remembered the solicitor making a funny remark to Alan as we walked into his office. "What's Alan got in his little box today?" I remembered it because I felt it was said in a rather sarcastic manner.

"Alan think," I said, "was it the little black case?"

Alan decided it could possibly be. It would make sense and yet he could not be certain. My mind was put a little to rest as I felt sure it was that black case. The strange case of the missing case brought home to me the massive strain that Alan is under. He never forgets anything; he always knows where everything is. It upset me to think we have such anguish and yet the case is no doubt safe with the solicitor.

FRIDAY JULY 3

The rate at which time is passing is incredible. I feel like I am on death row at the moment. Not a nice feeling at my time of life. And Alan, having worked like a pack horse all his life, should be enjoying a quiet time. He just enjoys his life so much and asks for so little it hurts to see him pawing over papers and evidence and phoning to find his witnesses. I long for the day we can just sit back and be. It's hard to watch his life's work dripping away through the hate-fuelled hands of his father.

Saturday 4th July

Our wedding anniversary today. 11 years married which makes my darling dog, Annie, 11 years old. Good age for a Great Dane, I am told. I always remember when Annie came to us shortly after we married. You just never forget the arrival of your first born! To think I was constantly informed that 6 would be a good age for her to reach. I have worried ever since! Here I am, 11 years later with my beautiful dog, my faithful friend.

I was also told:
Not to walk her until she was one year old
Not to give her milk
Not to give her eggs.

Naughty things we have given Annie

Walks every day, very long ones, twice a week since her arrival
Milk with an egg in every day
Chips
Fresh fruit scones (don't try this at home as a vet told me fruit
    poisons dogs)
Fruit cake
Regular cups of tea
A seat on the sofa with the humans.

I was not even going to consider going for walks and leaving my puppy at home. Hence, we enjoyed numerous long walks together, sometimes being out for two hours or more. This was right from puppy-hood. I got a dog to go walking with and walking we did. She would even accompany me and my horse, as we galloped around the fields.

We gave Annie milk and eggs to strengthen her bones and give her extra calcium. I have to say that my Annie has never had so much as a day's illness, lameness or otherwise. She has a scone or piece of homemade cake every night before bed. She likes a cup of tea and a plate of homemade chips. She has had what I consider a great time and has now reached the autumn of her life. She is now in a declining stage due to her advanced years. We have lived life to the full, Annie and I. She has nursed me through the most terrible loss of my life and she has protected me from anyone she considered a danger to me.

When I was grieving for my dear mum, Annie detected that a person I considered a friend was actually not. She had known my neighbour for two years and had gotten on well with her. I remember hearing her arrive at a time I did not want to see her. Although I was at the other end of the large house, Annie would not let my neighbour in. I can remember hearing her growling loudly. I heard my neighbour pleading, "It's me Annie, it's me."

Annie knew who she was and like me had realised she was not the friend we thought she was. Annie had detected that I did not want her near me at that time. My neighbour had to leave the house. This left me in no doubt that she would look after all my needs for as long as she was here. It is now my turn to nurse her with pleasure as she reaches her twilight years. As I write this, her fresh chicken is simmering gently as she awaits her special breakfast.

As I watch her stumbling clumsily around the farm it makes me so very sad. She has always walked beside me as a protector. Now I walk beside her as her protector.

July 7th to London and back

After hearing my dearest Uncle Paul had been taken ill again, we were up early and on our way to London. I had spoken to uncle's neighbour last night. She told me uncle was incapable of looking after himself. The way she described his living conditions so frightened me, we were off to see for ourselves (having already discussed trying to get him to come home with us if need be).

On route I phoned the solicitor regarding the mystery of the black case. Oh thank the Lord, they have it! I looked up to the sky and made the sign of the cross, "Thank you, God."

The trip to London was poignant as so many events in my life seem to be. We spent all our childhood holidays down here with Nan and Granddad and all mum's lovely brothers. I had not been to London since dear mum had passed over. I could not. It was strange as we travelled through the leafy suburbs. I had a permanent lump in my throat. On reaching Uncle Paul's house, another uncle, Shaun, met us at the door. It is 30 years or more since I have walked through the doors of this house! Anyway his neighbour had exaggerated terribly. Uncle's house was just fine and it is clear, although he may not be feeding himself as well as he could, he is keeping his house in good order and the cat is well fed. Uncle is obviously not controlling his diabetes very well.

The rain poured in buckets as the three of us made our way to the hospital to see Uncle Paul. I was so looking forward to seeing him. He looked thin and vulnerable and he slurred his words; I was a little shocked. After he had warmed up, my lovely Uncle Paul started to shine through. Stayed an hour or two then made our way back home to our beautiful dogs.

It will have been a very long and confusing day for them as we rarely leave them for more than a couple of hours. Thank goodness for my good friends, who have periodically called at the house throughout the day. If not for them, I don't think we would have dared go for so long. I have worried about Annie so much, I just long to see her face. I know we don't have long together now. I just pray nothing will go wrong when I leave her. It is so rare for us to leave the dogs for any length of time. It's hard when we do; I wonder how they feel about it?

Our usual greeting of wagging tails and cuddly toys thrust upon us, as welcoming gifts. It was good to be home. I do nothing but fret about my Annie while I am away from her. Crawled wearily to bed, pleased with our day.

THURSDAY 9ᵀᴴ JULY
WEEKEND IN NORWICH

What a week! Today I am off to Norwich to the Redwings Horse Sanctuary for a training weekend. I work for Redwings as a Support Field Officer. I cover Derbyshire and surrounding areas on any welfare reports regarding horses. I love the work I do and they give us regular training weekends, which are great. All expenses paid and we are treated so well.

Got up early and noticed Annie was tinged with yellow. I was shocked and upset and I really did not want to go away now. I went straight to the vet and he told me what I did not want to hear and yet I already knew what I would be told. I took my precious dog home and knew our time together would be short now.

Hated leaving to go to Redwings. I know Alan will take great care of Annie but I so wanted to be at home with her. Had I known how depressed I would become I would not have gone. I stifled tears all the way to Norwich and felt my heart slowly breaking. I went into the depths of despair at the thought of not having Annie in my life. I have worried about this for many years and now the time is nearing.

Everyone was in a pair at the training weekend, except me. I worked hard to remain positive throughout but found it difficult, especially when the coach drove off without me on one occasion (shows what presence I must have!). Felt a bit unloved at times. While I was busy I felt ok but once I went to my hotel room alone, I became very down without Annie. Annie was in my thoughts the whole time and I could not bear the thought of life without her. I missed home terribly and wondered if I would survive two whole days.

I enjoyed my active time at Redwings immensely but golly I was so pleased when I was on my way home. Alan and Holly picked me up at the station. The girls were pleased to see me; Annie was just as I had left her.

12TH JULY

Well it never ends does it? Me, Jack, Beth off to the Sheffield Dog Rescue Annual Dog Show. We did a brilliant tombola with a prize every time. We had got together 80 prizes last night, a mammoth task but we did it. I just had to wonder round the house a dozen times, collecting things from the shelves. It was a great day and we raised nearly £100 pounds for the sanctuary (not bad for bits and bobs). A long but satisfying day!

Alan went to a sale and bought two containers for us. He got them very cheap and was well pleased. One of them has a sink and fires in and Alan has the idea we are going to live in it! I really am not sure if he is serious. Carol thinks it's a great idea but said the dogs should live separately. Well there is no chance of that as my dogs will be beside me always. They are my guardians and my best friends and will live where I live. Although the containers are waterproof and warm and dry I am not really sure if I would want to live in one. At least we have a place to store our belongings, which has taken a lot off my mind.

20ᵀᴴ July

I was unaware when I woke up that this was to be the last day I would share with my Annie. I was as thrilled as ever to see her face when I walked into the kitchen. I was painfully aware of how tired she had become. She was tiring more with each passing day. I was just happy to see her each morning looking around to greet me. Her greetings had altered dramatically but they were still greetings, very special ones at that. I noticed also that over the last couple of weeks her urine has become very dark orange. I have seen this before with Cassie (my brother's lovely canine companion for all too short a time). I know the stages now; I know we don't have long. But I never thought it would be today.

Robbie came to see Annie as he had said he would. Annie's auntie, Lynne, came to see her. Only up till last week, Auntie Lynne had brought a little green bag into the kitchen on each visit. The bag would contain dog treats. Annie would spend the whole time fetching the bag off the table. She would drop it on the floor to make Lynne give her a treat. It worked every time and Annie always got extra treats.

I took Annie on her last walk across the yard to her favourite water trough at 11pm. I splashed the water onto her mouth and urged her to have her favourite drink. She was breathing very heavily. I regretted taking her across the yard. I guided her back to the house and she fell on her bed. She lay down and gasped for breath. Within minutes my best friend was gone. Her passing was as I had prayed for it. We were with her. It was quick and that is all I wanted. It seems only fitting that she started her life with us at Rufford House Farm and she finished it with us at Rufford. I could not ask for more.

My thoughts turned to little Meg; her mummy and her dearest friend was gone. She wagged her tail as she looked on, waiting for Annie to get up. My heart bled for Meg as she struggled to understand what had just happened and why her mummy was not getting up. In the morning, Meg and I looked on at our dear Annie. It was time to bury her on the farm where she belonged. We made sure Meg watched the burial. She watched but still looked out for Annie on the horizon for many days. Don't let anyone ever tell me that animals do not grieve.

JULY 25TH

First thing, off to Derby Market at what we both considered an early time of morning. However, when we got to the market, everyone was well under way with buying and selling horse tack. I placed all my tack at the end of the row ready for auction. As we were last, I did not hold out much hope for making any money. Not only that, we had to stand around for many hours. I was shattered and my knees hurt badly. They were constantly locking as I walked or stood. By the time our tack was finally auctioned, most people had gone off to watch the pony auction. We were disappointed by the results and had to bring a lot of tack home again. We could have sold Holly ten times over! Rob came to see us at the market and we all had chip butties. It was then time to part company, to make our respective ways home.

On returning home, I was immediately up to the ménage for my Saturday riding club. Alan, Jack and Blake burnt all the old accounts and letters from the farm business up to 1986. That was a good job done. Alan was really pleased about getting this done. It leaves loads of boxes for packing our goods and chattels.

JULY 30TH

A sad day for me yet again. Had to clear all mum's wardrobes, etc., in order to take them down to Robbie. I found the task poignant and therapeutic in many ways. It is work well done and will help me to unburden my soul a little. I found it hard to pack her clothes into black bags. Mum had so many beautiful clothes and many of them still had the price labels on them (i.e. unworn). I kept a couple of mum's dresses for myself.

As I sorted through the clothes, I visualised her walking about in her favourite dresses. I found the little track suit that my sister bought mum to keep her warm one winter. She was not confident enough to wear it as she thought she looked silly. In actual fact she looked really cute but, as warm and cosy as she felt, she could not wear it. I will wear it this winter in my mobile home.

I felt sure that the clothes in the black bags would bring great pleasure to the charity shop's shoppers. Mum's clothes will make ladies very happy as they will be able to buy elegant clothes for little money. That thought comforted me so much and I know it would make mum happy too. My mum was a lovely, kind, giving person, so I know she will look down and get pleasure from seeing others benefiting with her lovely clothes.

Hospital at 3.15pm, only to find my knee operation had revealed a broken bone. The doctor was very matter-of-fact when she told me that, if the pain got too much, I could have a new knee. Oh well, that's ok then!

Later, we went to see a solicitor to make our will. It was very complicated so we simply put it three ways. It was vital we had a will in case something happened to us before the court case is sorted out. If we died now his father, brother and sister would be laughing all the way to the bank. Not now they won't! Whether we are dead or alive, the fight will go on.

When you consider that these people have made two separate attempts to seriously injure me, or worse, it is paramount that our will is in place, especially as we have to set up residence next to the father-in-law! It will be a dangerous but unavoidable manoeuvre.

We have very little to leave at this moment in time but the horses are my main concern; when I die, they will become part of my estate and sold off the same as a car, house, etc. Robbie knows that they are to be found safe, caring homes, if I have nothing else in place at the time of my death.

AUGUST 2ND

Bakewell and Ashover shows are looming. I cannot believe the speed at which they have come around. This is very scary as the nearer these two shows become the nearer I am to becoming homeless. Amy is practising hard for her 'in hand class' with my beautiful Angel. Angel is doing really well also. We are all getting very excited. The Ashover Show is my yearly event and has been for several years now. There is just something so wonderful about being part of this lovely show. Ashover show is a real farmer's show with many interesting and affordable stalls. I just love to ride my horse at this show. We have never won anything but I really feel that, at this show, just taking part is amazing. You bump into all your friends (oh and enemies) and everyone has a good time.

I am working hard to get Bella ready for the show. Last year I entered her into the riding horse class. We had a ball and came second from the last. I enjoyed myself so much, showing my lovely horse off to the spectators. The only thing that let my horse down was when the judge got on her. She suddenly became a donkey and moved for him rather grudgingly. Having said that, she did everything he asked, but wearily. The judge yawned as he pulled up in the centre of the ring. I knew exactly why and mentally logged to have her full of oats for the following year. The following year is now here and she is well corned up.

Each night, I can be seen trotting and galloping around the field until we are both huffing and puffing. I am going to get this horse fit if it kills me, and it probably will! My knees are crying out in pain as we canter round. Who cares? You know what they say, "no pain, no gain". That is certainly true of my life; if ever I give in to pain, that will be the end of Gin Shirt.

Received a tip from Sara at the Hayloft horse shop. She suggested I give Bella a bar of chocolate just before entering the ring. Good tip by the sounds of it. I have a Double Decker on standby in the fridge.

Carol and I have cleaned Beatrice, the lorry. My little lorry is home from home and the best investment I ever made. She is a Bedford TK and over 35 years old. She attracts men, like bees round a honey pot. At first I thought the men were hanging around, having caught a glimpse of me. I felt sure that I must be getting more attractive with age. I was a bit deflated when I found it was my old lorry pulling them in.

I have to say she is rather beautiful and so many of these men want to buy her from me. The only reason I bought her was that I could make a cup of tea and a full breakfast inside the cab.

I have spent the last couple of weeks teaching Angel to load into the lorry. It's gone really well and I am totally surprised at how good she is. I started by just walking her up the lorry ramp for a bucket of feed. We did this for a couple of nights and then tied her in and shut the small doors. She was wonderful; we then eventually turned on the engine. The engine had a profound effect, as she raised her head in fear. She soon settled and was fine.

The next step was to take her for a drive, which was very scary for us both. I am not known to have the best nerves in the world around horses, especially when they are in and out of lorries. Anyway we went up to the Highwayman pub and turned back. That was about a mile and she was great. Felt elated on returning home, as Angel is, I feel, ready for Bakewell!

AUGUST 4TH

Sad day today as I had to attend a funeral. A dear friend's husband had died suddenly. I did not know him but needed to attend for the support of my friend. Like most people I do not like funerals but it was a moving service. However, at the actual internment, the rain and wind lashed at the mourners. The priest read out a lovely poem that brought tears to the eyes of most of us. The poetry brought dear Annie to my heart. I felt choked and so wanted to cry out. Held in the tears and carried on with a big lump in my throat.

Had a sit, a natter, a nice cup of tea and piece of cake at the church. Sat till my bum was sore and then hobbled out of the church. We went to Maureen's house for a cuppa and she presented me with £153 from her husband's funeral collection. I was overwhelmed and humbled. This has never happened before and it made me realise how valued the animal sanctuary is in the community—even if my wealthy and esteemed landlord wants none of it, and will see it shut down.

Mary and Amy bathed Angel till you could eat your dinner off her back. She looked amazing and was so well behaved I was rather shocked. I found I could not take my eyes off Angel as she hung her head over the stable door, chomping on Alan's beautiful hay. The excitement is mounting for the Bakewell show.

All Amy's family stayed overnight prior to the show. It was a pleasant bedlam in the farm house. Made supper and we all turned in to get some sleep.

August 7th
Bakewell Show

6am and all systems go. Everyone had a specific job to do on the morning, so we would get to the show on time. It will be Angel's first (of many) shows.

7am and for the first time ever in my life we left the farm on schedule. We were all very excited. We managed to get Angel across the mud filled yard; amazingly, she stayed clean and this gave us great expectations about the day ahead. Mind you, there was that much mud we had to put various rugs and blankets down for her to walk over. All her early training had paid off; all those weeks of walking her over bags on the ground, etc. It is only now I am beginning to see the results of my hard work.

As we trundled along in the lorry all was calm and well. That was until suddenly all hell broke loose in the back as Angel kicked violently on the sides of the vehicle. With the speed I could muster, I put on my hazard lights and then proceeded to make my way into a complete panic as I yelled for Amy to comfort the horse. I was on the 'thirteen bends', a stretch of road leading to Bakewell. The road contains, you guessed it, thirteen bends. I wracked my brains as to where I could pull over as Angel pounded at the sides of the lorry. Suddenly, she stopped and enjoyed the comfort of Amy's strokes across her head. I carried on with the journey and was surprised how quickly I calmed back down. Obviously something had frightened her and we figured it was a strap from her rug that had come undone, touching her legs and leading to unease. She can be a little over reactive, can that little mare. I wonder where she gets it from!

Arriving at the show, all was well apart from Angel being rather sweaty. She had also caused cuts to her hocks from kicking. All the lorries apart from my Beatrice had to be towed into the grounds. The ground was squelching with the rain that had fallen. Tying Angel to the lorry, we proceeded to make her look beautiful again. As I scrubbed and brushed and smothered Angel in chalk powder, I vowed I would never do another coloured class again.

As we dashed towards the ring at 8.30am, as instructed, the mud splashed up against Angel's beautiful white socks. By the time we reached the ring, the horse was covered in it. Well, everyone appeared to be in the same boat so it wasn't so bad. We dashed to the ring in anticipation; how would Angel and Amy perform together? We were surprised to find there was a coloured class well underway and, as we waited for the next class, Angel was a little fidgety. On entering the next class it became apparent that the judge was only going through the motions when looking at Angel. Super sleuth Gin Shirt got to the bottom of the problem with speed. It turns out we were in the wrong class. It was such a shame as I had never seen Amy work so hard with such good results. She worked her little socks off and showed Angel to the maximum. Yet another lesson learned.

Once the pressure was off, we enjoyed a look around the wet and sludgy show ground. Later on, the Sun came out and the weather took a turn. If anything it became a little too hot. Alan drove us home and Angel was pleased to return to her herd.

AUGUST 8TH

Off to Derby market a little earlier this week. I got my tack hung up nice and early. Called Rob to see if he wanted to join us for the morning. Rob arrived, so we were able to sit about sipping tea and eating ice creams. My knee was killing me and frankly I was too tired to live (yet again!). It was a struggle but I really enjoyed myself. Alan ambled around the tools and awaited the sale of his drills and other uninteresting implements. Everything sold well and, better still, Alan managed to buy a diesel generator for our mobile home. This was great and left me feeling a little happier about our move. Alan was well chuffed with his purchase. Late getting home. I had to dash straight up to the riding club for lessons. By the end of this fruitful, busy day, I was nick knacked!

I noticed the pregnant queen in the cattery was a little restless. I am hoping she is going to have her kittens tonight.

MONDAY 10ᵀᴴ AUGUST

Luckily it was a beautiful day for Carol and Amy to bath the horses ready for the Ashover show. Feeding the cats, I noticed the pregnant queen had disappeared. I knew exactly where to look and opened up the large cat kennel. Low and behold, there she was, curled up with four of the sweetest kittens I ever did see. They are so cute and the queen (Daisy) was so proud of her brood. The whole farm is buzzing with excitement around the new arrivals.

Robbie home in preparation for Ashover. As per usual, my lemon curd was a last minute rush and I knew it was far too runny to receive a prize. It was a pretty colour made with free range eggs from my own chickens. There is nothing nicer than using your own eggs from your very own chickens. I went with Jack to the allotment to pick our show peas. We hadn't a clue what constitutes a good show pea! My show eggs were a last minute collection of freshly laid eggs from the hen house.

I had actually been collecting my best eggs for three weeks prior to the show. I had a good selection for the mixed section and kept them hidden in a half dozen egg box. I had a pretty white one and a deep brown one along with a rare blue egg and more. However, upon finding my show eggs missing one night, it turns out Alan had sold then to Doris, our dear friend and egg customer. It crossed my mind to ring her just to see if she had eaten them. I decided not to and managed to collect a last minute but inferior collection. Oh well, it's only for fun, and you get free entry tickets to the show ground!

Alan was busy panicking about his red wine exhibit. He had entered last year and came first. He was so amazed as he had never made wine before. Mind you all our friends went mad over it. It was the nicest wine I ever tasted. It was so rich and fruity. Alan decided that he would bow out at the top and was not going to enter this year. Well bow out at the top my foot; I made sure to enter him in the red wine section again.

"It doesn't matter if I don't come anywhere," he said as he was frantically trying to find a cork that would fit the bottle. Rob and I suggested that the plastic one would do, as it was only for fun. But apparently it had to be cork or it wasn't right. Rob and I made a mercy dash to Miss Metta's. Miss Metta is our tiny little wine making friend, the one who prays for us all the time. She is so little, she is like a doll. She is Malaysian and is the finest of friends. Of course, she came to the rescue and gave us some corks to fit the bottle. She even gave us a demonstration of how to use it. I was alarmed when she started banging on the bottle with a lump hammer.

We dashed back home and Alan finished getting his bottle of wine ready, cork in place. The presentation was complete. Next, our annual dash to the Ashover show ground at 11pm. You have to put out your exhibits the night before the show. We were rather too late and, to our horror, the horticulture tent was closed up. Refusing to accept defeat at this stage, we decided to sneak into the tent undetected, to place our produce and of course collect our tickets for the show. Yes, it did cross our minds to nobble the competition but we walked away, resisting the urge. Oh, the stuff of which murder mystery is made.

Fell into bed, unable to function another moment.

ASHOVER SHOW

Managed to oversleep by one hour; jumped out of bed in shock. Pain seared through my body as I forced it in to action without warning. One thing my body needs when getting out of bed is time. Time to be gently nurtured into action. I had no time today, so the pain barrier had to be penetrated urgently!

I grumbled that nobody else had arrived, only to find that everyone was busy around the farm when I emerged through the back door. Oh well, how was I to know?

Started up the lorry with anticipation; she roared alive with two turns of the key. The rain fell heavily and looked to be set in for the day. It did not matter, I was still happy. I feel the rain equalises everyone rather. Everyone is wet and looks about the same.

Alan hitched up the cattle wagon for Dusty, our little pony that Amy was to ride. The hours we have put in getting Amy and the pony on the same wavelength is no one's business. They clicked last night; the little pony managed to canter on command, with the correct leading leg. Dusty was a little naughty loading, but we eventually got her in. Ed and Bella were brilliant to load, as expected.

The lorry was full to bursting; those who had no tickets lay low in the cab. The journey to the show ground was exciting, as I love to drive my little lorry. She is so old and so beautiful and thrilling to drive. The back of the lorry on show days becomes a changing room and a small café.

Optimism remained intact despite getting the lorry stuck in the mud. With lots of pushing and revving, Alan eventually took to the wheel and the lorry was free in no time.

Horses unloaded and the work began. Poor Dusty had cut her little face on the way but was still in good spirits. Ed and Linda were first to go in. I had to admire Linda as she had only ridden Ed a couple of times at home. She rode into the show ring and exhibited him well. You could see she was a little apprehensive but who would not be? Ed is a stunning beast standing at 17hh. Pure, unadulterated horse, that simply loves to go fast, very fast!

The judge got a much better ride as he was riding around alone, which calmed Ed down. However, as well as he went for the judge, he was a little bad mannered so we knew he would not be in the ribbons.

Meanwhile back at the lorry, Carol and her assistants transformed my lovely Bella to a beauty queen. Somehow (don't ask how) I managed to miss my class. I arrived for the final gallop. I figured that if I joined in the gallop as the competitors came past the entrance, the judge would not notice I was late. I waited till they came round and the judge had his back to me. I kicked Bella on and she galloped up with the rest of the horses and bucked all the way up the hill. We had blown it! I joined the line up feeling frustrated. Bella looked a million dollars (I didn't look too bad myself) and we had worked towards this for months and now it was over.

I had forgotten my camera and lucky for me a friend was watching at the side of the ring. He took many pictures (kindly presented me with them, all printed and tagged, at a later date). I was deeply touched by this and will have something to treasure from the day.

Later we visited the horticulture tent; Alan's wine had come first for the second year running. He could not hide the fact that he was over the moon about it. As the day drew to a close, we celebrated Alan's success and a fun day at Ashover by popping open the winning wine.

AUGUST 14TH

What an exciting day today was. We have had a couple of tents appear in our field this last two weeks. A week was fine without permission but Alan thought it was a bit rude to stay for two and more. Alan went down a couple of times to find out who it was. Nobody appeared to be there at all. The tent had been left untouched so Alan called the police. I have never known such a good response and they were with us in minutes. Rob and Alan accompanied them to the tents, which were searched. The police were concerned that the chap had left his ID and dole card. They contacted the police dog section. A team came up and went around all the fields to see that the chap had not hanged himself. Thank goodness they did not find a body or anything terrible like that. They have promised to keep us informed.

SUNDAY 16TH AUGUST

Today really was one of my lowest for a long time. I had received a phone call about a week ago, someone wanting a companion pony for their own pony. Their own pony had lost its own companion to old age. At the time I spoke of my beloved Peanut. He is my beautiful Connemara horse that was homebred out of my first ever horse, Lady. Peanut was a star of the future until a former friend of mine, through ignorance and lack of empathy, damaged him beyond repair.

This guy was fetching him from the field to ride; he got my lovely horse tangled up in electric fence. He then proceeded to put tack on poor Peanut. Peanut was always a willing ride and tried hard to please. This guy then proceeded to ride him, only Peanut made it clear by his behaviour that he could not actually move off the spot with this person in the saddle. He pawed the ground and pleaded for help while this person hit him. Bear in mind I don't condone hitting horses anyway, let alone when they are clearly seeking help. Being such a clod, this guy then found the horse could be pulled round on a very tight circle and made him do just that. After all this abuse, the horse was still unable to move forward.

Any horse person with average intelligence would have realised within seconds that this horse had injured himself while jumping about on the electric fence. The horse was from this moment damaged beyond repair and his career was over. My niece had witnessed the whole episode but, aged 10, felt unable to express her concern. She told me when he had gone. The irony is, this guy thought he was one of the best horsemen on the planet and I, foolishly, trusted him. Had my niece not witnessed the whole thing, I would never have known to this day what had caused my beautiful horse to be unfit for a working life ever again. During the whole nasty incident, my horse had torn ligaments to such a degree that he would never take weight on his back again. And be warned— that guy is still out there, talking the talk and persuading others of his 'expert horsemanship'.

Yes, a heartbreaking story that still brings pain to me this very day. Therefore, when a companion horse was sought, it sounded like a great future for Peanut. I chatted with the lady at length and she sounded a very caring person. Although I was sad, I knew this was something I had to do. Peanut deserves the one to one love he would have indulged upon him by this woman. He deserved a new life and it was an opportunity not to be passed over lightly.

I walked down the big hill to the field with a feeling of deep sadness, tears falling down my face. I knew what I should do but I was looking for any excuses not to take him. He strode towards me in eager anticipation, as if he knew what wonderful opportunity lay in front of him. I could barely see through my tears.

I loaded Peanut into the cattle wagon as the lorry would not start. I had hoped secretly that he would not load and then I would not be able to take him. He loaded just fine and soon we were on our way. I struggled not to cry during the whole journey. As we arrived at his new home a jolly lady waved frantically with a wide smile stretched across her face.

I knew instantly that this was Peanut's new mum and he was going to be very happy with this woman.

Peanut came out of the trailer and met his new companion. A tiny little fat pony ran over to introduce himself. They both had a good look at each other and wondered around the field eating grass together. I kissed my boy goodbye, wiped away my tears and headed for home.

AUGUST 22ND

Woke startled to find I had almost overslept. Managed to pull myself out of bed and get a cup of tea underway. We left the farm at about 7.15am. Gosh, by the time we arrived, the market was so busy that we were stuck way down the end of the auction stalls. Put all my gear out to auction. I must admit, what I hung up was pretty rubbish despite the fact that I had tried to clean it up.

I keep thinking that I ought to sell saddles and bridles but I will only need to buy such stuff again. When we do move I am still hopeful to start up a small riding school. So what is the point of letting things go at rock bottom prices only to have to go out and buy them again?

Alan had taken a few bits and bobs. The market was full of everyone's rubbish. Mind you, as I heard someone say, everything is recycled so that's good. We are both terrible at throwing things away so being able to pass them on even at a pound is good.

Robbie came to see us at the market. We sat and had hot chocolate in abundance and a good old natter. All this while Alan was out there bidding on things, despite the fact we are supposed to be clearing out. Mind you, it is all stuff that we need for our planned descent on to Syda Farm! He bought a large load of electric fencing for the chickens, so that's my mind at rest for my precious poultry. Oh, by the way, the poultry stall had my book for sale, "The Right Way to Keep Chickens", so I was well chuffed.

Home for around 4.30pm. Carol was giving the riding club girls a brilliant time. Alan took a borrowed tedder back to his farmer friend, David. I thought I would try and lessen his burden for night duties so I went across the road to check his stock. He has expected Lovebird to calve for a while now. All were present and correct and Lovebird looked in fine health. I decided, of course, to take a closer look as one must when they are expected to calve. I did not like the look of the discharge coming from her as it was tinged with red. Upon Alan's return, we ventured across the road again; the discharge looked even less healthy. Crunchy, one of our old cows, looked a little under the weather as well. She had not been to the water hole and was clearly dehydrating. Alan decided that we should fetch the trailer and give Lovebird an internal examination and fetch Crunchy back to the farm. First we had the dreadful task of walking round the field to look for a dead calf. Alan was sure the discharge was afterbirth.

With baited breath and other clichés, we walked the perimeter, hopeful of finding a live calf. We found nothing which meant there was a little hope she might not have given birth yet. Having said that, the discharge was not a good colour if the calf was still inside her!

We staggered back across the road, having been up since 6am and it was now 8.30pm, so we were both exhausted. We hitched up the trailer and emptied its contents from our morning at Derby. Meanwhile, I ran into the house to make a homity pie. Have you ever tried a homity pie? If not you must try it. Luckily, I had a lump of pastry left over so it was a quick job. Ran out again, leaving the kitchen looking like a bomb site. Jumped in the Land Rover and off we went.

Lovebird walked happily into the trailer blissfully unaware that Alan was about to put his arm up her bottom! Alan found nothing inside her, leaving us disappointed. We could not risk taking her from the field. She may have had a live calf and hidden it. We turned her down the ramp and low and behold saw a pair of ears through the long grass. The ears were erect and, as we walked across, we saw a beautiful live baby. Our mood went from solemn to elated in just a few seconds. The calf jumped to its feet and ran, still unsteady, to Lovebird, to find out what all the fuss was about.

Crunchy was next. Luckily, she too walked happily into the trailer. Getting her to the safety of the farmyard, she drank enough to sink a ship and settled happily with a wad of hay. It's always comforting to have the poorly animals close by. Ideally, they would be in the house but it's not possible.

Homity pie welcomed us home as we dragged ourselves wearily to the house. As I looked around at the bomb site I had left earlier, my heart sank. For this is the life of a farmer's wife. As hard as it is most days; I would not change my job for the world.

Homity Pie (a simple but delightful meal)

10 oz pastry
1 Ib potatoes (Cooked and crushed) and onions (sautéed lightly)
At least 4oz cheese (grated)
Couple of garlic cloves crushed (or garlic flavouring)
Milk and seasoning
Roll out the pastry to line a small pie dish

Add the cheese to the potatoes and mix evenly along with seasoning garlic and a drop of milk. Add to the pastry lined dish. Sprinkle with grated cheese. Cook for about 40 minutes on a medium heat.

AUGUST 24TH

Up early and dressed in a nice bright white blouse. Vowed to keep it clean for lunch with my friend, Miss Metta. I fed all the animals while Alan went to get the tractor tyre repaired. Alan arrived home, having picked up Jack and his dog on route. Blake was dropped off by Kelly and her mum. Got the boys lunch and then went to Mavis's. Although I did not think to look, I was certain my blouse was still pristine.

Mavis greeted me and took me inside her neat little house. Mavis is a dear friend who I have already told you about. Mavis stands at around 4ft 2inches. When she drives her car she has to view the road through her steering wheel. From a distance the car looks like a runaway vehicle as no driver can be seen. It was the first time I had been invited to her house, socially. She had gone to a lot of trouble to prepare what I thought was an Indian meal. However, she informed me it was actually a Malaysian meal. I sat down at the smartly laid table and looked down at my blouse. I had been under an illusion about it being pristine. I had a large dog foot print on the left side and several cat prints on the right. Added to that there were several little splodges of goodness knows what? I was ashamed of how I had turned myself out for this lunch date. Mavis had gone to so much trouble, bless her.

I ate so much of the lovely food and drank wine. I rarely drink when I am driving so I was a little worried. We chatted about cats and St Martin and how to make wine. She is a lovely lady; I only wish there were more around like her. The world would be such a lovely place if everyone lived life like Mavis. As I sat in her little dining room, I prayed silently at her little altar. The candle was lit as always and her rosary beads sat on her prayer list. It felt comforting to be sitting in such a spiritual environment. I don't go to church but I talk to God always and I know he does listen.

Home tired and exhausted but well nourished. All I wanted to do was rest. As usual I could not so I got a little depressed instead. A lady called and brought me two kittens. Pretty little things much in need of love and care. I fed and watered them and left them to settle. Felt emotionally drained and felt myself sinking into despair. Not a good place to be right now when I have so much to do. Alan came in and realised I was disabled with weariness and, yes, self-pity. He sprang into action as always and cooked me a lovely chip supper. I do love that man. I make a silent promise to pull myself together by morning.

25ᵀᴴ AUGUST

Up bright and early and straight into the shower, determined to start the day on positive note. Washed my hair and dressed smartly. I looked directly in to the mirror. I told myself how gorgeous I am and tried hard to believe it. I strode confidently into the kitchen and told Alan and the dogs how gorgeous I am! Alan looked up and declared that he already knew I was—how sweet is that?

A positive start to the day and the effect was profound. I had eight or more friends pass through my house today. Each and every one of them complimented my hair and how I looked. Each one asked if I had been to have my hair done. I am not exaggerating here; the power of positive thinking and making a small effort was unbelievable. I will hopefully try this more often.

Jenny, wonderful Jenny, came today. This woman is like a whirlwind and is one of the kindest women I know. She has sorted out my life and is helping me to pack all worldly possessions away in a methodical order. Everything we pack goes into boxes with clear labels of the contents on each one. She had turned my disorganised hell into an organised heaven. I have been dumbstruck by her organisational skills and have never met anyone like her. I cannot put in to words the effect she is having on my mental health at the moment. I am, as Alan puts it, very fragile right now. Good word, as I feel like a glass tumbler ready to shatter at the slightest knock. Alan has another carefully chosen word for my behaviour— excitable. I think that word sounds so much more endearing than hysterical!

When Jenny leaves my home I feel that she has lifted a weight. Not by her leaving of course but by the fact that when she leaves I look around and can see a result. When I work alone I seem to become lost in a world of chaos. Jenny puts that chaos into manageable chunks and I cope. She guides and gently pushes me to do what I have to do. Thank you, Jenny.

Later on I nipped to town to the knicker shop. I think it's called Bumps and Boobs. I bought some pants last week that are supposed to squeeze my flab in. They were not very good as they just moved it higher up my body. That's no good at all! The lady was happy to change them, leaving me only a choice of big, old lady's pants. I quietly laughed to myself as she handed me six pairs. I visualised myself with these big knickers falling down my ankles with every step. Oh well, I figured I could put them in the charity box as there is no way they will fit me. It was obvious as I held them up; they would be way too big.

For a laugh, I got home and tried on the big knickers. I was rather upset as I struggled to get them over my thighs. With a jolt, my laughter stopped.

26TH AUGUST

Started the big knickers diet and was really good up until dinner time. Went to see Lynne, my artist friend, and looked at her pictures in the art exhibition. She has done me yet another wonderful picture of one of my animals. She has done my beautiful Jaffa, my big impressive warm-blood standing at 17hh. Her coat is a beautiful rich mahogany and her mane, tail and legs are jet black. I need a mounting block to get on and she pulls up by the gate when I have to get off. She is my therapy horse. No matter how bad I feel, she will take me wherever I want to go and never complain. She will walk while I talk and never exhibits any unnerving behaviour, as a horse can often do. The only fault she has, if it is a fault, is no brakes, but hey who needs breaks. I just sit on board; no matter how much physical pain I feel, Jaffa will do the rest.

27ᵀᴴ August

A positive start to the day (well it's worth another try). Had a shower and washed my hair, even spared some time to apply mascara. Singing as I always do to help keep my spirit elevated, but never sure if my singing does that for those around me. Fed all my animals and was just finishing off when I heard the main gate open and shut. I looked up and to my horror saw the Prodigal Son stomping across the yard. I marched forward to stop him in his tracks but he just barged against me, causing me to fall against the gate. He marched around the yard shouting. I asked him to leave straight away. I asked him several times and he just shouted at me. He was very aggressive in his manner and the way he barged against me. I felt the jolt in my back and struggled to follow him further, while demanding he left. He just looked at me and shouted in my face. "I have come to see if you will be out of here in a month and it's clear you won't." The Prodigal Son is actually a born again Christian, by the way, only the kind that love to render people homeless, without even stables to keep shelter!

I kept asking him to leave and he pushed me aside again as I tried to stop him going in the buildings. I dialled 999 and requested police assistance. He even pushed me against the gate as I was on the phone to the police. He is a big, ugly brute and, though underneath a coward, he'll not hesitate to maraud around against the wishes of a lone woman. He must have suddenly realised that I really was talking to the police and also Alan had arrived back. The Prodigal Son re-entered coward mode and left rather hastily. I shouted after him that the police were on their way. He shouted back, defiantly, "Send them up to Syda, then!"

During this exchange, a man had stopped to admire the sports car the Prodigal Son was driving. Poor bloke thought I was the born again's wife, calling the police because he was looking at the Jaguar sports car. I think my display would have removed any feelings of grandeur the Prodigal Son may have been feeling about his 'modest', gas guzzling choice of mobility.

I was left shaken, unsettled and in a lot of pain. This was just a taster and I was painfully aware that there was more to come from this nasty family. It made me realise the enormity of the situation. Yes, we plan to move to Syda Farm and it all sounds like fun. Yet here I am confronted by reality and what this secret plan really does entail.

I was painfully aware that my two remaining Great Danes had allowed this brute to march onto the farm and in and out of buildings. I felt a black cloud descend as I realised my Annie was not by my side at the time I needed her most. Not her fault, I know, as she has always been there for me. Had she been here, she would have ripped his arm off in defence of her mistress. Even at her most frail I am certain she would have died defending me from this cowardly person. I was sad and down for the rest of the day. I miss my Annie.

SATURDAY 29TH

I did not sleep well and was in extreme pain all night. The incident yesterday had triggered panic attacks which left me feeling sick and shaky. I could feel myself hyperventilating all morning. I had to work really hard to control my breathing. I tried hard to overcome the panicky feelings and carry on with my day as per normal.

Had a shower and dressed smartly for my friend's 50th birthday party. Lynne is a dear friend and we enjoyed the party so much. Lynne and her husband, Andy, have worked all week towards this celebration and had really pushed the boat out. Of course, I ate more than any other party guest. It was a wonderful party which I did not really want to end.

MONDAY 31ˢᵗ AUGUST
THE HOPE SHOW

Woke feeling dreadful physically but mentally excited at the thought of taking Bella to Hope show. Bella is one of my beautiful rescue horses and she is a dream to ride. Well, a dream until I take her on a hack and we are stalked by a plastic bag. I haven't hacked her out since the incident about six months ago. I don't blame Bella for acting up in a serious manner. The bag did seem to have it in for her and it seemed very personal. The wind lifted the said bag up into the air where it stayed, following us down the main road. That was bad enough but Bella was going at great speed backwards while on her hind legs. Do bear in mind at this point that I am not the boldest of riders due to much physical impairment! We were heading backwards on two legs down the main Chatsworth to Baslow road and it was no fun. The bag would not give up and remained in hot pursuit while 12 ft off the ground. It did feel a little personal but I am not sure if it was after Bella or me. Had I been alone I would have sorted it out bravely. However, I managed to steer my horse backwards, still on two legs, onto the lane opposite and we lost the bag. We have never hacked out again since and I am not sure we ever will.

I am very lucky to have been given an entry for Hope show. I was rather late to get my entries in. I have never been to Hope show and I am really excited about it. This is another local show that has been going on for many years.

Off to Hope we go! The journey there was really pleasant and Linda and I chatted all the way. Linda had agreed to be my groom for the day, which is great. She really knows what she is on about with horses. On arrival, the atmosphere was great and we were both full of anticipation. Within the first half hour, I had already been verbally attacked by a very old man with a large chip on his shoulder. I only had my little dog in my arms as I made my way to the secretary's tent on an urgent matter. Out of nowhere came this old man who only had one arm. To make up for only having one arm he had the biggest belly ever and a temper to match. Having dashed over in an attempt to remove my dog from the warmup ring (she was still quietly under my arm) I was almost catapulted across the warmup ring by his gut. His eyes flashed and his teeth grinded as he hollered at me to leave the ring and take out my dog. Bear in mind he was still physically touching me with his belly and stump. There was no actual gap now between my belly (that's on the big side too) and his belly. Now, had he looked like Jean-Claude Van Damme, I would not have had a problem. However, as he resembled an overweight Steptoe, I took offence. I had to physically remove him from my person while pointing out that the amount of aggression he was using against me was totally unnecessary. Eventually, he began to calm down and stopped spitting and grinding his teeth. Towards the end of this incident, Linda returned and was rather taken aback by the whole thing. This chap then moved on to verbally attack another member of the public who then threatened to "Rip his head off!" if he ever spoke to him like that again. Well, this was all over by 9.30 am, so I was sure the day could only get better.

The day was fun and full of incidents that will entertain at many dinners to come. Bella was superb and in both of my classes performed in such a way that I was as proud as I could ever be. Home absolutely shattered so much so that I forgot "Coronation Street" was on! Unfortunately, this meant I had to fall out with Alan, as he had not reminded me it was on. Well, we reached an agreement that in future he will always remind me no matter what. Alan cooked me a lovely dinner of home made chips.

TUESDAY 1ST SEPTEMBER

Trip to Barnsley to look at field shelters for our animals. Alan's farm at Syda (I call it Alan's farm even though this is not official, yet) is apparently 200 feet higher than Rufford. This means it is colder up there. I was a little shocked to hear this as I have only recently adapted to the cold temperature at Rufford. I made one deal with Alan when we married in sickness and in health. I added onto the contract that he must promise to always keep me warm. Sadly, he failed on that one! Well, you can't have everything in this life can you?

So off we went to Barnsley to look at field shelters for our animals. Well, we can check out our accommodation at a later date. The buildings were really good but very expensive. The rain fell heavily, adding to the difficult time we are living through.

Alan has built me yet another lovely little chicken house. The chickens will be well and truly fine, what with the electric chicken wire Alan picked up at Derby auctions.

THURSDAY 3ᴿᴰ SEPTEMBER

After phoning the law centre many times, we decided to make our way down to see them. I have put so much faith in this organisation, having been given rays of hope in the past. We sat down and waited in the hopes to see the usual man. I will call him John although this is not his real name. John agreed to see us and we all went into a little room. I could tell from the outset that John was very agitated and I felt very uncomfortable. We tried to get just a little comfort from him due to the fact he had told us we could call and talk through any concerns. After a while, I felt so uncomfortable in the room I was beginning to feel tearful. I struggled as John became even more agitated. I had to ask my one question that I had waited all weekend to ask. I needed my mind put at rest as it was racing with uncertainty. "Can I still come down to see you John when we get the bailiff's letter?"

John just turned abruptly and he retorted in harsh tones.

"Why would you come here? What makes you think you can come here? Why would you come here?"

By this stage he was very agitated and I have to say I was most upset at his entire cold and heartless attitude. I just got up off my seat, scooped up my little dog and said, "Because you told me I could when we last spoke, that's why!"

With those words I flew from the room needing air and a damned good cry. I have to say his whole attitude shocked me and the coldness of manner. He should not have made empty promises to me in the months before.

Friday 4th September

My friend, Lynne, called for a chat. We talk endlessly about our animals as we both share a great passion for them. She took one of my most unhomeable of cats and gave her a home. She has turned the cat's life around and made her the most pampered pussy you can imagine. When she came into the sanctuary, she came as a group of three cats, Mummy, daddy and baby. I did not want to split them up, yet I knew that homing three big black cats together was unlikely. Sadly, little mummy cat would not use a litter tray and this caused problems for homing. Max, the son (well he was two years old when he came in with mummy and daddy), was a big lad who, overnight, developed epilepsy. He frightened his mummy and daddy to death, as a cat after an epileptic fit can behave very strangely. I had to bring him into the house where he lived happily for about a year. One night, as I was calling all cats in at bedtime, Max could not be found. After frantically searching the farm we found him in the house, dead. He had clearly died mid-fit and I was heartbroken.

His mum and dad, Naomi and Calvin, found the perfect home on a farm. Sadly, over the weeks, Naomi and Calvin decided they liked to be inside the house and not out on the farm. The litter tray problem reared its ugly head and for a long time went unchecked by the new owner. Before long, the problem had escalated out of control and the farm house became very smelly. Naomi and Calvin were sent packing home to me.

They settled in within hours and seemed happy to find themselves back in the security of the cattery. It was like they had never been away. We decided that in order for the cats to live happy, fulfilling lives, we may have to consider separating them. I hate to separate cats that come in together, but sometimes we have no choice.

Calvin was spotted on the website by a lovely lady who was looking for a companion. She came to meet him and they fell in love. Calvin went off to his new life and settled well. He is still enjoying life with this lovely owner today.

I was very worried about Naomi as I felt sure that nobody would want her. I decided that the best thing to do would be to let her become one of the resident farm cats. I let her out of the cattery to live happily on the farm with the other cats. I was so surprised that she did not like it one little bit. This was the first time I had encountered a cat that did not like living on the farm. This is where my friend, Lynne, comes into the picture.

Lynne has just had her whole house refurbished. She has carpeted the house out in white carpet and it looks beautiful. Lynne liked Naomi but knowing of her history and her inability to use the litter tray, she decided that it would be impossible for her to take the said cat. However the cat had other ideas!

Lynne called to see me on this particularly sunny morning and we had a chat and a cuppa. We had to keep a watchful eye on Naomi as she was not settling to life outside the cattery. When it came time for Lynne to leave we said our goodbyes. Lynne made her way down the lay-by to her car; Naomi went too. The future of this little dirty cat was sealed and she was taken home to the newly refurbished, white carpeted house. I dare not tell you how many times the white carpets have had to be cleaned since Naomi moved in. Lynne has stuck by Naomi, now called Aimee (Princess most days). No matter what this little Princess does outside the litter tray, she is now safe for the rest of her life. Thanks, Lynne. If only there were more owners like Lynne, what a wonderful world it would be for all the animals.

Alan took various antiques to Bagshaws for valuing. He took a commode and a monk's chest and a deer's head along with a butter churn. We are still trying hard to lighten our load ready for the move. I have placed the monk's chest and my wedding dress on eBay.

SATURDAY 5TH

Lovely day around the horses and ponies. That was of course until Carol decided she was going to throw herself off the mounting block. Well, maybe not by choice but, nonetheless, it was very traumatic for me as a witness. One minute she was preparing to mount Pudding, and the next she was falling backwards at great speed from a great height. It was not nice at all, not for me, not for Carol and not for anyone else. Her head hit the floor with such a thud that I felt the pain myself.

We got her to her feet and she was determined to ride the horse. Later, she did not look good and made her way home. She was sick on the way home and made her way to Accident and Emergency. Luckily, she is there so often with horse related incidents, I imagine they have a cubical with her name on it.

We had to get all the animals across the road in preparation for the forth coming tuberculosis test. We have to do this test in order to sell any cattle. It is a very stressful exercise for animals and humans alike. Traffic never seems to want to stop these days and will often attempt to drive through, no matter how hard you try to stop them. It will be so great to be away from this road. I always suspected it would be the death of me in the future so I am not sorry to leave it behind. I am getting excited at the thought of owls to sing me to sleep at night and the chirping of birds to wake me in the morning. Oh what bliss! Up at Syda Farm, life will be so much more tranquil and oh so peaceful. Of course, I am leaving the old man out of the equation at present!

TUESDAY 8TH SEPTEMBER

Took Poppet and Tommy Tucker to the vet. Poppet is there for a dental and Tommy has a massive abscess in his mouth. I think the vet had been reading up on cancer this week, as both cats apparently have it. It is unusual for our vet to overreact to ailments. As I say, he must have been reading up on it or perhaps attended a seminar.

THURSDAY 10TH SEPTEMBER

I went to town first thing as Alan has an eye test booked at Boots. It was a lovely sunny day and Alan was the most relaxed I have seen him away from the farm. We are a pair as we are both at our happiest at home with the animals and the farm. The Thursday flea market was in full swing and the sun was shining brightly. In town, everyone seemed to be happy and looked to be enjoying themselves. While Alan had his eye test, I ambled with Holly around the flea market. I have not looked around this flea market in years. I saw some lovely designer handbags, to which I nearly succumbed. They were fakes of course but I realised that to go out shopping with such a bag would require me to look very smart, thus making my wellies redundant.

Alan came out from his eye test unable to tolerate the sun. The optician had put a solution in his eyes to make the pupil open up. The sun penetrated to the back of his eyes. Sun glasses helped as we now explored the market together. Alan continued to be so relaxed. He went to have his hair cut and took me out for lunch, but not before finding a beautiful copper jam pan on the flea market, which he bought me for the princely sum of £25.00—what a bargain!

I don't understand how it happened but we strolled around town without a care in the world.

FRIDAY 11ᵀᴴ SEPTEMBER

What a day! I had dreaded it for some time as the vet was booked for TT testing. We also had new dog kennels being delivered along with two little rescue dogs. The kennel company was due at 8am but turned up at 7am (being early is not a bad thing). The vet was scheduled at 8.30 and Doreen and Alan (the dog fosterers) were scheduled for 9am. The vet was late which meant that there was a serious clash and everything happened at once, just like I knew it would!

The TT test was a four man job but there were only three of us. This is par for the course. Alan, the vet and I did the job of two people each but we still failed to meet the criteria. Anyhow, half way through the TT test, Doreen and Alan turned up and understood that we had to ignore them. I managed to dash across and introduce myself before running back again and banging my head on the crush (the implement the cows go into for the test). It is made of very thick, dense metal not ideal when meeting the human skull at great speed. It's strange how the pain tolerance level increases when people are around. Had I been alone or just with Alan, I would have collapsed in a heap and required immediate and sustained TLC.

The kennels (donated by Doreen and Alan in return for taking their dogs) were beautiful and very expensive. I think those around me felt I was mad embarking on such a project at this time. Maybe I am mad but animal rescue does not stop just because the Duke of Devonshire is exercising his bank balance. When I met the two delightful little dogs that came free with the kennels, I was instantly smitten—love at first sight. I may be mad but on meeting the two little dogs I realised I had done the right thing.

Meg is a beautiful terrier-cross and very hairy. Brandy is a very sweet little cross also, who looks a little like my Tango. Tango was one of my first dogs when I was a wee lass. He was a beautiful Fox Terrier Pedigree. I adored that dog so much and still think of him so often, even though he passed over some 20 years ago.

SEPTEMBER 12TH

Two cats homed today which is good in itself. One of those cats was a long termer who has been in the sanctuary for several months. He is almost a wild cat and I was never expecting to home him. He came in from my dear friend Mavis. She prays constantly for Alan, me and all the animals. A wonderful lady came with her daughter to see Star and the mother fell in love with Choc Chip. This was nothing short of a miracle, which is what I have come to expect in my life.

I called Mavis with the news and she was over the moon. I know from talking to the lady and her daughter that both cats will be safe for the rest of their lives. The two women said that no matter what the cats did they are now their responsibility for the rest of their lives. That is the sort of talk I love to hear. It is amazing in my work how often owners will just ring up and pass over the responsibility of a pet. There are some circumstances that leave owners with no choice and that is what rescue centres are for. However, when someone brings in a beautiful cat because they have a new boyfriend! That's the time I get a bit upset. Or the teenager who has got bored with their pet.

MONDAY 14TH SEPTEMBER

Up early to load more animals for market. Only able to go as their TT test results were a pass. I always feel sad to see our animals go but at this moment in time it is even worse. Alan brought a calf back for Daisy, as she is being suckled by three big yearlings and they are pulling her down. He brought her back a little baby to take the strain from her. She seems delighted with the little champ and they have bonded well. Alan just can't resist bringing little calves home.

I had to get a taxi for my hospital appointment as Alan was not home on time. The visit was a waste of time as the doctor wanted to put a tube up my nose and down my throat. I was out of there like a shot and headed to the canteen. I needed a hot chocolate to calm my nerves after this ordeal. If he wants to put anything up my nose, I will have to be well anaesthetised!

Home and had a cup of tea, but no rest yet again. Andrew came to load up yet more animals for the market at Beeston Castle. Our beautiful animals loaded as well as ever and were taken to the market in readiness for the morning. Jack stayed tonight as he has been given the day off school to go with Alan. The cows will stay overnight at the Castle, where they will be bedded down, fed and watered.

15ᵀᴴ September

Up bright and early to make sandwiches and fresh baked scones for the boys. Waved them off feeling a little glum; I never like it when Alan goes off for the day; I miss him so much. I had to make sure I kept busy organising bits towards our move. I kept going and made the most of my time. I had ridden two horses before dinner.

Alan arrived home earlier than I expected but he was disappointed by his day. He thought he would have been as well going to Bakewell with the animals. Well, you have to try these things.

Word is spreading about Alan's stockmanship. He is being recommended to people all over the place. He has a good reputation for the honest man he is. He is also apparently being recommended as a farmer who is good with his animals. It is a shame he does not have more stock to sell as people are ringing him from all over the place enquiring about his animals. It is time he was recognised for the brilliant stockman he is. The old man never did, despite working him like a slave for nearly fifty years, and he never ever gave Alan credit for his wonderful skills.

16ᵀᴴ SEPTEMBER

Today was the dreaded conference at the solicitor's office in Belper. I was dreading it as I found the idea of sitting at a table with these intellects rather daunting. Tried a bit of power dressing and we turned ourselves out smartly.

We had a mad dash around the farm to feed and clean all the animals before we left. We left in plenty of time in order to keep stress levels down. We are meeting with the barrister in order to find out if Alan has a good case for his claim on Syda Farm. Our future now depends heavily on the answer we receive at this meeting. It did not really matter so much when we had Rufford House Farm. Now it matters a heck of a lot and we need to hear a favourable answer. The old man has brought this all to a head by handing over our rights to residency at Rufford—he may well rue that malicious act. Hoisted by his own petard, you might say.

We arrived bang on time but were kept waiting for over half an hour. We were presented with the usual terrible cup of tea. I just have an insatiable urge to advise them to invest in a teapot. For all their airs and graces and training, you would think they would know how to make a decent cup of tea. I mean it is a very British thing, isn't it? Simple really and I pride myself that I will always welcome visitors to my home with a good cup of tea made in a teapot. And I don't charge over £200 per hour for people to see me. If they did pay this sort of money, they would drink my lovely tea out of gold plated cups.

The meeting was long and drawn out. Now I realise how innocent people can be made to confess to crimes they did not commit when subjected to long interrogations. Half way through this meeting, I wanted to suggest to Alan that he lets the old man have everything and put it to him that we went home and had a proper cup of tea!

Though long and drawn out, the overall conclusion was that Alan has a strong case. The barrister insisted that we forget any fight to save our current home as the landlord has far too much money for people like us to mess with them. We must leave Rufford House Farm and move to Syda Farm and make our home—in a caravan. We are to arrive unexpectedly and reside as unwanted neighbours!

After two hours that seemed more like twenty four hours, we left in high spirits. It felt somehow good to have it confirmed that Rufford House Farm, our home since our marriage, is no more. It made it final and left us both planning for our move to Syda. We had a nourishing meal on the way home and discussed our future.

17ᵀᴴ SEPTEMBER

Rob had sent me my missed episodes of "Coronation Street" to catch up on. Oh, I was so excited, but watching it with my lifestyle is not going to be easy. But I'll happily give it a go!

My first attempt early afternoon was thwarted by the arrival of a friend. Graciously, I switched off the DVD player and decided to wait until later, feeling sure I would fit it in before tonight's episodes were aired. Confident about this I decided to feed a few animals, before returning for a second attempt.

A good couple of hours later I put the disc into the player again and made my second attempt. Five minutes into my second attempt another friend called. I chatted politely, though feeling rather deprived at this stage. I turned off the disc again and suggested we walked the rescue dogs. This seemed like a really good idea at the time and the walk was rather pleasant. We headed over the fields and I began to worry that I may not get to catch up on Coro after all.

Upon returning to the farmstead I noticed Jack, Alan and Blake attempting to get some cows on to the farm yard. On approaching the scene it was automatic to intervene and help with the situation, like any good farmer's wife would do.

One of the cows in question was Ivory, a dear old cow who considers all calves born on the farm to be her responsibility. From the moment a calf drops out of a cow, Ivory will take over all parental duties. The mother cows all accept this happily and they seem to think it is a good idea to share the responsibility with Ivory. Ivory is barren now and will have no more babies of her own.

Now, I know she is very protective and I respect that. I think she is sweet, kind and motherly and I adore seeing her running down the field trying to keep up with her young charges. I was of course with the dogs and there was a lot going on around her as we tried to herd them into the yard. Suddenly, Ivory put her head down and came trundling forwards, before increasing in speed and ferocity. I found myself tossed into the air like a shuttlecock. At the same time, Ivory lost her footing and fell completely on top of me. As I lay on the ground, I felt her weight pressing down on me as she scrambled to get to her feet. Her knees dug into my limbs and bones and I was sure that I was not going to survive. I felt tremendous pressure as her hooves dug into my stomach. Pain seared through my body yet again as she tried desperately to get back on her feet. Eventually, I felt her roll off me and I looked up to see her about to attack again. I placed my bruised leg into the air and met her face with my foot. This was enough to deter her and normality entered the field once more.

As I lay on the floor with pain raging through every part of my body, I looked down at my watch. It was 7.15pm, only 15 minutes to go and "Coronation Street" would be on. Once more I had not managed to catch up on the week's programmes. I started to cry from sheer frustration of not having managed to watch my catch up. I cried from the frustration of yet more pain to endure for another week. After a few moments, I picked myself wearily up and brushed myself down. The pain was intense and I was aware my internal organs had been squashed. I could feel the pain of all my bits and bobs being concertinaed together inside of me. No time for drama, except on the box—I could hear the theme music and hobbled in for my dose of soap. Happy again, even if I was now unable to move a muscle, thanks to Ivory, our dear old mummy cow. And to think it all started with my attempt to stay indoors and catch up with continuing drama!

18TH SEPTEMBER

I woke up stiff and sore but a lot better than I expected. I was swollen in various body parts, particularly my hips and calves (very appropriate I think). My stomach was swollen and hard in places. I was a little worried that I should really go to the hospital as my internal organs did take a good battering. Still I could walk and nothing was broken (I don't think . . .) so that's fine by me.

Meg is beginning to show a sign of being herself again. We have nursed her through her grief and she has only now stopped looking for her Annie. She is back to carrying round her cuddly toys which, since Annie's passing, she has been too heartbroken to do. I know in her heart she will always think of Annie but will hopefully still have a lot of fun and many happy years to come.

19ᵀᴴ SEPTEMBER

Ouch! Now the swelling is subsiding the pain is increasing. My tummy is really sore and each time I cough I am in agony. I cannot believe that bruises are starting to show, as I never bruise. This is good news as I really need something to show for this incident.

I am selling some bits and bobs on eBay this week. My goodness, I do not know how people have the time or inclination to sell on eBay. It is such hard work and when you expect something to fetch good money it fetches nought and when you expect nought it makes a bit of money! Well anyway, I have received just one enquiry about the size of my wedding dress from a guy I assume is buying the dress for his fiancée. Well, let's hope he buys my beautiful dress.

One thing this entire problem with Chatsworth has taught me is to let go. I have always had a problem letting go of the past, with items such as my wedding dress a prime example. I always hang on to things and treasure the memories that go with them. I realise now that I cannot keep holding on to the past as it gets you down in the end. I consider the selling of many items a bit of a release. I am unburdening myself, lightening the load in preparation for the next chapter of my life. I am still struggling, don't get me wrong. However, the more I am letting go the more I am able to.

20ᵀᴴ SEPTEMBER

Jack came up early today and went to get the cows in. After ten minutes he came running in the house out of breath. He had found an extra calf in the field; good news, Lovebird has had her baby. We all marched up the field. I was still in my slippers and dressing gown. I could not wait to see our new born calf. She was so pretty and Lovebird is looking after her well.

SEPTEMBER 21ST

Lovebird and her calf were doing well in the morning and both thriving. In between feeds, the calf is tucked away in the bramble bushes. How is it they always look so cosy in their little cocoons?

Missy the cat is a little unwell today and seems to have a bit of a chill. I will observe her for a day or two and if she does not recover then a trip to the vet will be in order. Daisy, the new mummy cat that has just given birth, seems to be suffering from severe diarrhoea. A quick call to the vet and I was told to give her toast and fish for a few days.

Went to Buxton with Alan as he seems to think we need another container to store our belongings. Looked at a lot of smelly old containers and then we were shown a beautiful brand new one that we could actually live in! I fell in love with it immediately and decided, yes, I could live in a container like it! That was until I learnt of the price which was actually £15000. I think I will have to continue looking for a mobile home.

Tired and exhausted as usual upon our return home. I really don't know where Alan gets his stamina from. We had a cup of tea before feeding time. Lovebird is a little unsteady today and will need some Calcium Borogluconate to replenish the calcium she lost to the calf. Alan nipped to a neighbour's farm for the medicine, as the vet was closed.

September 22ND

Busy morning sorting out the animals. Missy is so much better now and eating a lot more each day. She is all but attacking me for her food. This is a very good sign, and the sickness and diarrhoea have also subsided. Daisy has the runs again due to me feeding her the wrong fish. Should be white fish and I gave her best salmon. I thought I was doing a good thing.

Lovebird is not so good today and Alan is rather worried and concerned. I am always able to cope with sick cows until Alan is concerned. Once Alan starts to fret, I know things are not good. Lovebird was unable to get up again today. I watched her as she raised her front end up just enough to allow her new calf to suckle. How dedicated is that for a mother who is unwell? Alan took water to her as she was unable to come to the trough.

I went to town with Robbie and we had a good mooch around. I was really tired but still enjoyed sitting and having a cream-topped hot choc with Rob and Holly. We visited the library to check out writing opportunities.

Went home and had a quick cup of tea. It was time to feed round and walk all my dogs, remembering that I now have two little rescue dogs that need lots of exercise. I went with Rob up the field with the first outing of dogs and bumped into Jack and Alan as they tended to Black Lovebird.

She was cold and Alan seemed to think she was in shock for some reason. Calling the vet, they both agreed it was milk fever. This is what Alan had treated her for last night. He dashed to our neighbouring farmer and borrowed another two bottles of Calcium Borogluconate. This he administered along with food and water, for which she showed little interest. We placed on her a warm horse rug to keep her cosy. Horse rugs are always on hand for poorly cows, as they warm them up with speed and help to keep in the heat.

Ate tea at 9.30pm, then it was time for Alan to take Jack home. They both decided to check Lovebird beforehand. Lovebird was gone. The saving grace was that she had died quickly but I was worried as to what pain she must have been in. Alan did all he could and we made her as comfortable as was humanly possible short of bringing her into the kitchen. Believe me, if we could have we would have done just that. Lovebird, another dear member of our herd/family, had passed away. She passed on where she belonged, at home. How sad that she had gone through birthing only to die. She was a good mum up to the time of her death. She had always been a very good mum and a sweet natured old cow. Offensive to no one, we shall miss her. God Bless you our dear Lovebird and goodnight.

Now we have Lovebird's little heifer to take care of. Alan took her in to feed from White Lovebird (this cow is Lovebird's auntie). White Lovebird was not too kind and slammed the little heifer against the wall. Alan fetched her out straight away and brought Daisy in for her to feed from. Daisy is a good old mother cow and has just weaned her three great big bullocks. The three bullocks were nearly as big as she was and she would stand patiently each day with these big beasts pulling and sucking at her teats.

Daisy took the calf straight away and stood quietly as Alan placed her on the teats. A mother cow has been replaced and I will say again, if only life were so simple. This little heifer has shown little or no grief and has a new mummy. I am glad we have not had to witness distress from this calf as I cannot bear to see animals in distress.

23ʳᵈ September

A local farmer came down to fetch the eight yearlings he was buying from Alan. As we loaded the stock, the farmer commented that he was not sure he had done the right thing. I guess this was because they were climbing over walls and plant pots as opposed to going into the trailer. They also knocked the indicator from my lorry, which I was not too thrilled about.

Well, the poor little sods didn't know what had hit them. I mean they are normally loaded in an area with no escape route, let alone several. I don't know what Alan was thinking of really, by even attempting to load them with so many exits. Once we had them in a single loading area, they went in like little lambs, bless them. It was a sad moment to watch them all going off to a new home, even if it is just up the road.

24TH SEPTEMBER

Out in my dressing gown to let the rescue dogs out and feed the cats. Missy is waiting at the door for her food which is great when you consider how ill she has been. I thought I was going to lose her but we have turned a corner and she is well again.

Daisy has overcome her diarrhoea and is enjoying motherhood again. It is so lovely to see her cuddled up with her babies as opposed to sitting, hunched up, looking so sorry for herself. It is always gratifying when my intensive care pays off.

Bell the cow came into the yard mooing and full of milk. We had not realised that her offspring was still feeding from her. Her two youngsters were sold yesterday and she was missing them. Milk flowed in abundance from her swollen teats. I dashed in to take Alan and Robbie a cup of tea. We now had to change our plans and go to the market. Bell needed a new calf and she needed it now!

After feeding hastily round and seeing all the animals were ok we left for Derby market. The three of us squashed up in the front of the Land Rover, we headed off. Alan dropped Robbie and me off at the shops while he went to buy a calf. He met us later at Rob's house and showed off the two little calves he had purchased. A little black and white one and a brown and white one. They sat happily in the back of the Land Rover on a bed of straw.

Home just in time for Doris to collect her eggs and the blacksmith to perform two trims. A lovely day culminating in a lovely evening.

Alan made us chip butties for tea.

FRIDAY 26ᵀᴴ SEPTEMBER

Daisy has had a relapse and her pen was awash with diarrhoea. I was very upset as it was a result of one of my volunteers feeding her cat meat. That's bad enough but I specifically asked the volunteer not to let a morsel of meat pass the cat's lips. I spoke at length about the effect it would have on her. Last night, after the volunteer had finished, I went to do my rounds before bed. Thank the Lord I did as I found a very large bowl full of meat alongside Daisy. I was really upset as I knew what this would spell for Daisy (and me!). Therefore, it was no surprise to me that she was very ill again. I shall have to keep the padlock on the pen and tend to her daily myself.

A strange feeling has occurred today. I am suddenly so excited about moving to the other farm. It was during my afternoon nap today that I first noticed the change as I lay in bed with my little Jack Russell and my deaf cat. I tossed and turned unable to sleep but I did feel much rested. I felt excitement rise in my tummy as I thought of living in my cosy little mobile home. I had warm thoughts of opening my door on to green fields and the quiet lane on the farm. I suddenly want to go and it's a really good feeling, despite the fact that we will be unwanted and unwelcome arrivals.

To leave behind the busy A619 and all its speeding traffic and fatal accidents will be a dream come true. The motorcyclists will miss me. Every time they screech past me I send them an Angel and a Blessing to keep them safe. I will still think of them daily though and add them to my prayers. I always worry about them as they are so vulnerable on this road. Sometimes they are silly I know, but I pray always that they will arrive home to their loved ones.

Up at Syda, I will have new territory to explore on horseback and with my dogs. I will have very accessible walks even off the farm. I will hear the birds singing and I will smell the fresh air. I will be able to open my windows when it's hot and not hear the traffic. I will be able to sit with friends outside my mobile and chat uninterrupted. Outside at Rufford, a conversation will always be staggered when the traffic interrupts the sentences. I feel bolstered for our daring and dangerous move and say quietly to myself, "Bring it on".

It could only happen to me. I have sold my wedding dress to a cross dresser! I was a little suspect throughout the sale as there was no mention of the fiancée or the wedding date. And reading between the lines I was sure there was no bride. It was confirmed when I received an email saying he loved the dress, it fitted him really well and it's the best dress he has in his collection.

I think it's rather sweet and I am happy to know my dress has a good home. It will be appreciated more than a bride wearing it for just one day. So it is what I consider a special home for a dress I loved. Thank you, Mike; have fun! I am sure you will look beautiful in your new purchase.

MONDAY 28TH SEPTEMBER

I took lots of phone calls today from friends who are thinking of us during this stressful time. Miss Metta rang to say she was praying for us and had offered a mass to us and the animals.

Today is the day we should have been leaving the farm behind, at least as far as our dastardly, wealthy landlord is concerned. We have to show we have some rights and so we will stay put for a little while longer, as an act of defiance. Our great landlord might have vast sums of money and power, but even he must be made to realise that he can't just play around with human rights (maybe it's the first time he's encountered such a concept).

September 29TH

My friend Jenny came over first thing to help me with my packing. Jenny is a very special person as I only met her a couple of months ago and she is organising me for the move. She is like a whirlwind and comes in the door, sorts me out and then goes. When I am on my own surveying the tasks I seem to become immobilised with the enormity of it. Jenny comes along and puts it in to chunks with which I can cope. I thank her from the bottom of my heart and pray that God will bless her in the way she deserves.

By the time Jenny left, so much had been accomplished and I was at ease with the world. Kelly and Lexee called and added more joy to my day. Lexee has to be one of the most beautiful little girls I have ever seen. She smiles for 24 hours a day (mind you her mum claims this is not so at home, but I don't believe her).

September 30th

Yet another day off the farm! Yuck, sorry but I like to spend the majority of my time with the animals. Spending so much time away is not only upsetting Alan and me but also our dogs. They are just not used to us being away for long periods. Meg cries with hysteria when we walk through the door after our long absences. This, I think, has come about since she lost her mummy, Annie. She would happily spend time at home with her mummy, while hardly noticing we were gone.

Today we went to see our new solicitor. Now that the case is moving forward we are with the same firm but with the litigation side of the company. They still serve the same awful cup of tea. I just have this tremendous urge to go into their kitchen and show them how to make a good cuppa. Today, I refused a drink, a first for me. I am known never to refuse. Now I have drawn the line! Well, things are certainly coming to a head. The old man has threatened Alan with court action on numerous occasions and never seen it through. Alan has not threatened court once, but now he has no choice.

The sun shone beautifully all day and I just wanted to ride my horse. Sadly, more pressing matters meant another day off the farm, sitting for too long in the Land Rover. After the solicitors, Alan took us all the way across counties again, with some rush hour traffic, to see a mobile home at Cotgrave in Nottinghamshire. The idea was to look at a static that we saw in the Ad Mag. It was priced at £2500 but was not really worth it. It was ok but I would not want to live in it. Probably, with my limited knowledge, it is worth a maximum £1000.

Headed home, a little disappointed, in time to view a static up the road from our home. Wow, I love it, it was like coming home. The static was spotless and cosy, like a little nest. I could happily come home to that each day. It is strange how one has become available just up the road. She was a lovely lady and, true to what I expected, she asked why we wanted it. I could not be truthful with her. I cannot possibly pass on our plans to a lady who lives in the tiny village of Wadshelf. Like any little village, gossip will soon spread. Wadshelf is only over the hill from Syda Farm so I had to keep the information to myself. This was frustrating as the lady and her daughter were very horsy and I could have chatted away. Oh well, maybe in the future I will get the chance for a proper chat.

I have to say my excitement for moving has increased upon seeing that static. I can't wait; Rufford has always been a bit of a burden, size wise. Don't get me wrong, I love the place, I love the freedom, the fields, the beauty of the land and the scenery. But the house, yes the house has always been a millstone around our necks. I will be sad to exit through the door one last time. But the thought of opening my new door fills me with a sense of adventure and anticipation.

OCTOBER 1ST

Alan off to Derby Market to sell yet more stock. I was dropped off at Pets at Home to wait for Robbie. One good thing about Alan having to sell stock is getting to spend extra time with Robbie. You see there is positive in almost anything. We met Alan at the market for lunch. We ate fish and chips and shared stories of our day.

Later on went to Salford to see a static that Alan fancied. We have seen it on eBay and I have to say it looks splendid. I am not interested really as it only has one bedroom. Alan seems keen so therefore I am more than happy to go with him to check it out.

The chap selling it met us in the middle of Salford and we followed him to the site. Oh my goodness, one thing we have learnt today is never to bid on anything on eBay by looking at photos alone. The static caravan was a complete mess. The lady who owned it obviously smoked like a chimney as the ceiling was dark yellow. The fixtures and fittings were dirty and sticky. Doors dropped off if you opened them. The floor was rotten and was sinking in places. Golly, we were polite and then left hastily. We were gobsmacked and it made others we had looked at seem more akin to Buckingham Palace.

Long journey home broken up slightly by a visit to a takeaway! Just for information, the static in Salford had a winning bid of £1450. Nobody else had been to see it before bidding ended, meaning that whoever bought what looked like a bargain was in for a shock!

SATURDAY OCTOBER 3RD

The weather was dry again but this meant that the dust from the ménage blew everywhere. The dogs were all covered in dust, making the white ones black. Everyone on the farm had black faces and grit in all crevices.

Michele came running into the house saying there was a cow on the floor unable to get up. I went running out in my slippers without realising that there were one or two wet, squidgy areas in the bottom yard. Anyway my slippers were a bit past it. Of course, it was our delicate Black Girl that had taken a tumble. She is the one that was hit by a car two years ago. She dislocate her hip when hit by the car and had landed on the same leg. Like all cows when they are stuck on the floor, she was using her head to try and lever herself up. The only problem with this is the force with which they throw back their head onto the floor. No matter what surface they are laid on (it is usually a hard surface), the head is thrown back with great force. I hate this as they always end up with severely swollen eyes as a result. I ran to get some hay to make some padding. Alan arrived and we managed with great difficulty to pull her to her feet. She shook herself off and walked away, seemingly unscathed.

Riding club was very difficult today as the wind whipped up in the ménage. The ponies played up a little as you would of course expect. The wind always gives them an excuse to tear around at great speed, pretending to be scared.

Alan is working so very hard as usual. I worry about him overdoing things. Neither of us is getting a rest at the moment. We are on the go all the time. We are going to bed shattered and waking up shattered. Alan is making a real difference in the shop (it's not a real shop; it is a room on the side of the house that was once a shop). He is clearing all the tools and bits from the shop into his trailer. I really don't know how he keeps going. We both seem to be on a hamster wheel right now with no chance of getting off.

SUNDAY OCTOBER 4TH

A poignant day full of so many happy memories. Rob and I sorted mum's lounge; the most comfortable room in this big cold house. A room that was once filled with laughter and warmth. A room that was the hub of the house, where we would all sit and relax. All the family news would be shared in this very room. A very special room with a large, plush settee and matching chairs. An open log fire that would burn so warmly, greeting all visitors. A dresser housed the little trinkets mum had collected since moving to Rufford with us, shortly after our marriage. A large brown wall unit sits on one side of the room and is filled with gifts and mementoes gathered throughout mum's adult life. The china and the Beswick pieces; the photos of her beloved children and grandchildren; even a small decorative piece of marzipan from a birthday cake—it sits decomposing on the mantelpiece.

It was an emotional struggle, but we managed to divide her treasures between ourselves and the charity shops. The shops would benefit so much from our misfortune. It makes it easier to cope, to think of all the charities that will benefit now. To think of the little old ladies, gents, children, mothers and fathers purchasing some of mum's wonderful belongings and enjoying their little treasured finds. It brings a warm feeling to know that we are helping others while we continue to sort through the preceding decades of our lives.

Alan is busy moving his valuable farm machinery to a friend's farm. I know I am a sentimental old fool but it is hard to watch him losing his business. Nearly all his animals have gone now. It is time for his machines to be put away for safety. It is so sad and so unjust to see a man and his life's work reduced to what I see before me by the greedy, the mean and the vindictive (our antagonists can sort out the adjectives amongst themselves).

FRIDAY OCTOBER 9TH

Most of the week seems to have been taken up by packing, sorting and looking at mobile homes and containers. We have been to a couple of sites to look for statics. It has opened up a whole new world. The sites are so welcoming and the homes so cosy. The more statics I see the more excited I become about the immediate future.

I think we have found the perfect one. It is on a holiday site but is privately owned. The owner is an old lady and she has to sell. It is all I have dreamed of and has central heating and double glazing. It is so neat and tidy and very clean. We made a deal with the site manager and Alan shook his hand to seal the deal.

We are so excited to have at last found the caravan of our dreams. Now we really are well on the way to our independence. They will hold it for us until it is time for our descent onto Syda Farm.

Saturday 10th October

My word, what a morning! The kitchen was rather like a scene from Piccadilly Circus. People were in and out like goodness knows what. Waited for one lady to collect her kitten and she was an hour late. Of course, this affected the rest of the morning seriously. Jane Keeveny called to take Tommy Tucker to his new home. This home for Tommy has come right out of the blue and is a prayer answered. Like so many of my prayers. Tommy is a dear old cat of 12 years old whose owner was taken into a home. When Tommy arrived he was so miserable; we nick-named him Victor Mildrew. Over many months he came to love being the kingpin at the rescue centre. He blossomed into the sweetest little cat I have ever known.

He liked his daily routine of walking down his ladder to meet me at the door. He would then walk up again to his feed bowl and turn to face me. I would feed him the best food I could lay my hands on. Sometimes if he did not want his food I would go in and fuss him. Fussing him as he walked back to his bowl, he would always continue to eat provided I kept rubbing his back gently. He just likes to check that I still love him. I loved him so much, I was hoping deep down to keep the old gimmer forever. But the home that came up was a wonderful opportunity; I could not let it pass by.

Sometimes, as in many things, you just have to love enough to let go.

Well Jane took him off in his cat carrier, once we had given his nails a good old trim. I was worried the last minute manicure would upset him. He is a delicate little soul really. However, apparently, at his new home, he woofed down a pouch of food and went to sleep. I am so happy for my little Tommy Tucker.

Chatsworth Estates have put us in court to get possession of the farm. This is despite the fact that our solicitor has spent time (hence loads of our money) instructing them on the phone that we intend to get out as soon as is humanly possible and we are already in the process of packing (us and over seventy animals). The court date is December, yet they have been informed we will be out by mid-November. I guess when you have as much money as they do, it doesn't really matter wasting it (though, of course, they intend to claim costs from us, we who have nothing . . . .). Both Alan and I want to be gone from this hell hole. I now see Rufford House for what it is—a big cold house. I see all its bad things now; I have removed my rose coloured spectacles.

SATURDAY 17ᵀᴴ OCTOBER

Up at the crack of dawn to feed the lame horses that are confined to the stables. Quickly cleaned up a load of cat poop and left for a fundraising morning at Pets at Home. Jack Wood came with me and Blake met us down there. We drew up outside, only to see another charity setting up inside. I was gutted and ready to go home for a cup of tea. Phoned Alan to check my diary to see if I had the wrong date. I hadn't so he persuaded me to go inside and point out what had happened.

It's a good job I did as this guy had only come in on a whim so they told him of their error and he kindly left. Felt a bit mean but I apologised to him and he was fine about it. The kids and I set up our tombola and off we went, raising over £70 for the animals. It was great fun and, thanks to Jenny (the red tornado), the tombola was absolutely tops. The funniest thing was, the Hired Assassin (see my prologue) came in the store. I suggested the boys asked him to have a go and I guaranteed he would not want to support the rescue. I was correct and he certainly did not want to. He was so horrible that a lady behind him commented loudly, "Well, what a miserable man." Yep, she got that spot on.

The tombola was all done by 12.30 pm. Everyone had a really good time. I went and spent half the money on cat litter and special cat food for the cats. I have to get special biscuits for Daisy, as she has to have food 'for sensitive stomachs'. Bailey, the nutty Siamese, has to have the best biscuits, so that he can graze on them all day. Home for a cup of tea and some well earned dinner.

Oh what bliss, a lovely afternoon up at the ménage, with kids and ponies. I don't know what it is about Saturdays but I love them. Set up my video camera on a tripod facing the ménage. We had two major events which might be a bit of fodder for You've Been Framed. Carol's sister, Lynne, lost control of Bella, who ran away with her, and little Hailey was thrown onto a jump pole by Dusty. Once I checked the camera was still rolling, I did check that they were both ok!

Had a nice shower in preparation for a special evening; Alan's wonderful fish and chip night, and it doesn't get much better than that. I popped on the bathroom scales just to keep a check on my weight. I appeared to have put on a couple of pounds. Moved the scales around the bathroom to a position where the weight was lost again, which makes me feel more deserving of my fish and chips.

Cola the cat sat on chicken pen

Hope the cat from Taiwan

Holly my puppy and Mimi my Great Dane

18TH OCTOBER

I went to see my new home again. Sad, I know, but I lay awake at night thinking about it. So warm and so cosy, a real little nest of a place. Just as we were leaving, we got a phone call from Pets at Home. Someone had walked into the store and dumped a dog! Alan took me straight down there. Lovely little dog it is, a small terrier type. Took her home and put her in the new kennels. Then, although a little late, we headed off to see the static at the caravan site.

Had another look around my beautiful caravan. Oh, I can't wait to get it home. It's so quaint and homely. It opens into a little hallway that leads to a lovely kitchen with all new units. Although small, it will be manageable for my baking. It then opens up into a neat little lounge with a television area. No expense has been spared on the abundant net curtains. The actual curtains are also of a good quality and rather thick. The pattern is bland but that's not a problem. The settee is large and stretches around the top end of the caravan. It looks ample size for Alan and me, along with our pets and any guests.

I got a frantic call on the way home. Tommy Tucker had pooped on the carpet of his new owner. I had to give him a call and a friendly chat in order to keep Tommy in his new home. Lovely chap but, with him being disabled, he could not clean the poop up. He was upset but I managed to convince him this would be a one off! All's well that ends well. Tommy has never missed the litter tray in all the time I have known him. I am thinking it was more than likely a fur ball. That can often be mistaken for poo.

Tuesday 20ᵗʰ October

Up early as Jenny is coming to help with more house clearing. What I ever would have done without her entering my life I do not know. I can't even think about it. Fed round all the animals and Jenny arrived just as I finished my rounds.

We went in for a coffee and Alan dropped a bomb shell on me. He had phoned the caravan site to discuss taking over a deposit and was told the caravan had been sold to a dealer, as he offered more money. Why I was shocked I don't know because it seems money rules everything now. The gentleman's agreement is no longer binding, except Alan did not know this. We were both shocked and upset as we had taken three months to find this caravan. We had been in contact with this site since the beginning of the month. We have waited patiently for the home to become available. We have been to the site three times in a week and then we are gazumped. The guy who sold us the caravan was out with his wife as it was his day off.

Not one to take things lying down, I rang the site office. The lady was lovely and very sympathetic. She told me to send the details by email and she would pass them on to the man in charge. This I did but it took up most of the time I had with Jenny. This meant that we did not get as much done and I felt I had wasted her time. She was, as ever, really accommodating and just carried on regardless.

Later, when the lady from the caravan park rang back, she had another offer to make us—a fleet static that was a bit cheaper. I don't think so! A fleet caravan is one that is hired out on the park weekly through the season. The one we had picked was privately owned, double glazed and centrally heated. I was very cross and told her so. She said she would get the boss to call me. I suggested he did not call until Alan returned home, as I did not really want to deal with it. I was very upset and would only have aggravated the situation. Alan always puts his point across quietly and calmly.

Later on the boss rang and spoke to Alan. The man was very understanding and is going to talk to the dealer and try to retract the deal. I could not understand why he could not say "Deal's off!" like he did with us. This is the bit I don't get.

Waited all night for a call from him but everytime I dashed to the ringing phone it was someone else. I had to sleep on it which was difficult. I asked my pendulum if we would get the caravan back. My pendulum said "Yes," so that helped a little. I often ask my pendulum questions and it is usually very good at giving me the correct answer. My pendulum is made of crystal that sits on the end of a chain. The idea is to hold it up between two fingers and ask the pendulum, "What is your yes?" It will then swing or rotate in a certain direction and this is the direction it will swing for yes to questions you ask. You do the same to find out its no. You then ask your questions and whichever way it swings, that is your answer.

WEDNESDAY 21ST

I woke up still worrying about our static caravan. Life goes on and the morning was spent tending Sooty's sudden foot abscess. Poulticing a foot is the worst nightmare for my poor old back. Gosh, Sooty had such a smelly foot, the stench would not leave my hands all day. After I had walked all the dogs, Alan called me in for a hot chocolate. I went over to the kettle and Alan told me he would leave the phone on the table incase George rang. I thought this a good idea as we did not want to miss his call. I felt sure that the dealer would not let our lovely static come back to us. "Leave the kettle for now, Gin, and come and have a doughnut," Alan said quietly. As I turned and looked at his face I suddenly realised the doughnuts were a celebration. I could see him attempting to conceal a grin. "Are we celebrating?" I asked eagerly.

"Yes, we are—the static caravan is ours!"

I could not believe it and was so happy. We had a home again and we could continue to prepare for our move. We were both worried that we were back at square one, having spent so many months looking for a static only to have to start again. I made some urgent phone calls to inform worried friends that we were ok after all. I guess we will appreciate our beautiful static even more than we did before we nearly lost it.

Crunchy, the old cow, is looking really well lately. She runs around all over the farm and covers more ground than all the younger stock. She has a big bowl of sugar beet every day. Alan had to fetch her up from the bottom fields today, as she had travelled so far. She had gone down the big hill to the meadow. It's a lovely walk down and so enjoyable. However, I think Crunchy had enjoyed the walk down but needed persuasion to get back up the hill. It's a lovely walk down there and I have enjoyed it so often myself. But like Crunchy, I always get to the bottom and think, "Oh my, what have I done?"

Alan fetched the two containers from Buxton this week. He has done a wonderful job sorting it all out. I don't know how he does it, so calmly and so efficiently. He never moans about all the tasks he has to do. I know I would have been doing a bit of moaning if I had been in his shoes. He just seems to love anything that involves setting off in his battered old tractor for a few hours.

He is very proud of his containers and has made sure we have plenty of storage space for our goods and chattels. Well, I think the containers will look smart alongside the old man's hedge.

THURSDAY OCTOBER 22ND

Busy day as ever, clearing out rooms in the house. Butler's pantry came in for it today. It's an old pantry type room, absolutely brilliant and has always been very spacious. Alan put shelves in it when we first married. It's very dark in there, which is the only problem. It was full of tins and packets of food that I had actually forgotten all about. It also contains lots of belongings from other people who have lived in the house over the years. This has been a major problem in Rufford House Farm; we did not start with a clean canvas. This has made life difficult at times and more so now.

Alan had to nip for a bale of straw for the crippled horses that need stables. We now have to include Ginny in this list. It is strange that two horses out of the same field have suddenly developed foot abscesses? Poulticing the horse's feet every morning is proving very difficult. It's not so bad in the evening when my back has loosened up. However, up till around noon each day, bending an inch is out of the question! The two horses are responding well to their treatment.

The day was given a brilliant end when we went to Kelly's house for fish and chips and "Coronation Street". Stayed for an hour or two enjoying the chit chat.

Saturday 24th October

Table top sale at The Old House, a local pub. Up with the larks; the morning was wet and misty and very miserable. Still these things need to be done to raise money for the animals. Emma met me there and we set up a wonderful stall. Then we sat and waited . . . .

Three hours later, and having managed to make a loss of four pounds, we packed up and went home. I was so tired from lack of activity. I can't say lack of stimulation, as Emma and I chatted endlessly and had a real giggle. Found out we have even more in common than I thought. We enjoyed the morning talking about our animals and other family members.

Monday October 26th

Took Robbie off early to Ashbourne Heights. This was to see our lovely static caravan. Alan wanted to pay for it today to make sure it is safely ours. Alan took us on our usual picturesque journey through Tissington. The drive is wonderful this way and takes us through the Oakover Estate. The scenery is so picturesque and green. The ground is undulated where the horse-ploughs have worked the land. This route also involves driving through a ford which is great fun.

Arrived on the caravan site, only to find them removing our caravan, not due to be moved until 2nd November. My heart dropped and I could tell Alan was worried, though he pretended not be. Alan jumped with speed out of the Land Rover and Rob was quick too. I just sat in a panic thinking we had lost it again. Rob signalled over to me that all was ok. I breathed again and got out to see my lovely new home.

During de-site, it had been made untidy. Not to worry—I did cope with this and skipped in to admire it once again. I love it and cannot wait to live in it. Mind you, I am aware that I am under a big illusion that it is going to be wonderful. I am sure it is a bit of an illusion as how can we, along with all our animals, cope living in this small box? I can't seem to picture the reality of it. I can only see the sheer joy of my first real marital home. Help me someone, please. I need a good slap to bring me off my planet and into the real world.

Once Alan had paid for the static, we left for home knowing that Alan would have to come straight back to the site. Alan and Jack headed back after a sandwich, in order to pick up the static's steps. The steps luckily come with the caravan and are worth a fair old bit. At least we will get in and out of the static safely.

Rob and I walked into town and had a coffee and did a bit of shopping. Alan fetched us at about 6pm. Home for our usual Monday "Coronation Street", double bill heaven.

Tuesday 27th October

Very busy morning carting various animals to two different vets. Dropped Alan and Meg (little hairy terrier) off at our own vet. Meg has been showing signs of incontinence. This has not been very obvious apart from unexplained little pools of water in the kitchen. It was not until she was laid fast asleep in the kitchen that we spotted her urinating in her sleep. She woke up in a big pool of water. Once we dropped Alan off, Rob and I had to go to Clay Cross to another vet for spays and castrations for the kittens. Three were old enough and one was not. Left the three and brought one home.

Alan was waiting for us with Meg at the Old House pub. Meg is not incontinent but has a very slack muscle in her urethra. Bruce, the vet, has given her some drops to put in her food twice a day. Would you believe that the first drops she had stopped the leaking urine? I could not believe it. Wow, what a vet!

We all squashed into the Land Rover and made our way home. Had to pick up a couple of little girl horse riders on route. I was a bit irritated, as this meant we hit traffic that we needn't have. Had dinner and then we started to clear my tack room ready for the move? Packed all my tack into the tractor bucket and took it across the road to my tack shack (a container all of my own). We managed to clear the tack room in two journeys. Once we had finished, we had to go to sign our wills. Once that was done, our minds were really at rest. Now, if anything happens to us, others will take on our fight.

OCTOBER 28TH

Rob and Alan took my wonderful ménage down today. I found this rather difficult to watch as I remembered the joy of seeing it built. The hours spent putting in the poles and the posts. It has actually only been up fully for two years. For several years it was fenced off with rope, which worked really well. It did not look ever so professional though. Two years ago, Alan bought all the wood to fence it properly. I will never forget the sight of it. It was so beautifully fenced by Kelly's husband, Dave. I can remember the pride I felt when I worked in it. I suppose I could liken it to power dressing. I am sure the newly fenced ménage improved my teaching. I can't say I noticed it improve my actual riding though.

To see the ménage coming down like this really hurt like hell. I felt sad to the core of my heart. This part of the farm was my little bit of heaven. I would climb the loft stairs on a summer's day and walk through my dusty old tack room. Once I had negotiated the rotting floor, an adventure in itself, I would open the door onto my little bit of heaven.

I would find such peace and tranquillity up there. The view was stunning. A dry stone wall surrounded the area and this was lined with many beautiful trees, housing a variety of different birds. Wildlife was abundant and the whole area was a sun trap. I remember when Alan enclosed the whole area, my area. This was Gin's world and it was being torn down before my eyes; my dogs' world, the horses' world and my friends' world too. As I watched Rob and Alan working, I waved and said I was going to walk the dogs. I was struggling to keep the tears at bay. I cried all the way on my private, reflective walk. My Meg stayed loyally by my side, knowing I was suffering emotionally. I wondered why all this was happening. Then I remembered that I was moving to a whole new Gin's World!

THURSDAY 29TH

Hell of a day! Off to the Royal Hospital for the dreaded mammogram. What an ordeal and only the ladies can understand this. I was so worried about this appointment but thought it was in a few days. However when I got up today, I discovered it was the day of my appointment. Girls, we need to get our heads together and invent a boob friendly mammogram. The one in place at present was obviously invented by a male of the species.

Out of the hospital and home again in no time. Packed Rob's last few things in the back of the Land Rover. This included mum's widescreen telly. Dropped them all off at his house in Derby and had dinner out on the way back. Went in a pub with two for one offer and had a lovely meal. Suddenly remembered the chickens were out in the dark. Hasty ride home.

Tombola to prepare for tomorrow which we put off until the very last minute. This of course being bed time. The three of us sat at the table, bleary eyed and barely able to talk. We somehow managed to put together an excellent tombola. Went to bed happy but wishing I had done the tombola earlier in the day.

31ST OCTOBER

What a wonderful day! Although getting up out of bed was the last thing I wanted to do, I had little choice. A fashion chain had offered us the opportunity to do a fund raising event. The plan was to do tombola and take Meg, the little terrier, to attract people over to us.

Carol met me and Rob and we drove to the back of the store. Emma arrived and we set up a really good event. Little Meg just sat on a rug eating a bone; she never moved. That is until someone walked in with what sounded like a tiny little bell ringing. Meg started running around the shop and all the displays, trying to find the mystery bell. No one could locate it but it became apparent that to Meg it held great significance. Luckily, after having Meg's incontinence problem sorted out we had no little leaks on the shop floor.

Rob and I went for a drink; I had a hot chocolate, with all the works of course (the works being a good dollop of spray cream and marshmallows). Also sharing a Panini, I left the shop feeling rather sluggish.

Back to work and what a pleasant time we had. The people in and out of the shop varied greatly. You had the animal lovers who would be drawn over to view our display boards. You had the serious shoppers who would spot our group and do a hasty U-turn to avoid us. We met a lovely Italian family who were so intent on winning a bottle of wine, they purchased numerous ticket until they had their bottle. A lovely old gent and his wife bought tickets just to support our sanctuary; each time they won, they put the prize back in the tombola.

By noon we had made an amazing £100 and had met so many wonderful people. As we packed away, we had very few prizes left, which was a good feeling. All the hard work had paid off.

WEDNESDAY NOVEMBER 4TH
IN WHICH WE
DESCEND ON THE FARM!

Today the cow pat really does hit the fan! I felt sure that fireworks would come a day early. This is the day we have waited for; the day that Alan takes me home. The day Alan returns to the farm he has worked all his life for. We are up early, ready for the start of a lengthy battle.

Although Alan constantly tells me everything is fine, I am sure this is not the case. As I said before, Alan tends to hide his feelings. Today, I could tell even he was fraught with the task ahead of us. This was a new beginning but not without its problems and dangers. I nipped off to tend to animals and failed to take my mobile. Rob came to find me to tell me that Alan was in a right state and was worried as to my whereabouts. When I went back to the house I tried to calm him down, as he seemed agitated. I was glad to see a bit of emotion coming out. At the same time I was afraid; if Alan crumbled now I felt sure there was no way I could keep it together. I had been recharging my courage through Alan's strength, yet it looked like my courage was about to lose its source.

We had tried to ring the caravan park in order to find out the arrival time for our static caravan. Alan was worried it would already be at Syda Farm, thus alerting the old man to our plans. Alan did a mad dash to the farm to find it was not there and that seemed to settle him a little.

Alistair arrived at around 10.30 am but sadly without the troops he had led us to believe had been rallied. I don't know how Alan felt at this point but I felt very vulnerable. How could we set up a static on Syda with no back up?

Fraught with emotion I called on some of our many good friends. Those that were available had no hesitation in heading straight to Rufford House Farm, to provide the moral support we so desperately needed. I felt honoured to have such support and loyalty. Carol, just made redundant, found a silver lining in the fact that she was able to be with us on this day. Our dear friend, Alan Keeveny, who was actually working when I called him, phoned back moments later and said, "I'm knocking off from this job, Ginny, I'm on my way." He left off the job he was doing and came over straight away, meaning he would have to fall behind on his own work. Ever dependable Kelly not only came along with our Goddaughter but she brought her entire family too (mum, stepdad, younger sister, et al). And my dear friend Lynne, who suffers terrible ill health, made her way over, once she had taken her hair curlers out. Alistair's girlfriend Katie, although heavily pregnant, joined the troops. I was completely overwhelmed by the support we received. I knew from this moment that we were safe.

Over the last few months we have often heard the expression "conflict of interest" when needing support or help. This has been from the top, most highly paid professionals. Many people use this term as a get out clause, I believe. This expression has been used by people that know the truth about Alan's treatment by his family, yet they choose not to get involved. When the dreaded phrase "conflict of interest" arises you know that is another phrase for simply not wanting to get involved, not wanting to help. But there we were, with our close friends who did not hesitate or pause for one moment in our time of need. Nor did I hear the cowardly expression "conflict of interest." In our hour of need, friends rallied and I was humbled. They know the truth and there was no question.

We waited anxiously for the call. We filled up on cheese sandwiches and tea. We sat and paced and sat; I felt more like I was waiting to go to the gallows. The call came; our home was waiting at the Highwayman pub, up the road. It was all systems go, go, go!

Suddenly all hell broke loose and we piled into the cars and vehicles. Alistair drove our most vital weapon, the Ford Case tractor! Alan and I raced off to meet the static with hearts pounding out of our chests. We were about to embark on the most frightening journey of our life.

Flashing the Land Rover lights at the lorry driver, Alan turned round and beckoned the driver to follow. Adrenalin pumping, I jumped from the vehicle and threw open Syda Farm's main gates, as Alan pulled out the heavy metal centre to gain access for the lorry. We raced against the clock to unload the static and get it in situ before anyone could stop us.

Our supporters arrived in droves and we felt safe at last. As the cars pulled in on the grass, I was uplifted at the sight of many of my good friends and my brother, Robbie, on this momentous day. From reading this diary you will understand what a potentially dangerous situation we were putting ourselves in. We had been left with no choice.

All was quiet on the western front as the static was unloaded from the lorry. The caravan swayed from side to side as it was slowly and precariously lowered down the feeble looking ramp. I felt sure this was the bit where it would all go horribly wrong. It continued to wobble and slid towards the lane, hitting the road as it descended. The driver asked us where we planned to site it.

"Oh, you won't get it up there mate, believe me. I have been doing this job for thirty years and I'm telling you. You put this static on that field and it will sink straight away."

On hearing these words I wanted to cry. I looked across at Alan as he listened to the driver. The look on his face told me he was going to get the static caravan exactly where he had planned to and nobody was going to stop him. The drivers turned their now empty lorry in the yard below and revved the engine. Putting his foot down, he roared across the field, passed the caravan and was gone. This indicated the ground was not as bad as all that.

Within moments, Alan had the static hitched up to his tractor, well before anyone could say "Get orf my land!" I have to admit I saw a different person at the wheel of the tractor. I saw the man I loved but suddenly beyond that man I saw my super hero.

As the tractor moved slowly across the sodden field, dragging my new five tonne static, my heart nearly burst through the walls of my chest. The static tipped to the right and at this stage I felt sure it was all over. Suddenly it righted itself and carried on up the field. The wheels began to sink into the ground just as the delivery driver warned us. Alan kept his cool, while I was ready to collapse in a screaming heap. He continued with his foot pressed lightly on the accelerator. The static caravan sunk lower with every inch it moved. The ruts on the field were becoming very deep and wet. I called to my friends to help me push the static. We were probably of little consequence but we pushed hard as the caravan tried to topple over. Alan dragged the static into position, reversed slightly and by a small miracle the static was in place. Alan Shirt had come home to the farm he built and he had brought his wife with him (that's me by the way). Everyone cheered and laughed as we realised (so we thought) that the worst was over!

The men spent hours getting the static sited. This was a shock to me as I was under the illusion that it would take maybe an hour. My plan was then to go in and make all our supporters a hot drink. This was not to be. As we stood around in the cold and bitter evening there was no hot drink. There was a lot of activity around the farm, with the old man and his new neighbours making frantic, emergency calls (the neighbours had bought 4acres of Syda Farm, despite knowledge of the dispute between father and son and, representing a lower branch of humanity, had seen an opportunity to exploit the dispute, to sweet-talk an old man in to giving away even more of the land—possibly all for next to nothing! Their resentment at Alan's arrival to make his rightful claim and thwart their plans for Syda-domination continues to this day, unabated!—more in future diaries). Various visitors sped past, peering at the caravan with shock and fascination. The large gate at the top of the lane was chained up by said neighbour, one Mr.Trog. No conflict of interest there, then. It is really nothing to do with them, but sadly they got involved from the outset. Fortunately, we have not come here to make friends—we have come here to claim what is rightfully ours. We will do our best to be peaceful and keep focused on what we need to do. The Trogs clearly have their own agenda.

The police arrived and entered both of the neighbouring properties. They eventually came to see Alan and listened as he put his story to them. The old man had not even informed the police that the static belonged to his own son. They were astounded at the lack of information they had been given by Alan's father. The two policemen declared we had done nothing illegal and would be returning to both sets of neighbours to inform them that we must keep out of their way and they must keep out of ours, until the matter is duly sorted through the appropriate, civil channels. The older of the two policemen was more interested in getting back to his car for warmth, such was the nature of the bitterly cold night from which we were still unable to withdraw.

Eventually, the static was ready for habitation. My friends began to drift away back to their own world, while I stepped inside with Alan and Rob, across the threshold to a new, exciting world. The evening was delightful as we sat by the little fire drinking tea. After popping out for those ubiquitous fish and chips (if ever there was a period in my life when I needed comfort food, it was these months covered in the diary); the evening could not get any better. The night was surprisingly quiet and we slept well. My brother Rob will be with us until the dust settles. I think he will be here for some time!

Stepped outside and found a hand delivered letter on the step. We must be off the farm by 5pm tomorrow and we must let them know if we need any help. Well I guess this is it; "Get the tractor hitched to the static Alan, it's time to leave." I don't think so!

Went to check on Rufford House Farm and see our darling dogs before bed. It feels terrible to be parted from all our wonderful animals. The dogs have to look after Rufford for us. They were frantic with the change in their routine. Holly was very aggressive and upset; I made the mistake of scooping her up and bringing her home to the static.

THURSDAY 5ᵀᴴ NOVEMBER
OUR FIRST FULL DAY
BACK AT SYDA FARM

I got a real shock this morning when I woke up and got out of bed. I had so much planned and so much to do. My head hurt as it rested on the pillow. This is not an unusual start for the day! However, as I raised my head and climbed out of bed, my brain seemed to be pounding to get out of my skull. I could barely move or speak as I attempted to dress myself. I opened the door of the static and breathed in the morning air. It was crisp and fresh and the fields were covered in silvery dew. The view was amazing with a beautiful sunrise; there was not a car in sight. I so wanted to soak up the moment but my head hurt so much. This terrible pain was to be with me for the rest of the day.

I went off to Rufford to let the dogs out. No sooner had we left the static, a Trog pulled up outside and proceeded to take photos of our new home. He got a bit of a surprise when Rob lifted the nets and waved at him. At least they now know that we have another person in residence when we go out.

FRIDAY 6TH NOVEMBER

A better and less painful start to the day. I flung open the static door and soaked up the sunrise and the tranquillity that surrounded me. I headed down to Rufford to meet a potential owner for Fudge the dog. However, as I fetched her out of the kennel they arrived at the same time. This was not good and did not endear Fudge to them. I was a little upset as Fudge is such a lovely little dog. I felt that this couple really wanted a perfect little pooch that ticked all their boxes. Fudge is hardly a perfect pooch and I sensed straight away that I was wasting my extremely valuable time. Rescue dogs don't usually allow you to tick all the boxes.

In the afternoon, I wasted my time yet again. Another potential home, this time for our little Meg. Again, as soon as the lady arrived I could tell by her demeanour that she was not keen to have a dog at all. Meg does tick all the boxes (rare as I said). This lady had clearly been persuaded to consider homing a dog by her friend, Mary. Mary is the woman that owns Sooty and she clearly was wasting my time too. I was a little disgruntled as I have so much on at the moment. To have to make extra journeys up and down to the farm is very demanding to say the least.

Alan was as busy as ever building decking outside the caravan. He is preparing for the arrival of our Danes. We need to be prepared and make sure that the entrance to the static is suitable for them. It is a little scary, the thought of bringing them to this small, contained space. I am just worried about the actual introduction to the static. Introducing them to a new farm with neighbouring dogs will not be easy. On Wednesday morning, little Meg will be fostered for a while. This will be the day we bring our babies home.

I will be sad to see little Meg go as we are very fond of each other. She has loved her time at the farm with us. I feel she has had such a wonderful time and I have enjoyed her stay. Had we not lost Rufford, I am sure she would have stayed with us forever.

SATURDAY 7TH NOVEMBER

Back down to Rufford for most of the day. I just want to spend more time in my little home at Syda. Alan and Alistair, along with Alistair's friend Les, moved all the big furniture into the storage container. I gathered up my two hall cats as I call them. Dotty and Scoop are two delightful rescue cats. They are mother and daughter and have been living in the hall for the last few years. They are very possessive of the hall and will not allow any other cats into it. Dotty is a pure white cat that is completely deaf. Scoop is a lovely black cat with a disabled paw. Having gathered them up for their own well being I took them to the safety of our static caravan.

Rufford House Farm is slowly becoming an empty, soulless, desolate building. The heart of this big old farm has stopped beating. I don't believe it will ever beat as a beautiful working farm again. I feel nothing for it anymore. My love for Rufford is packed away in the storage container. I have a new love now and it's time to move on. Thank you, Rufford House Farm, for the fun and laughter you have given us over the years. I shall never forget the happy and extremely sad times we have shared. I just want to go home now.

Driving backwards and forwards between farms is taking its toll. Both Alan and I are extremely tired. We have readily called Syda our home, which is funny really when you consider the welcome we have had. We are made to feel like outcasts, which we expected anyway.

The Trog male came at me aggressively on the drive (when no one else was about, of course), raised his fists in front of my face and yelled at me to get back to my "Gypsy caravan". What a joy it must be to be the Trog female (although, to be fair, they are both extremely well matched). He kept punching the air with his fists as he threatened to "Have me". He was like some wild animal and so out of control. His language cannot even be repeated. Spit flew from his ugly, angry mouth as his venom was let loose. What a charming man! It is so sad to think that human beings can behave so badly towards fellow human beings, knowing full well that we are homeless and in a very vulnerable place right now. Of course, the old man and the Prodigal Son engineered our plight in the first place (mere greed), and our landlord played along with it (for him, it's all about maximising profits. What price people, eh?). The Trogs are involved to, as a result of nefarious and unlawful land deals behind Alan's back, it would appear.

The Trogs have bought the old farmhouse at Syda, at a snip. The old man has squandered at least £150,000 to spite my husband, including a further reduction in price so the Trogs avoid paying full dues back to the Exchequer (i.e. stamp duty). Maybe that would have been fine, if the Trogs had honoured the pledge to pay the rest to the old man in cash, which they didn't!

The Trogs claim to have had all sympathy for our plight until we moved onto Syda. Oh damn! Had I known I could have retained their sympathy by staying until the eviction date, I would have done so. Well, do the Trogs mean that they would have brought us a cup of tea, as we sat on our suitcases outside the gates of Rufford House Farm? I can't believe I have missed out on this chance to see the better side of human nature. As a result of our moving before the eviction date, we have seen the low shallow side of a Troglodyte, and not a moment too soon.

Drat! Apparently we have particularly upset Lady Trog. She wants to try living like I have for months, never knowing who is going to turn up at Rufford and make trouble; receiving threats from the old man, the Prodigal Son and the grand old Duke's men; dreading the postie and the sight of the regular official letters, containing further threats, often in legalese, designed I'm sure, to intimidate. It must have been hell for poor Lady Trog to see a static arriving on land that is actually nothing at all to do with her. These people have purchased a farm knowing there's a dispute. They are happy to live on "a farm" but what I don't get is that they want it to remain a silent setting, with no actual farm life upon it (the noise from their commercial venture is no matter it would appear, because, with such people, as you know, it's one rule for one . . . .).

If the Trogs are truly so unhappy to see us homed and sheltered, then, from the bottom of my heart, I say to them— Life's a bitch (if that's the way you want to live)!

The Trog male was upset that we did not warn him what was going to happen and what we had planned. Alan pointed out that this was impossible as he would have gone straight in to tell the old man. Apparently he would not! Mmmmmm . . . . what can I say? Our mistake, perhaps. No. Let's not forget, the Trog male was quick to bolt the gates once we were inside. A pretty futile act, but not one of an objective observer of the unfolding events.

SUNDAY 8TH NOVEMBER

Another day of packing and storing. Thank God Alan got the storage containers in readiness for all our belongings. We worked really hard along with our friend Dave.

The Prodigal Son has been busy around Syda, chaining and padlocking all the gates on the fields. Having succeeded in taking them by surprise with the caravan, they are, I suppose, locking the stable door after the horse has bolted. However, I am sure they are aware that Alan and I come with a lot of baggage in the form of numerous livestock! They are going to great lengths to keep the livestock out (this Christian man begrudges part of 100 acres for his brother's homeless animals—where would he have them go? Silly question, as this saintly sibling was intent to see me and Alan and our many animals on the streets).

We are busy getting troops together for the next stage of our move.

My sister Katie invited us down for steak and chips—sounded good to me. However, we have to do it in two sittings. I went down first with Alan (no time for a shower), ate our dinner and watched "X Factor", ah bliss. Just before we left, Bill, my sister's partner, cooked Rob's dinner and put it in a foil tray. We then did a mercy dash to the static caravan so that dinner was hot when Rob got it. Well, I don't know how Bill did it; as I tipped it on the plate, it felt as hot as if it had come fresh out of the oven.

To bed around midnight. I am sure I was asleep before my head actually touched the pillow. Sign of a clear conscience, I feel. I wonder if the old man and our other new neighbours are sleeping soundly? I somehow doubt it!

Monday 9th November

I have often heard people say they are living off their nerves. Now I know exactly how this feels. It's not all bad though as living off my nerves has caused me to lose a couple of pounds in weight. However, on the down side, it is not a nice feeling. I feel very sick most of the time and I am very edgy. I am nervous and feel threatened at all angles. I go to Rufford and I feel sick, then I go to Syda and I feel sick, then I go to town and I feel sick. If I leave the static caravan, I worry until I get home again. I worry about my animals all the time. Have I locked my chickens up? Did I shut the door properly? Did I lock the house up? Did I feed the dogs? Did I lock the cat pens? Such are my nerves and my anxiety.

Tended to the animals and grabbed another cat on the way out. Murph the Smurf this time. He is my epileptic cat and needs to be at Syda with us. He shouldn't really be left alone as he can hurt himself when fitting. He has been in the family for around seven years and is a very special cat. His nose is very big and he is known affectionately as Jimmy Durante. Wiped Murphy's feet and popped him into the static and he fell asleep on the sofa. There he stayed in a blissful sleep for almost 36 hours.

We seem to be doing nothing but chase back and forwards. It is very difficult to look after the animals when they are on a separate farm to us. I am feeling shattered all the time and look forward to the time when I can sit quietly in my static caravan.

Had a pleasant visit from my sister Kate and my niece Jodie. They had even bought me a card welcoming me to my new home. They had also bought me some nice cups and a bundle of cream cakes. Had a natter and a tour of my new home. The tour took all of two minutes! They went out for a cigarette and found a silly note on the car. The note was calling them trespassers and demanding they leave immediately or else! So much for us all keeping out of each other's way! We just found it rather pathetic and sad.

Down to put the chickens away before the fox pays a visit. Rob came down to help me and he walked Fudge while I did the cats. Had a young lady and her daughter come to look at our last little kitten. The little girl was delightful and picked each cat up in turn to give them a hug and kiss. She would have taken them all home if she could. However, she picked the last kitten of Daisy's litter and kissed her goodbye till she picks her up on Wednesday.

I let the girls out for a walk and proceeded to walk towards the field gate. The girls were really excited. It is terrible to have to leave them at Rufford while we are in our caravan. I miss them so much and know that with them by my side I will be safe. We are both a little nervous of bringing them to the caravan, yet we are incomplete without them. I think we fear the filth that they will bring into our small home. However, having had Holly down here for a week, it has become apparent that the dogs will not get filthy like they do at Rufford. Holly has developed a really shiny coat and looks lovely. I can come in and out of the static without getting caked in mud and filth. At least I won't have to take my wellies off when I go to the bank anymore.

As I was about to begin our walk, I happened to notice that the lady who came to see me about the kitten had left the farm gate open. I was shocked and relieved that we only had old Crunchy in the yard. I looked across to the hay where she had been eating moments earlier. I thought she must have gone to bed. Thank the Lord I looked in the direction of the road and saw Crunchy had nipped out in the dark and crossed over the A619 to see her friends. I ran towards the road bellowing for Rob. Rob bellowed back, thinking I had been attacked by some mad axe man. I bellowed in the darkness for him to stop the traffic. Meanwhile, a driver had spotted Crunchy and turned his vehicle round to come back down and put his hazard lights on. He stopped the traffic as we danced around in the middle of the road. Once the traffic had stopped, we opened the gate opposite the farm and directed Crunchy to her friends. We thanked our hero who had stopped to help. The van he drove was full of young people who had watched his heroics with great admiration. We then tried to figure out how this old disabled cow with one eye could possibly spot an open gate in the pitch dark, let alone sprint hastily across the busy A619. No one can ever say my life is dull.

TUESDAY 10TH NOVEMBER

Sadly, had to say goodbye to our chief house sitter Rob today. Took Rob to the train station at around ten in the evening. Of course, this will take our freedom away but Rob has a life to live too. He has given up so much time to me and Alan and is set to give up even more of his valuable time in the future. His support for me and Alan has been overwhelming and without his help our lives would have been so much more difficult than it has been.

My friend, Linda, called up to see our static and discuss moving the horses and ponies. We have decided to carry out the move on this coming Monday. It will certainly make our lives easier when all the big animals are here. Of course, the old man has organised the chaining and padlocking of all gates around the farm. This has kept The Prodigal Son very busy indeed. There are many gates leading into the fields of Syda Farm but we only need one.

We have informed the solicitor of the locked gates and he has the ideal solution. Apparently we can break a link as opposed to the padlock. The gates are preventing us access to common land (I don't really get this) so we are allowed to break a link. Let's do it. Mind you, I was laughing earlier as we remembered one of the first letters the old man had sent on our arrival at the farm. He stated that he would like us to leave by 5pm the next day. And yet here we are without an exit wide enough to get our static out, thanks to the shenanigans of the in-laws. That is of course if we wanted to leave, which we don't.

As Linda was about to leave, Carol arrived with a Bakewell tart. You see things aren't that grim. We had a good old natter and catch up before taking a stroll around the fields. Upon Alan's return, I had to go down to the farm to feed the stock and lock up the chickens. I met up with the neighbour who works for Chatsworth. Of course the agents have kept him very up to date with our business. He now appears intent on ripping Alan off to the sum of £250. This is for hay, feed and general care of the horses. Apparently, he was unaware their horse was grazing illegally! Illegally or otherwise, we have taken care of the said horse for the last eight years. Well, they have recently been robbed so I put it to him that he was actually no better than a common thief. A few other choice words were sent his way. I told him I would go to the small claims court if he failed to pay in the next few days. When you are married to a man as kind and honourable as Alan, it is difficult to witness him being treated in a way that is so far removed from how he would treat people. They are mere opportunists, hoping to make a small gain from our plight. People, eh . . . .

WEDNESDAY 11ᵀᴴ NOVEMBER BRINGS A WONDERFUL NIGHT WITH THE WHOLE FAMILY TOGETHER AGAIN

Luckily, Alan had accidentally left the fire on all night. That was good news for me as I came into a lovely warm room first thing this morning. Oh, it was like heaven. Still no water today and this is making life difficult. Alan had to go off first thing for a shower at Rufford.

Dear Jenny came to Rufford at around 9.30am to help clear even more stuff. All the large furniture has now gone. The house should be looking empty and yet, with each large piece of furniture removed, a whole load of junk seems to take its place. Jenny had also come to take our lovely little rescue dog to a new home. The little dog, Meg, was very special to me and I think I was to her. We had bonded really well despite the fact she had killed two of my chickens. I reasoned that she could not override her instinct and I could not hate her for it. Upset though I was, I could not see her as a bad dog. As I carried her out to Jenny's car, my heart was breaking. I knew it was the best thing for her but there was something very special about this dog. I felt our relationship was special too. As Jenny drew her car away, Meg looked at me through the back window in a terribly longing way. I stifled the tears as best I could. I made my way into the house and broke down.

I sobbed for the loss of my little dog. I sobbed for the hell me and my husband have been put through and are still going through. I sobbed for each and every animal in my care that had, like me, become so vulnerable and so exposed. I sobbed for the changes that were being forced upon my life. There was a knock at the door; I wiped my eyes and went outside to home yet another little kitten.

The tears helped to release some of my emotions that I had kept locked deep within. I put them back in the little box and focused yet again on the positive. Our beautiful Great Danes, locked in a big, empty, cold kitchen for the last week, are coming home with me today.

Alan and I had been a little nervous about bringing them to the static. Leaving them at Rufford had been difficult and traumatic for both the dogs and us. Although we had not missed out on our wonderful daily walks, we had missed each other just being together. I called Alan on my mobile and announced happily, "Alan, the girls are coming home, get ready!"

Without hesitation or deviation, Alan welcomed my news. I loaded the girls into the Land Rover and, excitement and trepidation in hand, I drove them to their new home.

Alan and Holly met us on the fields. The girls went for a good run to hopefully let off steam—we did not want that in the static caravan. The moment came when they would step inside our small shelter. I somehow expected a massive explosion of energy leading to the static falling from its supports and rolling wildly down the big steep hill. Alan sat on the settee with a Dane perched on each knee. I noticed tears in his eyes. "Are you alright?" I asked, worried that they might be too heavy for his replacement knee.

He could only just speak enough to say, "We're a family again." Well, they do say home is where the heart is and we had just brought the heart into ours.

The dogs were wonderful and the static remained intact. We all had the most wonderful evening together.

THURSDAY 12ᵀᴴ NOVEMBER

What a hell of a night we went through!

We had all enjoyed a cosy evening. When it came to bedtime, Meg in particular seemed to be suffering from some form of separation anxiety. She cried and pawed at the door all night. I have never known her like it. She seems to have been seriously disturbed by the upheaval. I was shocked as she clawed at the little door between the kitchen and bedrooms. We listened to her whining until we could take no more. Alan went into the lounge and spent the rest of the night with the dogs. He always gets the best jobs.

Alistair came to see his dad and helped with some major jobs. One of the jobs was actually getting water supplied to the static. Although we have had a threatening letter saying not to touch the water, we have no choice. It was great to see father and son working side by side behind the static. Although working in top secret, the pair of them looked less than discreet as they dug behind. They would have looked much less conspicuous had they worn cream coloured clothing, which would have matched the caravan. Instead, the two comforting figures were kitted in conspicuous black. I had to laugh.

I went off early afternoon to meet Rob at the train station. I planned to sneak in a hair cut but Alan, as always, put paid to that idea. I was asked to go on a detour to fetch a gas bottle for the static caravan. This would have been fine, had the guy selling them not hurt his back. I had to jump out of the Land Rover to help him get the bottle in. Dripping wet and cold, I arrived at the train station, my usual dishevelled self.

Later in the evening we had to fetch larger farm implements from Rufford. With the implements strapped down to the trailer, we headed for Syda. Alan stopped on the top road and turned off his tractor lights before turning onto the field. I fumbled around to drop the sheep netting so that Alan could pass across it. The tractor chugged noisily across the field surrounded by the darkness. We could see the male Trog working in his garden. This garden backs out onto the field we were now crossing. The Trog was wearing a headlight so we were aware of his presence the whole time. We also knew the instant that he became aware of the noise of the tractor as it crossed the field.

It was comical to see his head suddenly rise in to the air as he was sure he could hear something. In a flash, Alan shut down the whole tractor and we waited in the darkness. All the Trog could hear now was any mischievous play by the Silence! After a moment of two, the headlight went down. We had not been rumbled. We set off over the rest of the field and made it to the caravan undetected.

The less these folk know the better.

Friday 13th November

Alan spent another night with the dogs in order to keep them settled and calm. There is no doubt that the recent week spent at Rufford alone has upset Meg. She is very clingy and will not let us out of her sight. We have taken the net curtain off the side window so that the neighbours are aware we have our protective dogs.

Fudge has settled well at Rufford and is now running around the farm yard. The animals at the farm seem bereft as they wander the soulless yards and buildings. Buzz, our cockatiel, looked isolated in the kitchen. Today was his day for coming home to Syda. I quickly washed the cage and cleaned his belongings out; I gave all his toys a good scrub. Bundled cage with Buzz into the Land Rover. He squawked all the way home.

I found the perfect place for him in the static and perched him happily there. Buzz sang and chirped till his throat was sore. He looked so content and seemed more than happy to be on the same level as us folk. At Rufford, he was on top of a big filing cabinet and was much higher up. He seemed really thrilled to be at eye-level and in a nice warm place. He is a lovely bird and was given to us when his owner became allergic. He was always a good guard bird at Rufford, as he would always sing a very loud warning when people came into the kitchen. He also impersonates different sounds. Last summer, gardening out the front, I was continually running in the kitchen to answer the phone. Each time I reached the kitchen, the phone stopped. It took many exasperating attempts to get to the phone before I realised it was Buzz mimicking the sound of the phone.

The neighbours have actually coughed up after my warning to them. They put the outstanding money through the letterbox and about time too. Talk about getting blood out of a stone. Anyway, my new life will mean that no matter what problems it brings, I have the advantage of never having to deal with that awful couple ever again. The new neighbours, on existing evidence, will be horrible but living next door to my old neighbours has taught me not to give a damn.

Sadly, I am now well rehearsed at ignoring the lower side of humanity. Most often, these depths originate in the excessively privileged aka spoilt brats but I refer to those who struggle with what to me are simple notions such as get a life, get on with it, enjoy, be charitable and kind and let all others enjoy their lives too.

Saturday 14th November

Up bright and early with a wake up bark from Holly. The dogs have now settled really well in the static. Down to Rufford at 8.45am, back to Syda at 8.50am. Rob had phoned me saying that the Prodigal Son had been snooping around the static and taking photos. I dashed home to see Rob was okay. I left the farm again but was back within five minutes as the oaf returned, the minute he saw me departing. An altercation ensued, resulting in a 999 call and all hell was let loose yet again. Lots of our valuable time wasted by a waste of space.

When I eventually made it down to Rufford, my head was in a whirl. I had a family coming to take some ducks from me. Lovely little family and I know they are animal crazy as most of my friends are these days. I was happy to see my ducks go to them but every time an animal is taken I feel a certain sadness.

I am happy for the animals as they are all going to good, probably better lives. I have done my best by the ducks but they do not deserve the mud they have to drag themselves through on a daily basis. Having said that, I like to think that they have had fun and lots of freedom here. Ducks are such a joy to have around. So easily pleased by a small bath of fresh water and a pile of freshly mucked out straw (nice heat generating dung!). They will sit on the piles of dirty straw to make the most of the lovely heat straw and dung produces. Ducks have amazing social lives—chatting, arguing and, of course, their extremely demonstrative courtships.

Little Fudge was let off her lead for the first time today. It was Carol's idea and a very good one I have to say. She ran around like a little foal just let out of her stable. The gaiety she displayed was such that words failed me. I have never seen such joy and grace in all my years of animal ownership. She pranced and danced and leapt and turned in the air. She will make someone a delightful friend. Carol threw sticks for her and Fudge could not get enough. When the horses came to investigate, it was time to take her back to the kennel.

Having been dumped at the local pet shop, Fudge was so called because she was a dirty fudge colour. A Fox Terrier like dog, we had many opinions as to her breeding. But one or two people said that, should we bath her, she will be white with a grey spot. We could not possibly bath her until now as she was unpredictable and needed time to settle. Up until now we were also aware that, living in a kennel, she would chill easily. Rufford Farm now stands virtually empty. Carol and I skipped to the house with only one thing on our mind-bathing Fudge. I was totally unaware of what we were about to find under that mucky little exterior.

As the freshly run water turned murky, Fudge became a white swan.We were totally amazed, as two washes and rinses later, a fluffy white lamb emerged. I was overwhelmed at the thought of where this dog had been locked away to give the appearance of being a fudge coloured dog! What story this dog has to tell will sadly remain untold. I shuddered to think what she would tell us if she had a voice. The texture of her coat, once coarse and dry, was fluffy and absolutely beautiful. We dried her off and left her in the big kitchen at Rufford House Farm. When all the other animals were fed, I peered in through the kitchen window, hoping to see Fudge curled up asleep on the settee. My heart sank when I saw her sitting as close to the door as she could, head bowed, waiting and listening for my return. In that moment, I felt so sad for all the abused dogs in the world, locked away, sitting and waiting.

I wish I could help them all. I wish.

Sunday 15th November

Rufford at 9am to feed the animals. Took Fudge for a nice long walk and then really started to sort out the house. Emma stayed an extra couple of hours and vacuumed the upstairs. This made such a difference and really spurred me on. I can't believe the energy that engulfed me as I sorted out our remaining belongings. We lit a hell of a fire for all the rubbish.

The upstairs of Rufford looked beautiful. I felt sad at the sight of beautiful Rufford, which I had not seen in a long time. I had forgotten how lovely the old house could look. I cannot remember when it all went horribly wrong. What day did I decide I could not handle taking care of the house anymore? What day did it all become too much for me to cope with? I cannot put a date on it and I cannot figure out why or when it happened. All I can say is that, however lovely it looks now, I never would have seen this again. Even if I had lived here another fifty years, things could only have become worse.

It's true that in life we don't always get what we want but we usually, God willing, get what we need.

It seems I have been too busy enjoying farm life and neglected my home. Well you know what they say, "Dull women have immaculate houses." Clearly I am no dull woman; I have simply enjoyed being a farmer's wife, tending the stock and making cakes, and one can't do it all. If I did housework and ironing as well I would never get to ride my horses, walk the dogs or watch "Coronation Street".

When I moved into Rufford, it was already full of other people's rubbish, from families that had inhabited this farm before me. I never did have a clean canvas from which to work. Despite this, I have done my best but it has never been enough.

Fed around the animals and fetched little Jack up from the field. Jack is another one of our rescue ponies and is on his way to make real the dreams of a little girl. Jack is a wonderful character and it is time for him to be the little girl's special pony. I am sure he will not be easy to master, as he never was. However, once you have won him over, he is putty. I loaded my woolly little pony into the trailer and kissed him goodbye. I felt the tears welling up in my eyes as I said goodbye to yet another friend. The ponies that are going out to foster homes are always sanctuary ponies and always have a home to come back to.

I got back home feeling too tired to live (notice how quickly I have termed the static as home), but had to get dinner prepared. Sat down on the lovely welcoming sofa, only moments later to be reminded by Alan of our proposed midnight fencing expedition. He had mentioned this but I was praying he would forget. Coated up to the hilt, torch at the ready, off we went to the top farm. This was the proposed destination for our group of horses. Tired and worn out, Alan and I headed up the hill in the darkness. The night was cold and blustery and all I wanted to do was go to bed. Alan knows this farm like the back of his hand. He walked all the perimeters, feeling the fencing like a blind man as he went, making a mental note of all the areas that needed repairing the following morning. Alan flashed the torch, occasionally, just to confirm what fencing was good and what needed repair.

The houses down below were lit up well, making even the quickest flash of the torch a high risk. If anyone was to get wind of tomorrow's plans, we would be in deep trouble. Not knowing the Morse code, I was concerned that someone might spot the intermittent flashes and receive an unintended message such as "Help" or, worse still, the dot dot dash might convey the message, "We are checking the fences for the arrival of the horses."

I was feeling very concerned about the darkness and the uneven terrain. Alan guided me by the hand through the long grass and uncertain ground. I lost the confidence in Alan as my guide, when he ended up flat on his face in the long reeds of grass. Suddenly we were confronted by a large vehicle full of men out lamping. This is when a very high beamed torch is shone around fields in order to find animals to shoot. It is an illegal activity that I certainly do not agree with. We had to quickly duck down behind the dry stone walls. As the torch beam headed away, we would bob our heads up again. Suddenly the beam would be swung round towards us, forcing us to duck again, sharpish.

I was uncertain as to whether we had been spotted or not. The beam seemed to be searching us out. I was nervous that the beam would catch our eyes and the men would shoot. Hiding behind the wall, we waited until the vehicle pulled away. After breathing a sigh of relief, we carried on with our midnight fencing check. As the mist continued to close in, we headed for home. Rob made us a welcome cup of tea and it was soon time for bed.

MONDAY 16ᵀᴴ NOVEMBER

Woke to the sound of rain lashing the sides of the static. The wind was swaying her gently from side to side. How could we possibly move horses today as planned? Ringing around my troops, I found they were all more than happy to go ahead. Today, I realised yet again what special friends I have. I have friends that have walked beside me on every step of this frightening yet adventurous journey.

My nerves were in tatters as I made my way to Rufford. The task was so huge I was paralysed by the enormity of it. I did very little that was constructive while I waited for the team to arrive. Once they started to arrive, I actually began to function. The horses and ponies were brought into a small holding paddock and the mountainous task began.

Linda and Donna loaded two of the bigger horses in their trailer and helped load my little lorry with a further two. This part of the operation went very well. Well enough, indeed, for my nosey ex-neighbour to follow us to our new destination. It was rather comical to see her driving past, to see where the horses were going. Rob and I laughed, as we soon saw her careering round again to keep an eye on the situation. How sad and desperate she must be to have such an obsession. Is her life so unfulfilling that she has to follow me to find out where my new one is?

The second leg of the journey was nowhere near as successful. The remaining horses were now frantic with worry as they had seen members of their herd taken away and they did not know the fate that awaited them. By now, Penny and Maureen, two more experienced horsewomen, arrived to help. This meant we had three horse transporters. However, the task had become extremely fraught as we also received a phone call to say that Alan's sister had pulled up alongside the fields to make her presence known. My nerves were in tatters, as I tried desperately not to let the horses pick up on my fear. Horses are very perceptive to the emotions and feelings of those around them.

I was literally only just holding it together. I felt like a time bomb ticking, ready to go off at the merest blip. The remaining ponies failed to cooperate. Penny held on to Dusty, as she reared in the little lorry while waiting for her travelling companion. Her travelling companion, Summer, was refusing to go into the lorry. We tried her in my big lorry but it was too late; she had been upset and fear had set in. Linda and Donna managed to get Summer into the trailer but dashed to help with Ginny, as she would not go in my lorry. Luckily Penny's son, a very experienced horseman and a newly qualified farrier, working locally, came within minutes to help us load the difficult ones.

While the group helped load Ginny, I was not far away from the trailer containing a restless Summer. I heard a crack and a loud commotion. Turning, I was just in time to see Summer limbo under the back bar of the trailer. Within seconds she was loose and running down the main A619. I ran into the road to stop the fast traffic. I made a grab for the head collar and led her back to the safety of the yard. After upsetting herself this badly, would she consider loading again? The answer was no! She reared and bucked and kicked and shook with fear. As the lorries thundered past, Summer showed no intention of going into the trailer. By now there were four of us trying to cajole her. Time was running out, with Alan's sister now on to us. We did not know for sure who had tipped her off but we had a fairly good idea that it was a Trogledite. Suddenly, as if by magic, Summer stood motionless at the bottom of the ramp. With one purposeful pull, she was in.

Ramp up and we were off on our final leg of the journey. Jaffa, Merry and Velvet were to be left till later. Jaffa would be ridden up as she will not travel. Merry and Velvet will then look after each other till morning, when they will go to their new retirement home. This is no ordinary home; it is a very special home for very special horses indeed.

Merry and Velvet will live in a small paddock behind the house of my dear friend, Shirley. Along with Jenny, they are both always working for animal welfare. These women have done nothing but help me and my animals, not only through this terrible time but prior also. Shirley is a wonderful character and more like something out of "Heartbeat". She is a very down to earth woman in her seventies, with lovely silver hair. She has clearly worked hard all her life in the farming industry and sadly this has left her lame and in constant pain.

After moving all the loadable horses, I was tired and weary. Despite this, I placed a saddle upon the back of my beautiful mare, Jaffa. Hoisting my aching, weary body into the saddle, I felt as if I was suddenly recharged. I bid goodnight to the two remaining ponies, Merry and Velvet. They clung tightly together, fearful of their fate. If only I could have told them that as long as they are my ponies their fate will always be good. As we walked away from Rufford, Jaffa cast off her last shoe—out with the old. A special moment when even Jaffa wanted to leave the past behind and move to a better, cleaner, safer life.

Off we went into the dusk, amidst the thundering Lorries. As the darkness closed in, Jaffa and I arrived at our new home. Alan held her bridle, while I lowered myself to the ground. Jaffa's herd was pleased to welcome her home. The field was safely padlocked and now it was time to take a break. I could not believe that we had carried out this major operation without any serious problems. Now we are truly reunited in our new home.

TUESDAY 17TH NOVEMBER

Up early after a very unsettling night. As the gale force winds shook the caravan, I was in fear we would lose our little house. There has been sustained high winds since moving to Syda. Alan did warn me that, due to it being higher and more exposed than Rufford, we would experience more extreme weather, and he was right! Looking out of the window and watching the sun rise over the valley made everything seem okay.

After a couple of cups of tea, we made our way to Rufford to feed our animals. It is very hard to see our remaining animals waiting to be moved to their new home. I find it heart wrenching to see my blind cat, Fluffy, waiting and listening for my voice. I find it hard to see Hoppy bereft of his usual dose of human contact. I have found this separation hard to endure—the emptiness of the kitchen, the desolation that the cats are wandering around in. The room that once could be heard to beat now stands cold and empty. At least now I can see an end and sense a new beginning. Soon this torture and deprivation will be over for me, Alan and our beautiful animals.

Merry and Velvet had stayed as devoted as ever to each other over the night. It was now their turn to find happiness, which for them comes in the form of a new home in Matlock. Although it took us an hour to get them in the lorry, the arrival at their piece of heaven was poignant. Merry and Velvet came down the lorry ramp and into the little field and headed off into the afternoon sun. They grazed side by side, unaware of the gap they will leave in my life. I was happy for them and content in the knowledge that my two little ponies were about to be treated like the treasures they are.

The next stop was a storage farm that would now be the home of my little lorry, Beatrice. It was an emotional day and I shed several months' worth of tears in a few moments. I wiped the tears away before anyone could detect they had been shed. Parking my lorry, I patted her wooden sides and walked away. Glancing back for one last time, we turned the Land Rover and headed home.

Passing the field at Syda where my horses are now kept, I noticed that the access had been well and truly chained and padlocked to deny me the ability to take my horses out. Oh well, I haven't time to ride now anyhow. I will just have to deal with that when the time comes. After all, I have some serious exploring to do and I am really looking forward to it.

WEDNESDAY 18TH NOVEMBER

First job was to get my lovely bed into the static. I have always loved my special bed as it was a wedding present from my darling mum. I really can't believe that it fits in so well but it does. Makes it a bit of a squeeze to use the en suite bathroom but it's worth it.

Next, the cows, and this was a rather daunting task. I felt much less edgy than when bringing the horses down. I guess this could be due to the fact that the old man does not hold a psychological hatred of cows. It was wonderful to think of bringing yet more of our family to the new farm. We transferred the cows in three trips. The cows as ever walked eagerly up the ramp. The first leg of the journey took Daisy, Lovebird, Black Girl and Ivory. Although all gates had been chained and padlocked to prevent any animals entering the farm, the field proposed for the cows had thirty foot width of wall missing. Alan could not fence it last night as this activity would have alerted the enemy. Hence with the first batch of cows, Rob and I were left in place as a makeshift wall.

Alan backed into the field but there was a drop that he had failed to take into account. As you will know by now my motto is to always remain calm no matter what situation I find myself in. I screamed loudly with a hint of hysteria when I saw Lovebird nearly falling out of the gap in the top of the ramp door. She was far too high, meaning that she must have been balancing on top of another cow. Still screaming frantically (don't worry Alan is used to my erratic behaviour when in stressful situations), I tried desperately to lower the ramp. There was too much weight on the door. Alan came round as calm as ever and managed to open the door. It was upsetting to see a pile of cows in the doorway, all the old girls at that. Cows are so resilient but I find it distressing to see them struggling or hurt in any way. Poor old Daisy was at the bottom of the pile with Black Girl in the middle. By now Lovebird had scrambled off the top of them both. As the girls struggled to their feet, I stood with baited breath. I watched them shake off the trauma and head straight for the grass. Heads down, it was as if nothing had happened; I just wish I could have recovered from the ordeal so readily. We took our place as dry stone walls and Alan left for the next batch of ladies.

I was rather surprised that the mummy cows now stood munching on the lush grass without a care in the world. Not one of them seemed to notice that their calves were not with them. It was bitterly cold as we stood in our designated positions. None of the cows even attempted to head towards the gap in the wall, leaving us feeling a little redundant. Oh well, gave us chance to have a natter.

The next few cows arrived, including old Crunchy and Erica. This time, the unloading went without a hitch, so I could remain calm. Alan backed the tractor up beside the gap, this time allowing the girls a better exit. By now it was getting extremely cold in our capacity as a wall. The Great Danes had now joined us and were having a lovely, if frosty, time prancing around the field.

As the trailer made its third and final journey full of the little calves, we all breathed a sigh of relief. Although the trailer was still a considerable distance away, the cows headed frantically towards the drop off point, fully aware that their children had arrived. The bellowing was poignant, as the trailer headed towards us and youngsters called to their mummies. As the trailer door came down, the reunions were beautiful to watch. It was amusing to watch the mummy cows, as if they had only suddenly realised, "Oh, with all this lush grass, I had forgot the kids!" Well it's easily done, I suppose. I guess I would do the same but in a pizza field.

As we all looked on, the babies drank frantically from their mothers, sucking and butting and sucking till their hearts (and bellies) were content. As they all slowly ambled into the distance, Alan, Alistair and Dave set about fencing the gap in the wall.

All was well and our mission was almost accomplished, but then we noticed the Prodigal Son driving menacingly past the tractor and trailer. Oh, the cow pat hits the fan again! The men carried on fencing, unperturbed, as the light was fading fast. Rob and I had to head hurriedly to the farming shop to purchase a dozen more fence stakes, to fully enclose the field and protect the stock. As we left the farm, we saw the Prodigal Son driving slowly back towards the fencing team. He pulled in and appeared to wait. However, as Alistair and Dave approached his vehicle, he sped off up the hill again. Moments later he telephoned Alistair on his mobile phone. We now realised why he had pulled in—to take down Alistair's phone number, as written on the side of his van. He was offering Alistair (his nephew) some advice. Alistair made it plain that he did not require any advice from this man and called him a name I had best not repeat.

The final bit of fencing to be carried out was exactly outside the old man's window. The Prodigal Son seemed to be in full control in the house. Even when the sister turned up the Prodigal Son appeared to be giving them both a sermon. As the men hammered the posts into the ground, the atmosphere was electric. I was a bag of nerves waiting for the bomb to go off. As we finished and headed home for a cuppa, the police finally arrived. They went into the old man's house and we never even saw them again, thank goodness.

As we settled for a cosy evening in front of the telly, we all discussed the day's events. As we turned in for the night, Alan commented that the old man's kitchen light was on late. "Something's afoot," he said, "we will probably get a letter tomorrow?"

As the generator died down, I whispered my usual plea to God and St Martin. I prayed for them to protect all our animals and keep them safe.

THURSDAY 19ᵀᴴ NOVEMBER

Up early as usual. After a couple of cups of tea, Alan headed off to Rufford in the tractor. Within moments of leaving Syda, Alan came hurtling back to the static alerting me to go and check the horses. He noticed that they were in the wrong field. Alan dropped me at the gate and I ran across to see why they were out. It suddenly became apparent as to why the kitchen light was on next door. The Prodigal Son was simply waiting for the generator to be switched off, so that he could sneak up to the horses. He had taken their gate off its hinges and thrown it on the floor. As it was still padlocked at one end, it was in a very precarious position. The horses had been running in and out over the gate. I was very lucky to find them all safe and well. With the gate at such an angle, I was blessed not to have some injured horses. The wind was fierce which was just as well; I had an abundance of steam coming out of my ears that needed cooling before reaching the atmosphere. I was furious. I could barely breathe. I managed to pick up the gate and remove the immediate danger. The man is greedy, selfish, cruel and an absolute liability; I headed home and called the police straight away.

The police don't really want to know as this is a civil matter. They did say they would contact the R.S.P.C.A. The Prodigal Son was at work so they also said they would contact him there. I am sure, knowing the coward this man is, that he will not try anything in the immediate future. This will not stop me fretting and worrying of course.

Frantic calls from Tommy Tucker's new owner. I have to pick the cat up straight away as he cannot tolerate him anymore. I was saddened to hear these words as Tommy is a special cat and does not deserve to be spoken about in such a way. I assured the man I would get there as soon as was humanly possible. Gosh, I don't know, moving house has been so hard because all the farm work and sanctuary work needs to be done in between moving animals and machinery. Still the animals need to be fed, cleaned nurtured and re-homed, etc. Life at the moment for us is just one long stream of chasing back and forth. I really do not know how we are managing, as we are both a pair of physical wrecks.

Tommy Tucker was on my mind all day. How would I find the time to pick him up? A phone call later that day set my mind at rest. My dear friend, Jane, sorted it all out and Tommy was taken to his new owner's mum. Thank God for friends like Jane, thank God for all the special friends with which I am blessed.

I managed to nip to town for a few errands. I hope I won't be feeling the way I do forever. Once I have left home for an hour I start to feel very edgy and nervous. I am filled with dread and anxiety. I just hope this will pass as we settle fully in our new home. Anyway, I tried to put my anxiety behind me and continue with the job in hand. I could not wait to return to the homestead. I seem to have had these feelings of anxiety for a long time now. I guess they have become so ingrained they are now a big part of my life.

FRIDAY 20ᵀᴴ NOVEMBER

A busy day still sorting out the massive Rufford House Farm! Will this ever end? I am beginning to doubt it. We have told the landlord that we will be out for mid-November. Well, as he has put us in court anyhow, we have an extension of sorts, as the court date is set for December 10th. However, I do want this move to come to an end sooner, in order that I can start my new life.

Little Fudge, the abandoned dog, is walking well off her lead. She is one of the sweetest dogs I have ever met (well almost). She does have a quirky streak running through her. She can be a little aggressive but in a harmless way. I have a potential new owner coming to see her today. One problem, they have kids. I have explained her minor problems. We don't know any history about this pretty dog. What has she been through? Why was she abandoned?

The potential new owners turned up bang on time. They were excited and thrilled to meet Fudge. We all went up the field for a play. Fudge was such fun as always and everyone loved her. The couple had two children and they adored Fudge and she adored them. That was until she got overexcited and nipped the little girl. Oh heck, that's it, I thought. The parents were really good about it and explained to their little girl that the dog did not mean to do this. We waved the distraught little girl and her family off and then walked Fudge back to her kennel. We were sure she had blown her chances of a lovely home.

A call early next morning surprised me immensely. The family wanted to give our little Fudge a chance. We were so thrilled, as it was the good news we needed. Having left half of our animals at Rufford, I fret daily for them. They need our presence and that of our friends on a daily basis. At the moment I am in and out between moving fully, so it is not good. Life looks so cold and empty for them right now and this is hard for me to see.

A call from Tommy Tucker's carer causes me more worry. He needs to see the vet. I arranged to pick him up as soon as possible, if not before.

I decided to get Tommy Tucker straight away as I needed to see him. I made the trip to Arkwright Town with Rob to fetch Tommy home. I was saddened by what I saw, as he had lost virtually all his fur and had inflamed red sores all over his back. It looked like stress had taken its toll. Tommy is such a delicate little soul and often becomes ill when upset. I knew his condition meant a long wait in the vet's surgery the following day.

Saturday 21ST November

Took Tommy to the vet this morning. Though I really did not have the time, I knew he had to be a priority today. His skin is inflamed and he has scabby lumps all over his body. I always try to time my visits to the vet carefully in order to avoid too long waiting. With the vet I use you cannot make an appointment so you just sit and wait . . . . and wait. As I walked in to the surgery I knew I was in for a hell of a wait. This was something I could have done without. It was standing room only and five of the standing spaces were already taken.

I booked myself and Tommy in and called at the shop for a magazine. By the time I got back, I managed to squeeze myself next to a man and his puppy dog. The surgery was bursting with every pet you could imagine. One lady had a container full of puppies. Another little boy sat wearily with his mum and their little puppy. A lady sat opposite with a miniature hedgehog, for which she had recently paid £300. I actually enjoyed studying all the lovely animals as I sat waiting my turn. My enjoyment faded when I saw a lady come out without her pet. Tears were streaming down her face as she paid her bill and left. Any fellow animal lover will understand the devastation losing a precious pet can bring about.

After two long hours and thirty minutes the vet called my name. I had finished the magazine several times. Tommy had flea dermatitis possibly brought on by stress. Four injections later, Tommy and I headed for home—home of course being our little static caravan.

Alan went to town and bought a large amount of wood to make decking for the catteries. If I had known the work those catteries were to cause Alan, I would have sold them and started again. As usual, Alan made light work of the job.

Sunday 22ND November

Wilma, my lovely horse, went on loan today. For some reason I was pretty shaky during the whole process. I guess the tears have to flow at some point during this time. The girl who is having Wilma is delightful and I know will look after her well. It is still hard to have my family of animals all over the place.

Alan as ever made light work of cutting the link on the chain to get Wilma out. I sobbed ridiculously throughout the ordeal. When Wilma was presented to the ramp of the lorry, she stopped to take stock of the situation. Within moments, the transporters had lunge lines round her back end. Horses need a few moments when entering lorries and trailers, especially a strange and unfamiliar lorry. I immediately became defensive; after all they were upsetting my baby. Wilma was very agitated, wondering no doubt why she was being forced urgently into the lorry. Rushing a horse before they have time to think is a definite no. It causes them to become suspicious and can bring on fear and apprehension. I asked the transporter to remove the ropes and give Wilma a moment. Wilma, having being given time to collect herself, strode up the ramp happily. The doors were closed and my little Wilma was gone. I wiped away my tears, put my chin up and carried on forward to the next in a long list of things to do.

Jack and Blake came up to help for the afternoon. They had a great time and of course enjoyed the big fire Alan built on my ménage. Those boys always bring a smile to my face. They even took Annie, Meg and Mimi's sofa out to burn. They sat on the sofa while Alan lifted it up on the tractor bucket; it was a funny sight.

TUESDAY 24ᵀᴴ NOVEMBER

Alan really seems to be in the loop again with some of the local farmers. One or two of them are being really supportive and helpful. They seem to have genuine compassion and sympathy for his situation. These are farmers that have seen Alan build Syda Farm and put his whole life into it. He has three farmers that are more than willing to store his bales of silage. In "Darling Buds of May" style, Alan is to pay them with a bottle of Whisky! My kind of people. I know Alan has been very fretful about his silage so I am really pleased to see it all coming right for him. Everything is as always falling into place in a very magical way. As always, we are constantly having our needs met.

Alistair dismantled my catteries which was rather sad to see. The FIV pen (Feline Immunodeficiency Virus) was very hard to dismantle and had certainly been put up to last. The FIV pen has saved so many cat lives. Before I suggested this pen, cats with FIV were routinely put to sleep by the organisation I once volunteered for (a high profile cat organisation). Some rescues still do this. When the pen was built it was a safe haven for cats with this virus. They no longer had to be put to sleep. All this was due to a little cat called Blue. She was wild and had a lovely litter of kittens. I volunteered for the cat organisation when Blue came to me. I was told by the boss to take Blue for an FIV test. I dutifully did this and was later phoned by the vet. I was told the cat had the virus and I had no option but to let them put the cat to sleep. I was devastated to say the least. This cat had trusted me and I had betrayed her!

Owners are led to believe by vets and other experts that FIV means a death sentence; well it does not. I read around the subject and it is clear that it is definitely not a death sentence. When I found this out, I did not want Blue's death to be a waste. Hence the FIV unit was born. Thanks to Blue, many cat lives have been saved. Now here I am watching Blue's unit coming down.

WEDNESDAY NOVEMBER 25TH

First thing this morning Alan noticed Erica missing. She is one of the old cows due to calve. The realisation that she had left her herd indicated that she had gone away to have her baby. Although she is an old cow and likely to be fine given her birthing history, it is vital to always check on them as soon as possible. Alan had to meet Alistair and the other men and therefore dropped me off to find Erica. Holly came with me into a small field known as the spinney. Erica was quietly and calmly hidden in a corner of the field, starting her labour. She had the usual small sack hanging behind her, which indicated the birth had begun. Holly and I crept quietly away and left her in peace.

I arrived as all hustle and bustle at Rufford was underway. The men worked tirelessly to load up catteries and other animal buildings onto the trailers. With the sight of the catteries on their way to Syda, I really felt like everything was falling in to place. As I continued to pack and organise the house, I was aware that the end of this leg of our nightmare was within view.

Nipped back to Syda and checked on Erica, who had given birth to a little baby boy. Both mother and son are doing just fine. The arrival of the animals and especially today's birth has breathed life back into the old farm again. Holly and I again checked that all was well and backed away quietly. It is sad to see Rufford having life sapped away, but oh so wonderful to see life put back into Syda.

Now I know with all my years of experience with people that the way to get a good day's work from folk is to look after them. So I was off to the chippy for fish and chips all round. Well of course I like to encourage myself as well! The men loved their fish and chip break and seemed to be spurned on by the treat. Rob, the house sitter, enjoyed his within the warmth and cosiness of the static caravan. Boy, did I envy him. All I want is a little time to fettle my caravan and perhaps sit in front of the fire too. My time will come I guess.

Once darkness fell, it was back home for tea and a welcome sit down. Wednesdays never have been the same since "Coronation Street" was moved to Thursdays. But we still enjoyed the evening, which was rounded off with a long dog walk. Rob and I decided to go up the bank to check on the horses. We walked around the field in the pitch black looking for the entrance to the steep bank. The mist was beginning to come down and we had given up finding our way. Would you believe, just as we were about to turn back the dogs, who incidentally have not been this way to the bank before, went through the bushes and showed us the way? We can only assume that we had left scents as we have been up and down a couple of times during the day. However, they managed it and we were really pleased and managed to walk up and check the stock.

My beautiful horses were dotted all over the top farm and I suddenly saw, yet again, a little bit of heaven. I had not even seen where my horses were living as we have been so hectic. I was so happy with the beautiful place they now live. Soon the cats will arrive, then the chickens. I can't wait for us all to be together.

Alan had walked down to check on Erica's calf. Only Alan can do a proper check, as he has a brilliant eye that knows if all is well or not. It was not and Alan was quick to notice that the calf had not drunk from his mummy. It is vital that the calf gets what is known as the first milk. These are the colostrums and contain life saving antibodies without which the calf would not survive. The calf needs this first milk as soon as possible, preferably within eight hours. There is only a certain amount of time after birth that this milk can be absorbed through the calf's gut. Alan got the calf on a teat and got him suckling the first milk.

Thursday 26ᵗʰ November

Today promises to be a great day for us. The tasks for today are daunting but once carried out will be a major milestone on our journey. The containers are coming! Well I do get excited over the silliest of things. It's just that Alan has worked so hard to source the containers. Once he got them, we have then had to fill them with our life. I have a whole container for my horse tack, which is full to bursting. Carol is more excited than I am about that one. We can't wait to spend a day sorting our horse stuff out.

Another container is holding all Alan's worldly goods. All his tools and bits and bobs; he's excited about that one for some reason (I think it's a man thing). We then have what we now call an office and a feed room. This is an insulated container that splits into two separate halves. We have the fourth and final one that is all our furniture and belongings. The furniture one was actually filled a couple of weeks ago and is kept in storage.

Of course, our arrival with the first containers coincided with a Trog in-law coming down the lane. Dutifully, he went immediately and reported back to the old man. We knew straight away that this would immediately bring the Prodigal Son running, and it did. He performed his usual behaviour of writing things on a note pad. He also told Alistair he was trespassing, to which Alistair replied that he himself was actually the trespasser. The Prodigal Son looked really furious that we had delivered our containers onto the farm through the padlocked gates; that's not supposed to happen I guess. I had to laugh as Alan and Alistair just carried on working as if nothing had happened. All Alan's months of planning and mapping out in his head paid off. All the containers and catteries just fell in to place like a jigsaw.

"Well, I am a chess player," he joked, quite proud of himself.

I wish I could have guessed what the evening would bring us!

This could possibly have been one of the most exhausting days we have had. Rob, after helping outside with the containers, made us a beneficial cup of tea. Looking forward to a cosy night in our static, I decided to unload the Land Rover. It was pitch black when I headed outside. I was suddenly aware of glaring headlights coming from the direction of the Trog dwelling. I figured they must be going out and shining the lights at the static as they were leaving. I carried on unloading but became aware of furtive behaviour behind the old man's hedge. The lights still beamed blindingly onto and into the static. I decided to stay still and observe from the darkness. The next minute I saw a figure dressed completely in black, including a black hat. The figure marched up towards the static in the darkness, with the glare of the lights showing him the way.

I walked boldly towards the figure until he saw the whites of my eyes. He turned tail and walked hurriedly away. I trotted on and shouted, "Can I help? Who are you?" The figure turned to me and started using the foulest language I have ever been subjected too. I asked again, "Who are you?" More expletives followed; whoever it was began gesturing wildly with his fists and screaming threats at me. I still did not know who this man was as he screamed he would "have" me. He thumped his hands with his fists and was totally out of control. He claimed he had purchased all the land and it was his (he paid next to nothing for 4 acres but claims to own 100 acres, which really, really is deluded). I saw the Prodigal Son rushing to his father, as this ranting man in black made his way to the Trog dwelling. Ah, Mr. Trog, what a charming man, what a delight he must be as a husband! He turned towards me with his eyes still flashing wildly, "I'll have you and your gypsy caravan off here quicker than you can say . . . ."

I will leave the rest to your imagination. The realisation dawned on me that I will be unable to sell pegs and lace to that vile man.

By this time, Alan and Rob were making their way down to see what all the shouting concerned. I realised that this mad man had been fired up by the Prodigal Son and that Trog himself was clearly showing off. The Prodigal Son, having been warned for wasting police time, called the police to say there was an altercation outside. Well, I suppose that's one way to get the police up here again. I really do think it is time he grew up and started acting like the Christian he is supposed to be. And as for Trog, this affair is absolutely nothing whatsoever to do with him. What sad, sad people; how I pity them all. You would think a couple with a young daughter would have better things to do with precious time. And what an example they must be as parents. God help the little girl as she grows up surrounded by such materialistic and selfish parents.

Friday 27th November

Another day trying to keep it all together. It feels like war has broken out up here. Do you know, the funny thing is, war or no war, I love it on my new farm? I am so used to ignoring unpleasant neighbours that it does not bother me one bit. I simply wake up in the morning, look at the view outside my static, thank God for all I have and I just enjoy myself. All the animals are settling well and look happy. That is all we are bothered about now. The views here are amazing and the fresh air has resulted in my breathing improving each day. At night, the stars twinkle so closely that I am sure I could touch them if I really tried.

Started the day with a lovely walk taking Fudge all round Rufford. Holly had to sit in the Land Rover when we got to Rufford. She never did like all the mud and I will no longer allow her to walk in the filth of this farm. It is sad to see Fudge get so dirty but not for much longer. She will be going to her new home tonight. I will give her a bath so that she can smell sweet for her owners.

Fudge was collected at 5pm. I was happy to see her go off to her new life. This is what makes my work worthwhile. Fudge is a lovely dog with minor behaviour problems. The charming family that have taken her will give it their best shot. I am sure with their love and determination, Fudge will overcome all her problems and blossom into the dog I know she can be.

SATURDAY 28ᵀᴴ NOVEMBER

The dogs have woken up every morning at 5-6am and yet today when we depended on it they slept through. Since moving into the static the dogs have become unsettled very early in the morning. I wondered why this was and I think today I was given the answer. During the night, Robbie went to the bathroom and found Dotty, the deaf cat, had opened the door and was outside his room. He took her back to bed with him and she snuggled down into the duvet. The dogs slept through so it is obvious that Dotty is the culprit for waking them up. She does this by digging at the door to get to Rob's room. Well at least we know now.

We woke up at 8am which was a disaster. Alan was supposed to be meeting Emma at Rufford to hand over the tombola. Emma is kindly doing this charity event as I simply do not have the time. I will look forward to next year's event as this one is annual. It's a lovely little do. Thanks to Emma, I was free to go down to Rufford and help Alan collect scrap. I hate to think of him doing these tasks alone. Mind you, it was hard work. There were little bits of scrap metal all over the farm. Alan was very reluctant to let a massive steel door go. "Hell of a door this you know?" he said with a wistful look on his face.

"That's as maybe, but it's a hell of a door that takes some carrying. Let the darn thing go, Alan," I pleaded, in vain.

We struggled to drag this door towards the trailer. Alan struggled to get it on to the fork. Next minute the door ended up dropping on my toes. The pain was intense, as my feet were extremely cold. Alan fetched me a chair and sat me down. I sat rocking backwards and forwards for about ten minutes. The pain in my foot faded and somehow became a headache? I don't get that either.

I had to help Alan move some wooden decking pieces. They were quite heavy and awkward to hold. Suddenly, Alan lost his grip when the wood was high in the air and it fell down and hit me on my cheek bone. By this stage I was not happy and was beginning to wonder if he had it in for me. I ended up with a severely sore and bruised cheek bone. Talk about abuse, I seem to be getting it all ways. I am a little concerned as we have, as you know, only recently made up our wills and since then Alan seems to be constantly clumsy around me. Well, if anything does happen to me please make sure it is fully investigated.

Alan left with a trailer full of scrap metal. Carol arrived and we decided to go to see the horses and sneak to the static for a cup of tea. As we clambered over the gate to the horses and struggled across the field against the fierce high winds my phone rang. Alan had broken down just moments from the scrapyard. This was all too much and I am afraid I became petulant, as Carol put it (I must look that word up as I have a feeling it's not a compliment). Time was of the essence and I had to be in Brimington with diesel, post haste. Carol and I said a brief hello to the horses and struggled back to the Land Rover. Neither of us is exactly the world's best example of 'peak condition'. I looked across at Carol as she battled up the incline towards the gate. The poor woman had come to see the horses and now she was performing the minute mile with me. Breathless and hardly able to speak, we headed in the vehicle to the petrol station. Alan was not going to make the scrapyard now. This was a bit of a blow as we had the day mapped out to the last detail. Now it had gone horribly wrong.

Alan managed to get the tractor going and I followed him home. He broke down a further three times but eventually we made it home. Our friend, darkness, had arrived and so it was time to clock off. I wasn't sorry. Luckily, one of Rob's friends, Rita, had made him a lovely meat pie. We had this for tea with vegetables and it was beautiful. Emma called to say the tombola had netted £70. I was thrilled.

SUNDAY 29TH NOVEMBER

I walked the dogs with Rob first thing. We peeped over the wall to see Erica and her baby. Erica had come out of the spinney and introduced her baby to the rest of her herd. Erica was grazing and we had to look around for the baby. As we peered over the wall, I expected to see the calf under the wall in the long grass. I was just about to go and look elsewhere and Erica looked at me and Rob and then she looked at her baby. Although she was worried we might find her baby, the look led us straight there. The calf was tucked away under the wall in the long grass. He looked so cosy and protected, we walked on, nonchalantly, so as not to alarm him.

Lots of work at Rufford and then I went into town with Rob. He starts a new job on Monday so needed some bits and bobs. I really did enjoy the break and I enjoyed our stop for a burger even more. Carol had taken over from Rob as chief house sitter and she tidied up the caravan while we were away. Sadly, Rob went for his train at around 8.30pm. Not only will I miss him but our home becomes vulnerable too.

Although Alan requested that the sheep are not grazed during this dispute, they did appear. The whole field was fenced off but at least the sheep farmer had the courtesy to leave substantial space around our caravan. I actually love the idea of seeing sheep each morning as I draw back my curtains.

MONDAY 30TH NOVEMBER

Oh, it's wonderful to see the end of our journey is in sight. I really cannot believe we have come this far. When we found out we were going to have our home taken from us in March, I cannot describe how I felt inside my heart. It was certainly a task well beyond my own capacity. I felt sure we would not survive this ordeal. Here we are nearly touching the finishing line and I am waiting to open the champagne!

When I came out of the caravan this morning, I noticed several large pads of flattened grass. It seems several of the sheep had come under the wire and slept beneath our caravan. I thought this was lovely and am more than happy to share my home with them.

Alan had a real struggle tonight as he delivered troughs and metal tanks and other machinery to Alistair at Barlow. Alistair's girlfriend, Katie, has a livery yard there and she is kindly storing items for Alan. I stayed behind in my lovely static and had a well earned snooze. I was happy as the clock ticked towards "Coronation Street". As it slowly ticked, the sound almost amplified in my ears. I started to get agitated as I had no electricity to work the TV and failed to start up the generator. I made several attempts to ring Alan and then my battery ran flat (phone battery as well as personal energy supply battery). I went out for the second time to try and start the generator.

This turned out just another failed attempt as the clock ticked closer to Coronation O'clock. I pulled the generator lead several times. Frustrated and in the dark, I headed back in to the candle-lit static. The clock struck "Coronation Street" and my life was over. Whenever I miss "Coronation Street", I am really agitated until the start time and then, after five minutes, I start to calm right down; weird. Anyway, I decide to use the time to write up my diary.

Alan eventually turned up and had been through a tough time unloading the tackle at Barlow. Apparently, Alistair had also gone a cropper and nearly broke his neck slipping on a plank of wood. It sounds like I was lucky to get Alan home.

I cooked a lovely tea, still using up our home grown potatoes and beans. The small kitchen has not detracted from my culinary skills, limited though they may be. Made some fresh scones (or as Rob calls them "wow pats", due to the lack of rising power in my little oven).

TUESDAY 1ST DECEMBER

Not a great start to the day as the weather was freezing and Alan had to use boiling water to open the front door! I must admit it was not ever so cold in the static, not like I would have imagined, being frozen in and all.

Another rather unpleasant surprise when a Chatsworth agent turned up at Rufford out of the blue. We were so busy working, trying to get a cattery down. I was mortified at the cheek of the man and his sidekick. However, Alan, being a gentleman, was as pleasant as ever. I guess you could say we complement each other well. Alan is the Mr. Nice guy and I am, well, what am I? I am sick and tired of the rat race and the dog eat dog attitude of so many of the rats.

Alan asked me to accompany them all around the house for inspection. I told them I would rather tend to my chickens, thanks. I did my chickens, while Alan politely showed them the now empty house. The agent took pictures of everything. They then came out to the sheds. I make no apology for telling the agent that he was not a nice person. "I am just the agent," he whimpered.

"Don't give me that rubbish," I retorted in annoyance. "Anyway I don't want to listen to you or I will say things you don't want to hear. What are you taking pictures for?"

He looked sheepish as he replied, "These are to show the progress from the last pictures."

"Oh, and when did you take the last pictures, pray tell?"

"Oh, er, last time we came . . . er, in April I think?" he stammered.

"Well, well, Alan did you know they had been here taking pictures?"

"No I did not."

"No me neither, so obviously it was behind our backs as usual."

They (the privileged and super-rich) just don't get it about rights and privacy, do they? I stormed off, aware that I was about to start going off on one!

I had a large fire going and was in and out stoking it up with all the household stuff that had no use to anyone. I could not resist the urge to shout across the yard, "Is there any more rubbish for the fire, Alan?"

Alan just politely shook his head. I was in and out several more times and had yet another urge. "Any trash for burning, darling?"

Oh, by now I could not stop myself and was on a bit of a roll. Besides, they had already put us behind by over an hour. I called to Alan once more.

"Alan don't waste any more time with them, we've got a lot to do. And anyway, they can manage on their own as they have before when they took photos behind our backs. That's how they like to work, behind people's backs!"

Alan tried desperately to disguise my loss of sanity with polite nods in my direction. Oh the poor man, bless him, it's not easy having a highly strung, very excitable wife who's just lost the plot running around the yard throwing bin bags on a raging inferno. Oh well, life's a bitch. I do make tasty scones though.

The icing on the cake came in the form of several wonderful explosions from my inferno. Somehow it was timed (not by me I hasten to add) just as the agent and his sidekick were behind the fire. I think it must have been a light bulb or empty cans or something. The bangs were so loud, they sounded like a round of gun fire. Our intruder and his sidekick turned in shock. I think they assumed the crazy farmer's wife had gone berserk with a shot gun!

Of course I was very concerned and looked across and asked, "Oh dear, has someone been shot?"

WEDNESDAY 2ND DECEMBER

The young chickens are coming home today. I have two lots of chickens—the old ones (I have obviously had them longer) and the young ones. The young ones are in a little Wendy House that's really cute and was only recently built by Alan. He built it with the knowledge that we may have been moving. Alan hired a flat bed trailer and we went down to Rufford to begin the manoeuvre. I am never the best person to help during stressful operations. As you already know, I can get rather excited. Anyway, we boxed up my dear little chickens and then placed them carefully back inside the house. Alan then placed ratchet straps around the house and began to drag the hen house on to the flatbed. I was okay for the first part but then I noticed that the hen house was being tilted to quite an angle. I started to panic and had to keep rushing forwards to check on the chickens. As the hen house tilted, the hens obviously tilted with it. Each time, I lurched forward screaming, "Careful with the chickens". Alan, as ever, carried on regardless, having lived with me for 11 years. I think he considers me somewhat dramatic. We lurched and pulled and pushed and tugged until the chicken house was firmly on the flatbed. After checking the chickens, we set off home to Syda.

We had to bring the trailer across the field where the sheep were grazing. This was a necessary evil as Alan would be unable to get the trailer and the house over the small cattle grid. Unfortunately, this involved having to lower the three-strand sheep net, driving over it and then putting it up again. Twice! Oh well, I have always enjoyed obstacle courses.

Oh, it was so lovely to see the start of my flock arriving. I won't be truly content until the old chickens and my ducks are home with us. The chickens came out of the boxes and went straight to roost.

Fed around my cattery, which by the way is still on top of a trailer! The cats do seem rather unsettled which is sad to see. They are used to a life of luxury and heated beds. I am making them as comfortable as possible right now. Lots of thick blankets knitted many years ago by my dear Grandma. I am so pleased to have found a good job for Grandma's blankets, as I did not want to lose them in the move.

THURSDAY 3ᴿᴰ DECEMBER

Golly, I thought we would be well finished with Rufford by now. The hellish pressure of the move is over but I am still finding the tying up of all the loose ends rather difficult. I am sure I have been carried by some amazing force up until this week. Not only have I got fed up with the move dragging on, but so to *the force* carrying me. The Force has well and truly dropped me from a great height. I am now on my own and don't I know it. I am tired, weary and in severe physical pain. My body has been punished and is now revolting. I am stuck between my old life and my new life. I so want to get on with my new life as I like the feel of it. But my old life is keeping me back, as we struggle to clear the farm and buildings. I worked out that we have been withdrawing from Rufford for nine months now. It's been a long hall, a marathon, and I can just see the finishing line. The problem is, I just can't seem to get to it.

I looked forward to meeting Rob from the train station tonight. Rob has been our rock these last months. He has protected our caravan like a reliable old bulldog! It is thanks to him that we can now leave the caravan at all. When I went off with Alan, the Prodigal Son and the Trogs, et al, would snoop round our home. Rob kept popping up through the net curtains and reinforcing the idea that, whenever they think the static is empty, it's probably not. Met Rob off the train and had a good old natter. This evening we enjoyed a pizza and "Coronation Street".

Friday 4ᵗʰ December

Now it's just lots and lots of bits and bobs and this that and the other. This seems to be more time and energy consuming that all the massive manoeuvres we have carried out. I can still see the finishing line but it seems to be moving away. Help!

Saturday 5th December

Along with Rob and Alan, I delivered my beautiful ducks to their new home. I have halved my numbers which should please Alan immensely. He has been rather concerned about the large number of ducks. Called at my friend Lynne's on the way home. She has completed a pastel picture of our beautiful Annie. I am afraid when I saw it I was reduced to tears. I tried so hard to keep them inside, as I normally do, but I felt like Annie was in the room. The picture was totally Annie and it came across as a very spiritual picture that was created with Annie's help from the other side. Sorry, Lynne, I know you were on the end of the brushes but Annie appeared to have done most of the work.

SUNDAY 6ᵀᴴ DECEMBER

Yet another day of this never ending marathon. Backwards and forwards to the house with all the finer little bits of our life. I am having great difficulty with one of my old dolls. Many of my dolls have gone to charity shops or been placed in our tombola events. I have also kept several of my favourites to take with me. I even have one or two on display in my little static. However, I have one very old doll that has no eyes. His name is Howard and I named him after my first love. Well, in my teenage dreams he was my first love but it was only a dream. Anyway, Howard was a beautiful big doll and very cuddly. He must now be over thirty years old. I have not been able to find a place for him and he just keeps popping up. I could not bear to put him in the bin (he is blind). I could certainly not put him on the fire. I decided that I would sit him in the house and walk away. However, as I took the last bits and bobs from the hallway, I spotted Howard. His head and shoulders had slumped and he looked so lonely and rejected. I just could not leave him; I scooped him up in my arms and brought him home to Syda!

After a bite to eat, we returned to Rufford and set about clearing the garage and small stable. We had a massive fire and cleared so much stuff. This was all stuff that would not be fit for charity shops. We had to be a little tougher while clearing these sheds. We have recycled so much and yet there is still so much rubbish. I left Alan to it at around 3pm and went into town with Rob. Had a well earned hot chocolate and hobbled around Chesterfield with only one of my hips cooperating today. My body is crying out for rest but I do have to say my mind is calming down a lot. My mind has been working so hard for these past months. I have also noticed Alan's mind has been overworked. He has become forgetful and absent minded during this time. I do hope that he too will find a more peaceful existence soon.

On Thursday we are in court, having been taken there by our landlord that was. Alan is busy preparing his case in order to defend himself. They are taking us to court to get vacant possession of a farm that we have already vacated! Not only have we already left but we kept them fully informed of our plans to leave. Poor things really; when the agent called this week he said that they were worried about costs. Ah, didums. I don't ever remember our name anywhere on a rich list, so I guess it is the two of us who should be worried. As we both feel we've been treated unfairly, we will have our day in court and hope some justice will be forthcoming.

MONDAY 7TH DECEMBER

Alan and Alistair got an early start to bring the final cattery to Syda. They worked so hard and did a brilliant job. I collected my ducks and remaining cockerels and took them to Syda. These are the final animals to arrive and it rather made my day. I think the ducks and cocks thought we had abandoned them.

Called to see my friend Jenny and had a coffee and a natter. Left at around 3pm as Alan was going to pick me up. I started to walk in the direction he was coming from. I felt like a complete wreck of a human being. I have not been able to shower for days and my hair's a mess; added to this I was dressed ready for the tramps' ball. I suddenly heard someone call my name. Well, I dreaded turning around for fear of who it could be that caught me looking like a complete vagabond. It happened to be someone who was once a dear friend. We had parted company some time ago and she was the last person I would wish to see. It was obvious she had come this way to view my living arrangements. I was shocked at the outpouring of sympathy and have no idea where it came from. This person was aware of my predicament at the start (nine months ago) so I could only put her current concern down to human curiosity. Alan arrived moments after this woman drove away, with the proverbial flea in her ear. The last time I had contact with her, she had placed manure through my letterbox in a fit of pique.

I was so pleased to see Alan and told him about the situation I had just found myself in. I expressed what a mess I felt and that it was not the best time for me to meet this woman, considering I looked such a wreck. Alan chose his words carefully, as ever, and soon made me feel good about myself again. He turned to me with his obvious concern and declared, "Darling, you don't look a mess, you never look a mess." He paused and I felt instantly better and felt myself grow confident again. However, these feelings were short lived as Alan continued. "You just look like you've been through the mill!"

Well been through the mill I have, we have, and we are about to emerge from it. We have survived and the future looks great.

TUESDAY 8TH DECEMBER

Oh, what a beautiful morning I got up to today. I looked out from the static and felt a warm glow inside my tummy. The fields were covered in dew that glistened in the morning sun. The cows were stirring and emerging from the spinney (where they shelter and get their water). The little calves were frolicking and kicking up their heels just for the fun of it. I could not help but burst into song:

Oh what a beautiful morning, Oh what a beautiful day, I've got a wonderful feeling everything's going my way.

I feel sure that everything is going our way. I put the kettle on and sang gaily as I waited for it to boil. Today was an extraordinarily exciting day! We were to take delivery of our portable loo! Life just seems to get better and better, there is no doubt about that. It came complete with two loo rolls and some paper towels. Alan set about finding a place for the toilet that would be most accessible from the caravan.

Alan got offered a job today. Yes, at 62 summers old, he was asked if he would like to do some relief milking. He went down to see the farmer about the proposal but decided, at this moment in time, to decline the offer. I think he needs a little bit of a rest now, time to collect himself and step away from the treadmill we have both been aboard since March 25th 2009.

Bless my sister Kate; she and her partner came up this morning to help Alan. The idea was that one of them would accompany Alan to his father in order to hand the keys of Rufford back to him. Alan felt concerned about going in alone. He was worried that his father may overreact and possibly accuse him of untoward things. Bill was more than happy to accompany Alan into the house. Bill, being an ex-copper, was just the man for the job. Katie and I had a natter with Kelly and her mum, who arrived just after Alan went in to see his father.

Alan and Bill were gone about half an hour. Apparently his father was fine and very amenable. He told Alan that he should never have left Rufford and that he would have been fine to stay there. That's all well and good to say that now. We have numerous solicitor letters informing us that Stan is happy for Chatsworth to take the farm back! That's the problem with the old man; he tells lots of lies and I think he believes many of them himself.

As I lay in my bed at night, I feel so cosy. I am in my little home and it's mine and Alan's little place. It's not his dad's and it's not the Duke's, it's ours, our very own. We bought it and paid for it and it belongs to us. That is a great feeling. Ever since I have known Alan, the old man has threatened him with the withdrawal of Rufford. Well, it's been withdrawn now so he has nothing over us anymore. It feels great to be free from his dark cloud. Although we are now next door to him, it is irrelevant. We are free. We are independent. We are happy.

As I asked God to look after us and I asked St Martin and St Francis to protect our animals, the moon peeped in through my window; it felt so peaceful and so tranquil and surprisingly so safe. I felt as though the moon was watching over me in my little world. I drifted off to sleep, feeling more peaceful than I have felt in months.

WEDNESDAY 9ᵀᴴ DECEMBER

Wow, it's so refreshing not to have to keep flying backwards and forwards to Rufford House Farm. I am starting to feel so relaxed and at home. I am settling down and feeling rested. I do feel so very tired, now the journey is coming to an end. I guess the adrenalin is no longer pumping around my body and I am no longer being carried by some amazing force. I am on my own and feeling it. I'm not complaining, just telling it how it is.

Having handed the keys back to the old man, we have been rather naughty and held on to one of the keys. Well, we still had a couple of bits to fetch but more importantly needed our last shower at Rufford. In the darkness (knowing what nosey ex-neighbours we have), we made our way cautiously to the shower room, only to find that the Prodigal Son had been down to clear the place. His efforts amounted to having removed our shower gel, shampoo and conditioner to the bin. By 'eck, that lad knows how to work. I crept out into the darkness and tip toed to the large black bin. Taking out my toiletries, I headed back to the shower. Oh, it was good to feel like a human again once I had been in the shower. We left everything as if we had never been there in the first place. Had it been up to me, I would have left the shampoo by the shower. However, Alan did not want to raise suspicion. Oh, I felt so naughty and so rebellious but it was fun all the same. Now we are ready to face the court in the morning.

Thursday 10th December

Alan seems ready for his trip to court. I think I would be better off not going at all. On arrival we were met by Uriah Creep, solicitor for our former landlord. This person turned out to be a pompous little ass and was most objectionable. He spoke to Alan with a small degree of respect as he was trying to get him to sign to accept all costs, thus avoid either party going into court. He presented the papers to us for signing, as if he was doing us a favour. He was left outwardly shocked when Alan said, "No chance, I am going into court."

This pompous little man crawled back to sit alongside the Prodigal Son. They were clearly as thick as thieves as they gazed into each other's eyes. The little man had no doubt been given a preconceived idea of the sort of person I am. Not to worry, this is something I am perfectly used to with any person coming into contact with my in-laws. He was most rude and every time I opened my mouth he shot me down in flames, accusing me of being aggressive. Poor man has clearly led a sheltered life. I put him well in his place when I exclaimed, "You are a strange man, what a strange man; Alan don't you think he is rather a strange man?" Tail firmly between his legs, he skulked off to rejoin his new best friend, the Prodigal Son!

The strangest thing was when we actually went into the court room. The Prodigal Son sat silently trying to frighten us with his smouldering expression. Creep just looked like he was on the verge of a nervous breakdown. This man costs his employees £275 per hour and here he was facing my husband, who had failed to bow down to his pathetic scare tactics on arrival at court, and now he appeared to be having a mental breakdown. Anyhow, the judge said, "You've got possession of the farm, so what else do you want?"

Uriah Creep stammered with sweat pouring down his brow. "Well, we want lost profits and costs, sir."

The judge turned to Alan and asked, "Do you agree with this Mr. Shirt?"

"No, I certainly do not, sir."

The judge turned to the quivering Creep and declared, "Well, this will have to go to trial!"

Creep looked like he was about to be led to the gallows as he nervously stacked up his papers. What would he tell his boss now?

We headed straight to the pizza diner and ate as much as we liked. I wasn't sure if this was a celebration or not but I sure enjoyed the pizza. For now, at least, the pressure was off.

With the keys handed back, our detractors will hopefully leave us in peace. We have nothing left to give to them now; we have no money and no income, as they have taken the lot. We only have a home because we bought a static and plonked it on unused land (it just happens to be disputed, Syda land). The expenses for our move were colossal. However, we have never been happier. We have our little static caravan which is bought and paid for. We have all our animals around us, safe and sound. Alan has come home and made his claim. By the end of this, who knows what will be left? Alan's father will only rest when all the assets Alan built for them have gone. One day, we will be left in peace to enjoy our simple pleasures of life. But for now we are taking things one day at a time.

Rufford House Farm is gone and Alan and Gin have come home. The stars are bright at night and tranquillity surrounds us. The moon peeps in through our window at night and the sun shines through in the morning. The silence is beautiful and the sound of the wild animals far reaching. I tilt my head at night to listen to the silence that surrounds me.

Rufford has given us some very happy memories and some very good times. Now it is time to move on and start afresh. As I look around the old farm, memories come flooding to me. Happy memories and sad ones too. Rufford House Farm has never really been ours. These last nine months have given us chance to grieve without even being fully aware of it. Our grieving is done and our hearts are mending fast. We have withdrawn our soul from Rufford, since March this year. It's time to enjoy pastures new. The cows are grazing in the beautiful fields and the horses are roaming freely on the green meadows. The cats are sleeping soundly, with blankets to keep them warm and cosy. The chickens are living again, free from the thick, pungent mud that haunted our lives at Rufford. The dogs lay by the cosy little fire with glossy coats that have never had the chance to shine before. Our lives have changed forever in the most positive and wonderful way. Wish us luck on the start of our new journey; I am so glad to be at the end of the last one!

Some of my ponies enjoying breakfast

Rob's special dog, Cassie, shortly before she died

Holly playing in the snow

DECEMBER 2009: we have now started our new life at Syda Grange farm. I now understand how essential it was to listen to Alan night after night, as he discussed the various manoeuvres over and over again, until I wanted to leave him and move to another country far away! I now realise why he sat so often with pen and paper, making notes. Many of the notes surface even now as I sort through our belongings. As all our kennels, cattery and storage units were put in their places with such accuracy, I realised what miracles Alan had concocted and why, if an army goes to battle, they must plan each and every manoeuvre on paper and verbally. We had carried out our invasion as planned and to the letter. We had made it safe and sound but a new war is about to begin.

11ᵀᴴ DECEMBER

We had a lovely day today as we worked to settle the chickens and ducks into their new home. The poor things have been locked away since their arrival. Needless to say we are only collecting three to four eggs per day. The chickens need a chance to recover and settle. The humans are far from the only ones to have suffered during this ordeal. In fact I should say the animals have probably suffered more. At least Alan and myself have known what is happening, why and when? The animals have had to simply go along with it and hope for the best. It is just so wonderful to see the poultry on the farm. They are enjoying the new area where they live as it is full of lush green grass, something they know little of.

Mavis always prays for us. She called today, as she was rather worried about me and Alan and wanted to see where and how we are living. I met her at Rufford, which was the last place I wanted to go. I suggested that she followed me to the new farm. She asked me not to go too fast and of course I agreed. However, what I did not realise was that she meant not to go above 15 miles per hour! As Mavis and I tootled along the busy highway, the disgruntled lorry drivers slammed on their air brakes in dismay. Well, I figured it would do no harm for them to slow down a little for once.

Mavis is such a tiny woman that, when she is driving, her car looks like a runaway vehicle. Yes she is <u>that</u> small and can only just peep through the middle of the steering wheel. This probably helped today as we snail paced down the A619. I imagine the other drivers were a bit confused with the apparently driver—less vehicle.

Mavis parked down the lane and came to see our little house. Her face was beaming as she saw our little static; she smiled more upon stepping inside. As she walked through my tiny kitchen, she felt the warmth and cosiness of our caravan. She sat upon our comfy sofa in front of the glowing gas fire. The cats made their way to greet our visitor. Mavis fussed and petted each and every one of the cats. She smiled and laughed at our little nest full to bursting with all its livestock!

"I am so happy," she exclaimed, "I was so worried and thought you would be cold and uncomfortable; it's beautiful and so cosy."

Mavis was genuinely happy that we had found such a lovely home and was happy now in the knowledge that her friends were safe and God had answered her many prayers. She told us how brave and courageous she thought we both were. And of course she was right. We have been brave and we have shown great courage but there is a lot more required of us yet!

12ᵀᴴ December

Doris, my friend, came to buy eggs. I could not provide her usual amount as the chickens are not laying well. Doris and Dennis, her husband, are really only coming to see our new home. Again, as with Mavis, I met them at Rufford and they followed me up to the top gate at Syda Grange farm. They got out of their vehicle and looked down the lane towards our home. They too had been so worried about our living accommodation and could now see we were doing just fine. Having seen where we were, they happily went on their way.

Had a call from Mavis; I was to go to her house when I had finished shopping in town. She had cooked me a proper curry dinner to take home to the caravan. What a woman, what a friend and what an angel. Well, I dutifully called at her house and was handed a large bag. Inside the bag was a fragrant, full, authentic curry for me to pop in the oven, as required. This was a wonderful addition to our Saturday X Factor night. I heated the dinner and it tantalised our taste buds good and proper. There was plenty for us all to share.

13TH DECEMBER

I went off early with Rob to call at Shirley's and see the ponies. We also enjoyed a cup of coffee and some lemon puffs, which I have not had in years. The ponies looked really well and had put on a lot of weight. It was so nice to see them happy and settled. They are fed special old timer food daily and have access to a salt lick, which they so enjoy. After feeding them some apples, we headed home.

14ᵀᴴ DECEMBER

Off to the launderette, another thing I have not tried in years. Well my life has certainly gone backwards recently. Mind you, I am not complaining as I am still happy with my lot. The washing was done really quickly today; it was the drying that seemed to take a long time. As I waited for the drying, I even managed to pair up our socks. I have not paired socks in years. Alan and I have become well known for wearing odd socks! As I paired our socks, my sister, Katie, walked in. We were both shocked to see each other. Katie has not been in the launderette for many years either. What a strange coincidence that we should both pick the same day. We had a natter and then Alan picked me up for home. It was a really good job done and in such good time. I will look forward to getting my washing and drying done at the launderette in future.

15ᵀᴴ December

I had a lovely day today mucking out my chickens. Alan normally does them for me but I am trying to have a bash myself. It was hard work but I was really proud at the end when they all looked delightful and clean. Wormed them all with the first of a three day course and added cider vinegar to their water. The chickens all rolled around in the fresh sawdust and clucked merrily.

Lynne came up and helped me with the rescue cats. Things are not good at the moment in the cattery. We no longer have the good amenities available to us. The cats are in a cattery on top of a trailer. This makes it difficult to access them. Once inside, the cattery slopes, which makes it very difficult to clean as I do suffer from vertigo. I seem to find the small inclines becoming big inclines when I am servicing the pens. The cats are not looking as cosy as they once did. I am doing all I can but it is not enough.

The cats in the static are living in heaven in comparison to the cattery cats. They sit by the fire all day and it is left on for them at night. If I had my way, I would keep all the cats in the static but I think it would spell the end of my marriage!

Alan got a plumber to look at our central heating boiler, as we really do need it working. He was a man in his thirties; he seemed a little agitated, to say the least. I guess it was a shock for a young man to have to service a boiler in a static in the middle of a field! Such was his compassion and kindness; he spent an hour having Alan run round for tools, then left. He promised to order the required parts and return the following week. We never saw him again; I was surprised that a young person could leave two old fogies freezing over Christmas.

17ᵀᴴ December

We took a trip to Bottington. Took an hour or so but it was a pleasant run. The purpose of the journey was to buy a large amount of cheap cow food. Alan had informed me that the food was purely belly filler for the cows and would put fat on them thus keeping them warm. It is apparently made up of cookie and cake mix; wow, that means I can use some of it.

On arrival, we had to go onto a weigh bridge so that the food would be put in the trailer and we would pay for the weight of the food. I realised promptly that I would not be using the cake mix, as it was obviously all the sweepings and left overs. It did smell yummy and we looked forward to getting it to the cows.

On arriving home, we eagerly filled up buckets of the new food and took it to our eager animals. The cows and young stock enjoyed their feast. Once the winter starts to set in, the cows need extra concentrated food to keep them warm. It somehow gives me a warm feeling when the animals are happily eating. In a lovely moment of spirited slapstick, they pushed and shoved one another to get at the mix; once finished, their faces were covered in cake mix and they wandered off to chew their cud.

18ᵗ ᴴ December

Alan had to go to town to see Alistair; poor guy's had his tonsils and adenoids removed, and cannot be left alone so soon after the operation. Alan really enjoyed relaxing with his son. They chatted and watched a film together. Later, Alistair's partner, Katie, came back and cooked a full English breakfast for them both.

Tonight the snow was thick on the ground. Although we have had all obstacles placed in our way to hinder the management of our animals, they must be given silage today. Cows are not the best foragers in the animal kingdom so will go very hungry when snow is on the ground. They now also require more food for warmth. All gates providing access to the farm and fields have been locked since we arrived. Although Alan has managed to overcome this, it has meant extra work. Today, he had planned to cut a link in the chain to provide access for the tractor into the cows' field. However, the gate was frozen into the earth and could not be moved. In the darkness, with hands and feet frozen to the core, Alan and I battled to pull the gate free. We could not! Alan had no option but to place the bale over the gate. This was not ideal but we had no choice. Cows being cows, they could not care less where we serve it so long as it's served. As the bale was lowered over the gate, the cows all tucked in and ate heartily. Checking them later on, we found them content, chewing the cud. What silage they had not eaten was then used as a very good quality bed!

The lights in Stan's house usually went out at 6.30 pm; it was 10pm when I commented to Alan that his father's lights were still on. The snow was thick on the ground and getting thicker by the minute. Whenever his lights are on late it means just one thing. The Prodigal Son was home, so we thought. We have to know when he is home as it is the time to watch our backs and the backs of our animals!

We had settled down in our little caravan. The kettle rumbled for our last cup of tea before bed. I poured the water in the pot, just as a fist pounded at the front door.

"Oh who the hell is that Alan?" I cried, my nerves being somewhat frayed round the edges. I stood rigid. Nobody knocked on our door at this time of night. Alan made his way tentatively to the door. I listened as I held my breath with fear. I could hear my heart pounding through my chest. I heard Alan responding calmly, which calmed me immediately. I heard Alan leaving the caravan and talking as he went. I popped my head out of the door, to see three policemen. Alan looked back at me. "It's dad, his bleeper has gone off and the police cannot locate him."

Alan went around to the house and peered through the window. His father lay motionless on the hearth. The police attempted to kick the door in.

"Break the glass to get the keys," Alan cried. "You will never kick that door in."

Once inside, an assessment was made and the ambulance was called. Stan lay semi-conscious on the floor. It was apparent he had taken yet another fall. Alan was asked by the police to open the large gates (the ones locked by the Trog-male, apparently at Stan's insistence). We made our way to the large heavy gates and pulled one side off its hinges. We struggled to drag it around to allow the ambulance access. We sat waiting for the ambulance, so we could guide them to the farmhouse. We sat for nearly half an hour in the bitter cold. We didn't see a single car before the ambulance arrived. We are so far removed from the busy A619 we've recently left behind.

The ambulance arrived and took Stan away to the hospital. We returned to the static and I made a second pot of tea. Alan seemed pleased to have had the chance to help his father. We retired to bed tired and exhausted from yet another long adventurous day.

19ᵀᴴ DECEMBER

The Christmas spirit has really come to Syda Farm.
Like Hell! It seems that not only do we have Alan's family
to contend with, which we were fully prepared for, but the
Trog-clan are even worse. They are obsessed with us and seem
intent on making our lives as miserable as they possibly can.
I hope if you have shared this much of my journey, you see
me as a very positive person and agree it takes a lot to get me
down. We are living our lives and living well, having fun and,
despite many obstacles placed in our path, we are overcoming
them. I feel deep sadness for the Trog-clan and their
inhumane nature. They are a couple who should be enjoying
their life and teaching their young daughter different lessons
to the ones she is getting from them. How sad to think that
they are wasting their chance to put a young caring human
into the world. Instead they are leading by example and
teaching her that when people are struggling, you must NOT
help and if possible make things worse for them. God help
you, little girl. God help you, dear.

If we were not so strong then we would have gone under.
It does make me sad to think that a fellow human being can
behave in such a way with those less fortunate. The Trog-clan
are the type of people you would expect on the programme
Neighbours from Hell. It is no small wonder that wars break out
and, on a smaller scale but equally tragic, that people commit

suicide through hounding and intimidation. I thank God each day for all my blessings and especially for all our good friends. Although I am planning to cook a traditional Christmas dinner, my friends have done nothing but ask us to join them on Christmas Day. It has been such a wonderful time to be surrounded by people who really do care. Luckily, they turn our aggressors into the insignificant beings that they are.

Lady Trog pulled into the top gate at Syda and proceeded to manoeuvre her car. She then got out of her car and carried her young daughter down the icy lane, as a fierce wind battered against her daughter's flimsy little dress and bare legs.

"Oh, how nice, she is going to show her little girl the calves," Alan exclaimed in his usual naïve manner. He sees the best in everyone but, sadly, this has not always been for the best.

"Do you really think so, Alan?" I replied, saddened to have to point out what she was really doing.

"Actually, Alan, she has parked her car in the gateway!"

We watched as she strode past our static, looking defiantly in our windows as she went. I felt so sorry that a little girl had been carried down a treacherous lane in such blustery conditions, wearing barely any clothing of significance. Just simply to make a point to me and Alan. That poor little girl!

She had parked her car in the gateway because we had opened it for the ambulance the night before. Because earlier in the day Alan had fed his stock, we figured that they did not even tie the act in with the arrival of the ambulance but decided in their sad little minds that we had removed it to feed the animals. Moments later, Stan was driven home by his daughter. This is the fastest I have ever known him come out of hospital after a fall!

After popping out in the dark, to enjoy my new, uncluttered view of the stars, I noticed that the Trog-female's car was still in the gateway. Yes, alright, it did cross my mind to put a brick through the windscreen but thinking about it is not a crime, is it? I fought the urge and headed off to buy some petrol for the generator. Driving home up the desolate road, I could detect a pair of head lamps glowing in the darkness of the distance. Not car ones but the ones you actually wear on your head. I was aware of them from the bottom of the hill, through the occasional illumination of repeated digging movements at the top gate of Syda. As I approached the gate, it became apparent that the Prodigal Son and the Trog-male were working side by side yet again. The Prodigal Son was blocking the cattle grid and I saw him glance furtively sideways to see who it was. Once he saw the Land Rover, he carried on and made out he did not know anyone was there. I headed for the main gateway from which the Trog-male had just reversed his wife's vehicle. He tried hard to get it back into the gateway to prevent my entrance. I simply put my foot down; I was going through no matter. I could not afford to get out of the vehicle, as this would have meant confrontation. He failed to get the car back into position. With my whole body shaking with anxiety, I made it home and had a well earned cup of tea.

We put our problems behind us to meet our good friends, Jane and Alan, for dinner. We had a lovely evening as always with these two kind, generous people. Mind you, we did spend a long time talking about cat poo and cat litter! It makes you wonder how you get on to such topical discussions.

20ᵀᴴ DECEMBER

Looked out of the window only to see the Prodigal Son walking up the snow covered lane. This man never walks for pleasure so this meant only one thing. He strode towards the cows and began to take pictures of each and every one of them on the snow covered fields. Who will these pictures be for? The RSPCA, perhaps? He seemed to want us to see that he was photographing the cows. Alan was not bothered in the slightest, but I was rather upset as I felt violated by his actions. Some of our cows are old and do not always look at their best. Crunchy for example is a very old cow and has lost one eye and looks like a relic. But she is happy and content (although the harsh weather is not nice for her). She loves her food and sits happily many hours of the day chewing her cud. She can even be seen to be running in the fields some days. Ivory is retired and had lost her quarters (teats) and she enjoys running round the field, mothering all the young stock. But they do not look brilliant at this time of year! To see these cows, day in and day out, is the only way to truly judge their quality of life, as with any other old animals.

The behaviour from the Prodigal Son today indicates that not one of them had tied in the removal of the gate with the arrival of the ambulance! Are they really that stupid? Yes, they are!

The snow was thick on the ground, making feeding and management of the animals more difficult but more vital. A hungry animal is a cold animal in this weather. Alan managed to force open the gate into the cabbage field that the cows live in. We took down a big ring feeder and placed it down by the Spinney. The Spinney will provide warmth and shelter for the cows. We fed them as normal and watched them tucking into their cake mix!

With the snow falling so heavily, the Trog-male had to open the big gates at the top of the lane, but only for his convenience, of course. They can only just get their own vehicles out in ordinary conditions. The lane is becoming difficult to manoeuvre on due to snow drifts.

21ˢᵀ DECEMBER

I'm dreaming of a white Christmas and it looks like we are going to get one! The snow is inches at least, with drifts around the farm up to two feet high. The dogs love it. The cows and horses are reasonably happy if the wind drops and it stays dry. A combination of wind and wet to the larger animals spells out their worst nightmare.

Everywhere is frozen including my net curtains. The nets are frozen solid to my windows and tear if I try to remove them. The cats in the house are well happy as the fire is on low for 24 hours a day. Every time I walk in the room I am confronted by a pile of cats. Literally! The dogs will squeeze in between the cats. Cats may end up climbing on top of the dogs. The idea is that first thing in the morning I bring my clothes into the lounge and dress in front of the fire. However, there is never any room for me and I end up just as cold as if I was in my bedroom. The cats in the cattery are not so lucky. The cattery is frozen solid and so are the pipes to our caravan. We have to get water from our friend's houses or the local garage. I am at present melting snow for the chickens as we have nothing but ice today. It is a laborious task and takes a long time collecting the snow and melting it in a small pan. Basically we are suffering a severe water shortage!

22ND DECEMBER

I nipped to town with Rob for our last minute Christmas shopping. The snow was falling thick and fast and Rob was so excited about the thought of a white Christmas. I must admit, once he got excited about it I realised how lovely it would be. I mean the thought of it is scary as I do not like the cold. But I have to think how cold it used to be at Rufford. My goodness, I had to put my clothes on a radiator by my bed so that I could face the thought of getting dressed. The windows would be covered in frost and I would be able to see my own breath. Alan could always jump out of the bed and into his clothes; I never knew how he was able to do this (he still does). Only once have I ever heard him cry out in shock as the cold clothes embraced his warm body. I remember it well as he let out a high pitched shriek. I just pulled up the covers and refused to leave my bed. Yes, I am well qualified to face winter in my static.

Alan picked us up from town and we headed home. Alan mentioned in passing that he had seen the Trog-male driving into the spinney. With his usual naivety, Alan thought the visit to the Spinney, in the dark, was innocent. He thought the Trog-male might be picking some Holly! I tried keeping positive but I am well versed in some of the realities of human nature and I was certain the visit to the spinney would be far from innocent.

23RD DECEMBER

I could not help but laugh to see Trog-male being towed out of the Spinney first thing this morning. And the fact that he had to get a tractor in to fetch him added to my hilarity. Not ones to gloat, we simply carried on trying to thaw more water for the chickens.

We had planned for our final yuletide trip into town early today. Sadly, the Trog-male successfully put paid to that one. We all went down to feed the cows only to find the real reason the Spinney had been trespassed, in the dark! The rotten swine had been down and fenced all our animals out of the Spinney. This meant they had no shelter and no access to the brook for water. We were all three of us shocked to the core at the low and despicable behaviour of this nasty person. Alan immediately phoned his solicitor while I phoned our local RSPCA Inspector. Both parties made it plain the fence was to come down. Alan called at his father's house. Upon requesting that the fence be taken down, it became clear that there is a huge control issue going on with the Trog-clan and Alan's father. Stan said that the Trog had been after the Spinney for a while. Alan informed his father that the fence must come down and the Trogs cannot have the field. The old man said,

"Well you will have to tell them."

Alan got the impression that his father was actually afraid of the Trog-male. Since moving here it has been obvious to us that the Trogg-male has a lot of control. During the visit to his father, Alan was informed that I needed a belt taking to me! Not only that, I have to stop effing and blinding over the fence all day long! Apparently I am performing this behaviour all day. Alan of course knew this was not true so the old man protested, "You want to hear her when you are not around."

Well really, Gin, this has got to stop, you naughty girl! The only problem is for me that I am not aware of what I am doing and when I am doing it. I really must see a doctor about my split personality, and soon.

Alan and Rob removed the fence and the cows regained access to their shelter. How many people would be able to deprive a few old cows of their shelter at this time of year?

Although a little late, we headed off into town.

The evening was cold outside and the weather was freezing. The decking outside the caravan is treacherous. We have a hand rail that we can hold to as we step outside. But the hand rail has a good coating of ice so, as you put your hand upon it, off you go down the ski slope! It's very nerve racking and I am so worried that one of us will come a cropper.

CHRISTMAS DAY 2009

Christmas morning has arrived at last. It started with a hot bacon sandwich and a cup of tea. I sat around in my dressing gown opening gifts. I had given Rob a list of ideas and so he went and bought me everything that was on my list. Could not wait to make a fresh cup of tea in order to use my new chicken shaped tea cosy!

The sun was shining and the snow was crunching beneath our feet. The horses were fresh and lively with the wind in their tails. I had decided today I would carry on my tradition of a lovely Christmas morning ride on my beautiful Jaffa.

Since arriving at Syda I have not yet been organised enough to start my horse riding. I guess I am a little worried about the reaction it will cause with this lot up here. But once I am organised there will be no stopping me!

Rob and Alan helped me to get my tack together. The wind was cold by this time, biting through my trousers. The horses peered over the wall as we approached the fields. I knew what they were thinking as they scrunched up their eyes to get a better look.

"Whose saddle are they carrying?"

I imagine it felt a bit like a lottery, especially as my saddle can be used on three or more of them. Poor old Jaffa got the short straw as I bribed her with a big red, extremely cold apple.

I hated removing her thick warm rug and questioned whether it was fair but I needed my ride. Alan held her bridle as I removed the rug to expose her beautiful mahogany coat. She stood still and quiet as the wind whipped around her limbs. There are not many horses you can pluck out of the field after two months and jump in the saddle safely.

I placed the cold saddle upon her back and she did not flinch. That is the nature of Jaffa, my wonder horse. I twisted the stirrup iron and placed my foot inside it, all this while also pleading with Alan not to let her go. I have not ridden for two months and Jaffa has been left in a field during that time. I trust her with my life but still I felt a tiny bit nervous. With my feet firmly in the stirrups, I permitted Alan to let her go. I squeezed her sides twice and we were away.

I walked in the crunchy snow and revelled in the sound of Jaffa's hooves. The wind blew and the sun came out and shined down on us. I asked her to trot and off we went through the virgin snow that nothing except little wild rodents had been on. I decide to head towards Rob and Alan in a lively but collected canter. Next minute, Jaffa hunched herself up into a little ball and exploded into the most humongous bucks ever. I gripped with every muscle possible and managed to stay aboard. Jaffa rarely bucks but, boy, when she does, she sure as hell bucks.

I realised she had bucked due to the wind hitting her hind quarters. I was desperate for another canter so I turned her into the wind. The feeling was exhilarating. The cold wind picked up her wispy mane, the untouched snow crunched under her hooves. Have I just died and gone to heaven? I looked across and saw Alan wrapped in Jaffa's fleece lined rug and realised I was still on this Earth. This was good news as I had a turkey cooking and I should hate to have left the men dealing with that.

Rob ran ahead with his camera looming towards me and Jaffa. I laughed and punched the air. Me and my Jaffa had just completed our first ride at our new home. I lowered myself out of the saddle and hastily flung the rug over her back. What a Christmas morning!

Ambition fulfilled, we headed cold and excited back to the homestead. Moments later, Katie and Alistair arrived with their family of dogs. Pandemonium broke out of course with our three inside the static and their three outside. We made the visiting dogs a bed in the cattery and went inside to sip champagne and orange juice (Bucks Fizz, I believe). After exchanging gifts, we went on the most delightful walk with the six dogs. The ground was beginning to ice over and I was so worried that Katie, being heavily with child, might take a tumble. The dogs had such a good time and ran across the fields full of the joys.

Waved goodbye to Katie, Ali and the dogs and headed yet again back to the caravan. It was time to finish my preparations for Christmas dinner and turn them into a good festive meal. We sat for a well earned dinner at around 6pm, just in time to enjoy "Doctor Who"!

I have to say the dinner I cooked was lovely despite emerging from the static's little oven. Once dinner was eaten I then proceeded to make an apple pie. Oh, it felt like heaven (again), apple pie with fresh double cream. What more could one ask for in life? Maybe a little peace!

26TH December

Pleasant start to the day! I had opened a gate to let Alan come in to feed the cows when the Trog-male drove past. Of course, being the gentleman he is, he stuck one finger up at me while scowling nastily. Oh, what a charming, well matured man.

Nevertheless, we continued with our tasks as the cows looked eagerly on. They all came trotting down the field after the food. It is so easy to keep the cows happy. A bit like me really, as food heals all.

27ᵀᴴ DECEMBER

Very wet today, with snow and cold, a bad combination for livestock living in the fields. Hence we had one casualty who had rested over night but slipped while getting to her feet. We found our dear Daisy in a heap shivering with the cold. We ran towards her to tend her as quickly as we possibly could. There is nothing worse than seeing a struggling cow and one that has got cold is even harder to bear. She had got herself facing downhill and her head was resting under a gorse bush. Alan hurried to fetch choppers to remove the gorse. We gave her a bucket of feed as this would help to warm her. When all the branches were chopped, we pushed and heaved to get her comfortable.

Cows tend to lie flat and have great difficulty getting up, especially so when reaching the grand old ages that our girls are. Once she was sitting up and covered with warm horse rugs, she began to recover. We could see she was not ready to get up yet and left her to rest.

Upon returning under an hour later we could see she had tried to get to her feet again and failed. This was not good; as the more they try and fail the less likely they are to ever succeed. I find these situations heartbreaking and worrying, as the end results are rarely good. When a cow goes down, downer cows as they are known, they either get up within 24 hours or, tragically, they don't. The next 24 hours with Daisy are critical.

Firstly, in light of where she had gone down, the first step was to get her to safety. She was now heading down a big slope that led to a brook. The worst thing about a sick cow is that you cannot scoop then up in your arms and lay them by the fire! The tractor bucket is the only way to get them to safety. It is a lot to put a cow through and you have to weigh up the pros and cons. Why put a cow through it, unless you are sure they are going to recover?

Daisy had only been down a couple of hours. We had hoped that once her strength was regained she would get to her feet. Helping Alan get her into the tractor bucket was not pleasant. I try my hardest to keep calm, really I do. But when I see cows or any animal in distress, I get extremely upset. Unfortunately for Alan, this involves a lot of verbal outpourings from me!

Once in the bucket, the stress of the whole situation rose to crisis point. I can just about bear all this if I know the outcome is what I am wishing for. Somehow, I knew in my heart that Daisy was not going to get up. I cannot even say she'd had enough. She still wanted to tend to her babies and was still full of spirit. But I knew deep down she was not going to get up. I held her beautiful head in my arms, as the tractor carefully made its way up the hill.

Upon reaching the top of the field and what we considered to be safety, Daisy was gently eased out of the bucket. We sat her comfortably, fed and watered her and left her to rest. We covered her with blankets and waited for her to warm through. She talked endlessly to the rest of her family and her babies. I walked away knowing in my heart that this was her time.

I prayed and prayed and hoped that my prayers would be heard. I could not settle through the rest of the day. When a cow goes down with that much spirit, they will try to get up. They put themselves in danger trying. We were in and out for the rest of the afternoon, having to sit her up again, just once. After that she sat contentedly chewing her cud.

She was not up by nightfall. This meant a restless night for me, as I could not bear the thought of her getting stuck flat out without her blankets. I prayed all through the night; still, in my heart, I knew that my prayers would not be answered in the way I wanted them to be.

My bedtime check was at midnight. She was sitting, warm and content with another cow, Erica, by her side. The rest of the group were not far away, as Daisy responded to my goodnight call. I went to the static and turned in for what I knew would be more of a restless night.

Woke at 1am and sneaked out of the bedroom and into my freezing Wellies. The door was frozen shut, but with a sharp shove it pinged open. I could hear the low rumble of Alan's snoring as I walked across the crunching snow in my fluffy pink dressing gown. The air was still and the night was calm. I peered over the wall and Daisy was still upright, under her thick blankets. I called to her and she called back, still full of spirit. I was glad she had not tried to get up but I was disappointed too. Why had she not tried to get up? Daisy was in full conversation with the babies of the group and it was sad to see she could not go to them. For such a wonderful mummy cow as Daisy, this must have been hard for her!

6am I placed my even colder wellies on my shivering legs. To be able to get over to Daisy in my dressing gown is a good sign that the temperature must be reasonable. The air was very still; this must make such a difference to how much cold you can actually feel. Daisy called to me as I spoke her name.

She was still in the same position and looking content. I went back to the caravan, with the snow still crunching beneath my feet. The view was beautiful and the silence was startling. It was broken by the mooing of the cows and an unexpected call from the one of the horses. I would have been so happy had I not been sure we were about to lose our beautiful Daisy.

Alan went out at first light. By this time she had attempted to get to her feet. Sadly, she had failed. We knew what we had to do. Over the years, we have had many downer cows; in the summer, you can give them plenty of time and cling to hope a lot longer. In winter the weather gets too harsh to have a cow disabled for any length of time. We had to let Daisy go. Such a decision is never easy to make.

Alan made the dreaded call to "the man". Daisy ate her breakfast heartily, after being made warm again. Her family ambled round us. It was sad to see her looking so happy and well and yet unable to stand.

I saw "the man" arrive. I had dreaded this all morning. It was a bitter blessing that he had come so promptly. The sun shone brightly all morning for our Daisy, as she enjoyed her last hours on this side. In that sense my prayers were answered as the sun shone down on her for the whole morning. Her passing was pleasant compared to what it could have been.

"The man" came along the top lane towards the farm. Being the coward I am, I took Holly to see the horses. I noticed a seemingly innocent child asleep in the front seat of the man's vehicle. I was worried that this child might wake up and see something no child should witness. I walked with Holly and said a goodbye prayer for Daisy.

With Daisy now in a better and warmer place, the dark cloud made its way from my soul. I felt sad that we had lost one of our family members but I know that we have always done our best by her. She was at least able to die at home which is a comfort for man and beast in their final hours, I am sure. Not only did she pass over in her own home but she enjoyed her final serving of food. This is a tradition that Alan will always carry out to make their passing as pleasant as possible. Goodbye, Daisy, thank you for all you have done for us here at the farm.

As the day went on, the weather changed drastically and for the worst. A bitterly cold wind was followed by yet more snow. As I have said before, praying to God and St Martin doesn't always bring you the answer you want. Instead of helping to get Daisy up, they sent the sunshine for her final hours. I was grateful for this and I know she was too.

28ᵗʰ December

My concern now is for Black Girl. This is the young cow that had the car accident on the A619 when we lived at Rufford. She walks with an awkward gait and can sometimes lose her footing. She seems to be managing to get about but I always watch with baited breath as she follows the tractor down the field for her food. When the ground alternates from frozen to thawed, as in Daisy's case, the worst can happen!

My dear friends Alan and Jane called at my caravan for the first time. They absolutely loved it and were sure I was much better off here than at Rufford. Jane was amazed at how cosy we were, sitting by the little fire.

I went to the laundrette later in the day and seemed to have a load of washing again. This is a little odd as we seem to walk around in the same clothes all the time! Well, I must admit I rather enjoy my visit to the laundrette, once it is under way. I usually put my first load in and then nip to the shop; I buy a magazine and a newspaper then a hot drink, so it's not such a chore really. Never in my life have I been so up to date and organised with my washing. I even paired the socks again, as well!

I found it rather difficult dealing with my washing as there was a young man in front of my machine. I had to stretch across to get a hold of my washing to bring across to the dryer. I was rather embarrassed clinging tightly to all my smalls. Anyway guess what spilled all over the floor. You guessed it, knickers and bras in abundance. Mind you, he could only take so much. As I grappled on the floor picking knickers up as more knickers fell, he decided at long last to move. At last, I thought to myself as I threw my washing over my shoulder, only to then whack him in the face with a pair of briefs!

29ᵀᴴ December

We took a trip to Matlock to see our little Merry and Velvet. I always enjoy a visit to Shirley as she is such a wonderful character, so full of life. Always a tale to tell and it's usually about some animal or other. Merry and Velvet looked a little miserable today due to the terrible weather. I fed them apples and went into Shirley's kitchen for a bowl of homemade tomato soup.

Walking into Shirley's house is like stepping back in time. I don't think the house has been touched for fifty years. It is really old world and there are pots and pans hanging from every available space. A small formica table sits in the corner, with two old chairs beside it. The floor is made of quarry tiles and the tops of the surfaces are all old formica too. A little cat climbs up on your lap the minute you sit down. The tomato soup was lovely and warmed me to the core; I must get the recipe.

Headed to Alistair and Katie where we were fed yet again. A most beautiful roast dinner fit for royalty. Alan and I had a lovely time and were made very welcome and at home. The house is full of excitable dogs, so it is rather like being at home.

30ᵀᴴ DECEMBER

Alan took me to Derby House Saddle shop for my new boots. I tried some on and finally found a pair that fitted and were really warm. I decided to keep them on and carry my old ones home. I was just about to go to the Land Rover in them to fetch Alan's wallet. Luckily, Alan decided to go to the vehicle while I walked around the store in my new boots. Thank goodness Alan went out as we discovered he had left his wallet at home so we could not pay for them. That could have been so embarrassing had I gone outside. As it was, I took them off and placed them back on the shelf for another day.

31ˢᵀ DECEMBER

Friends called up today and I was whisked away on an excursion. Usual round of saddle shops etc. We ended up at Sutton in Ashfield which meant I could pop and see my Peanut; he is out on loan to a lovely lady. He looked really happy and content and much loved. I hugged him tightly and inhaled his wonderful aroma. We had a kiss and a cuddle. I reluctantly said goodbye and we headed back to Chesterfield.

Alan was waiting with a boiling kettle ready to make us a cup of tea. He was very eager for our return so I was aware he had something to tell us. As soon as we walked in he produced a large envelope for us to peruse. New Year's Eve and Stan had put us in court for trespass!

We enjoyed ending New Year's Eve sending Greetings by text. I had some wonderful replies, including a lovely picture of Hugo, a rescue dog we homed last year. Hugo came to Angel Wings last Christmas Eve. He was an adorable little dog and did not deserve to be abandoned the way he was. He was homed in no time at all to a delightful couple who fell in love with his photograph. I had placed his picture in the vets and by the time I got home the couple called to enquire about him. They came, they saw, they fell in love. I got a nice picture of Fudge too, asleep in front of a fire. She looked very content but the text reply suggested she is being a bit naughty.

I was concerned about this but will leave telephoning the owners for a week or two; I am not ready for bad news yet.

We saw the New Year in together on the front porch of the static. We could see for miles and watched as the fireworks went off in the distance. The display was wonderful and we raised a glass of homemade Blackberry Gin. We are hopeful for 2010 and, let's face it, things can only get better.

1ST JANUARY 2010

Alan went out early to start the tractor only to find it would not start. He checked the battery and it looked like the terminals had been loosened. This coincided with a letter from the Driver and Vehicle Licensing Agency; the letter stated that a problem has arisen with the records of the tractor. We don't know the full details as yet but we are certain it is to do with next door. Time will tell.

Alan had to take the battery to a friend as we have no way of charging it in our static. This just made the job a lot longer than it should have been. We could not feed the cows their silage, which was distressing all round. Alan gave them a double ration of their cake mix.

2ND JANUARY

Alan fetched the tractor battery, thus enabling him to feed the cows their silage. He is now going to park the tractor nearer to the caravan in order to make it less accessible for the neighbours. We also have the advantage of our indispensable guard dogs, who miss nothing.

I went on yet another excursion to the saddle shop. Rob came with me and we all piled into the Land Rover. We had a bit of fun and enjoyed the beautiful scenery as we drove steadily along the tops. The whole of the scenery was pure white and very picturesque. We were rather in awe of the views. The dry stone walls looked like paintings, with carefully placed white and artistically placed brown stone peeping through; it was just the most amazing sight you could ever see.

I met Linda and Becky at the saddle shop and I invited them up to my des res. Becky, the cheeky mare, burst out laughing when I termed my caravan as such. I told Linda about the accusations of me running around Stan's garden swearing. As serious as you like she looked me in the eyes and exclaimed,

"You run, as if?"

4TH JANUARY

Up and out early in order to pay a visit to the Citizens Advice Bureau. Rob sat and waited at the centre while Alan and I carried out other errands. Met Rob back there and took him a large black coffee (I know how to keep him happy). I took a large pack of yum yums too. Sat in the waiting room and low and behold Carol's dad walked in. Soon after, Carol phoned me so I asked her dad to answer the phone so as to confuse Carol. She took it in her stride and made out she had meant to call him! What a coincidence that Carol's dad should walk in the CAB today.

I called at the the council offices to speak to the planning enforcement officer. This is the man that the old man and his Prodigal Son and no doubt the Trogs are dealing with too. They have told yet more lies as I am told I am running a livery business! Apparently they approached a lot of our visitors and were informed they were the horses' real owners. The owners were apparently running around shouting, "Where's my horse, I kept it at Rufford and now it has gone." Hence the council are not too happy with me. Well I put him in the picture and he was actually very nice. Once he came off his high horse he was very helpful. It was strange really because I was not overly aware he was on his high horse until he got off it. Once he got off it, he was very positive and very helpful. I felt a lot better when I left the council offices.

I am feeling unsettled again and very worried about what is around the corner. It is just like Rufford all over again. I just wish that Alan and I could be left alone to get on with our lives. How can a father want to torture his son in this way? I really cannot understand this man; I only know he is not a human being in the true sense.

I was so happy in my little static and I have put up with no heating, no water and an outside portaloo and they still won't leave us alone.

5ᵀᴴ JANUARY

My esteem is low yet again and I decided I would make a real effort and put a bit of slap on. A bit of slap for me simply means a bit of mascara. Well it usually makes me look and thus feel a little more human. I pulled the brush from the tube only to be confronted by a frozen blob on the end of the wand. Oh well, perhaps I will have another go in the spring. Until then, I will have to make do with running a brush through my hair.

7TH JANUARY

It was a lovely sunny morning with the snow still crisp beneath my feet. It crunched loudly with each footstep as I set about feeding my animals. Managed to muck out my ducks but it was not easy. I bedded them down with some fresh sawdust. Tried to muck out the chickens but with so much snow they are refusing to leave the coop. I just put down some nice fresh bedding for them. They seem happy enough; I was worried about them getting cold at night until I stood inside with them one freezing night. Their coop was actually a lot warmer than my bedroom!

Alan and I are both suffering with our feet at the moment, among other things. We went to Stony Middleton to try and fit ourselves up with some decent boots; Alan purchased a pair of rigger boots. They slip on and off his feet, which will make a huge difference to him. I tried on several pairs but decided to wait and not rush into buying a pair. At £40 a pair, I have to be really sure I like them.

Dashed into Chesterfield to the Law Centre; this was to attend an appointment at 2pm. The meeting was to discuss the court papers and to declare ourselves potentially homeless. The discussion left me feeling rather down I am afraid. All the talk was of our health problems (of which there are many) and how we should plead our case in order to avoid being on the streets. Oh what bliss. This is just not the kind of chat I want to have at my time of life.

After taking a phone call from my friend, Lynne, I realised I was blessed really, despite everything. She asked me and Alan to call down for our mail (it is redirected to her address). She also said we could have a shower and dinner. This was such a treat out of the blue and was very welcome. Needless to say, as soon as I sat on her big, squidgy sofa, I went to sleep. I was in the land of blissful nod and yet was painfully aware that my mouth was wide open and there was nothing I could do about it.

The shower was amazing as Lynne's is new and state of the art. It was so powerful and so hot. She had every conceivable flavour of shower gel and shampoo. While I was in the shower the wonderful smell of dinner wafted through the bathroom door. The garlic bread smelt so good and I got hungrier by the minute. We sat and enjoyed a wonderful meal with a wonderful friend.

Having left the static for several hours, we arrived home with trepidation. Upon opening the door, we were met with chaos. The cats had clearly had a mad half hour and the two Great Danes had joined in. Cushions were scattered all over the floor, along with my beautiful crocheted throw of many colours. The net curtains had been pulled from the windows and they too were scattered around the static. But one thing I was extremely grateful for was that none of them had soiled the carpet.

I am so pleased with my animals at the moment, especially the cats; down at Rufford, they were very dirty cats that seemed to totally ignore the litter trays I supplied for them. Here in the static they seem to be much cleaner. I must admit my management of the trays has been much more efficient than it ever was at Rufford. Maybe that has got more to do with it than I care to admit.

8ᵀᴴ JANUARY

Up early to be greeted by Alan with my usual cup of steaming hot tea. Without Alan, I would not be able to get out of the bed. Without him putting the kettle on, I would not be able to contemplate such a manoeuvre. My bed is so cosy and yet the bedroom is so cold.

Once I am up out of bed I open the static door and admire the wonderful view. Today, as I peered out into the winter wonderland, the cows were just beginning to emerge from the Spinney. After my morning cup of tea, Alan toasted me a couple of tea cakes which I smothered in butter. I warmed my clothes by the fire and got dressed in the little bit of space left by the cats and dogs. Once the animals have huddled around the fire, it is difficult to get near it for a warm. I must admit I do like to see the cats stretched out in front of it. We have to be vigilant though as Murphy and Hoppy are unable to detect when they are about to go up in flames. They sit as close to the fire as possible without actually getting in it. Luckily, they start to smell of burning before they go up in flames. I am then able to dive across the static and throw them hastily out of the way, while smoke rises from their little bodies. This is the reason why we can never leave the fire on full if we are out of the room. Both Murphy and Hoppy have bald patches and lots of singed hair.

We went to see our solicitor at 11.20am but it was a very long session. It seems the blue torch paper has now been lit. This trespass case could be the answer to our prayers. We still have a long and rocky road ahead but I think I can just about see a light at the end of the tunnel. At 2.40pm we left the office and went for a late lunch.

Called at Derby House Saddler's for the boots I should have had last week. They still had them thank goodness. I too am looking forward to a bit of comfort in the foot department.

Rather late home so we were very worried how we would find things. When I opened the door there was the usual scattering of cushions and throws but no damage done. Maybe the dogs and cats genuinely think they are making it nice for when we get home. It's a pity they don't put the kettle on instead.

9ᵀᴴ January

My computer decided to crash at the time I needed it most.

This meant that I could not open the document Rob had sent me from the Chatsworth House solicitors. We had to go all the way to Derby in order to get the document that has to be sent off as part of the court case. Our life just seems to be one long court case right now. We enjoyed the visit to Rob as this obviously involved a couple of pizzas.

When we got home and fed the cows, later on in the day, I managed to have a little amble around the spinney to have a look at the area where the cows sleep. The area is extensive and made me feel a lot happier. I could see the large area where they settle down at night. The cows are clearly very cosy and have found the most sheltered part of the area. The snow covered ground has large, black patches where the cows have slept. At the edge of each patch is a large pile of cow pats from each cow; I would call the area a definite cow bedroom. The site made me very happy and content in the knowledge that they make themselves comfortable through the night.

The cows are doing extremely well on the cake mix that we are feeding them. I am delighted to say they are actually putting on a bit of weight. The small calves have both cake mix and growers pellets. They need the proper food, high in protein to help them develop. Alan thought a bit of cake mix would add variety (and obviously cheaper food) to their diet. The funny thing is they always eat the cake mix first and save the proper pellets for when there is no cake mix left.

Jenny phoned me with the sad news that she has lost her beautiful dog Rosie. Although Rosie was old, it was still a very sad time for Jenny and her husband. Rosie was a very beautiful, regal and graceful dog; she reminded me of my darling Annie, who I lost last year. When we called to see Jenny she did look so very upset. Alan and I had a couple of cups of tea with her. When we left, she had a little more colour in her cheeks. It is so hard when you love your animals; their life spans are always so short, relative to their owners.

While at Jenny's house we received an urgent phone call from our solicitor regarding the papers for the trespass case that the old man has brought against us. As my computer is down, we were lucky enough to print the papers off at Jenny's house.

Alan read the defence that our solicitor had prepared and he was very positive about it. This is the big one! The old man has told so many lies to the locals about both of us and he now has his side kicks by the name of Trog and also the Prodigal Son. However, I pray a judge in a court room will not accept his lies. This is the action that we have waited for. The truth will out! Now we have to read it, check it and send it back. Sounds easy. Time is of the essence. We have to act quickly but we have no computer!

I booked a visit to the doctor as my breathing has become terrible. Although initially when we settled on Syda my breathing improved due to less vehicle fumes, once the damp set into the caravan, it's deteriorated. At night our bedroom sounds like a cat sanctuary due to all the wheezing from my lungs.

Self-esteem low as usual, I made my way to the doctor's surgery. Unfortunately, the ground was very wet from the thaw so my boots were rather muddy. I was too tired and breathless to make too much effort as to my appearance. I knew that once I had my prescription I would start to feel a lot better.

The lady doctor called my name and I walked cheerily into her room. She looked me up and then down in a most discerning manner. That was bad enough but she then repeated the manoeuvre yet I think her actions were meant to be discreet! Well, not one to miss an opportunity, I felt that she needed to know that her attempt to be discreet had failed enormously. One thing I had in my favour was my designer handbag (one Rob had bought me for Christmas). I just looked her in the eye and declared, "Yes I know, glamorous don't you think? But remember I am living in a caravan in the middle of a field. And besides, I have a really nice handbag!"

"Oh yes, it is a nice bag," she replied, rather taken aback.

I just wanted to be sure she knew I had noticed her condescending manner at my appearance. She was rather horrified at the noise from my chest and gave me a prescription and I left.

January 12th

Every morning I get out of bed and look through my window. The view is just so beautiful and I don't ever want to take it for granted. I look down to see the cows emerging from their sleeping area. I will then go into the hall and open the front door of the static. Again the view is just too amazing to believe. The fields are so green and far reaching down the valley towards the little village of Holymoorside. Dry stone walls divide the fields as they rise up to meet the Chesterfield town in the far distance.

After opening the door and peering out into the distance it all becomes too much for me. Something inside me stirs and my heart starts to sing and then my voice joins in.

"Oh what a beautiful morning, Oh what a beautiful day, I've got a wonderful feeling, everything's going my way."

So that is how my days begin and I love it. The cows raise their heads in response to my morning chorus. I close the door and head on in for my early morning cup of tea.

Today's morning chorus was hampered slightly as the door was frozen shut. The ice was over an inch thick on the inside of the door. I gave the door a couple of good shoves and away I went. There was a heavy mist so I could not see the cows and I am sure they could not see me. However, they will have heard me and I am sure that would make them happy.

Despite the terrible weather and the radio stations warning us not to leave home, Alan wanted to attend his hospital appointment. It was due to take place in Sheffield at the Royal Hallamshire. We called at my sister's for a shower and scrub up and then we headed in the treacherous weather to Sheffield.

The solicitor rang to check we had received the email he sent. It was the document which he had amended for Alan to authorise. As we have no computer right now, this was another prelude to a load of dashing around, although I did not know it at the time.

Alan and I thought long and hard as to which of our friends has internet access, etc. Carol was the first port of call, which involved an hour's round trip. Upon arriving at Carol's, we were informed that her internet was not working. Oh well, we will just have to go back to the drawing board. The situation is that we need to sign the document and send it back to the solicitors as soon as is humanly possible. Easier said than done!

Alan's daughter is a trained IT expert and has all the required equipment available. No worries, we simply made arrangements to go over and print the document from her computer. All went according to plan. I managed to open my email and download the document. I sat back to enjoy "Emmerdale" while Hannah went upstairs to print the document.

Five minutes later, our cosy world was rocked again with the words, "Sorry I can't get it to print. Don't worry they will do it for me next door. Won't be long." After a further ten minutes Hanna came through the door looking rather fed up. "Oh sorry they don't have a working printer."

Back to the drawing board as the document is a matter of some urgency. The trespass case is to be heard on 21st of January and we need to get these papers sorted before then.

Decided to call on my niece who of course welcomed me to her house to download and print the papers. What she did not realise is that the electricity on her street was off until late evening for repair work.

I phoned my friend Lynne, who said I could come down immediately. We rushed to her house and yet again downloaded the document and set it to print. It would not print! You can imagine by this stage I was feeling rather despondent. I was meeting Carol in town for a coffee so she suggested we go to the library. Alan dropped me in town and he ambled down to the computer shop to enquire about getting mine fixed. We had realised how badly we needed a computer. Half way to the library, Alan phoned me to tell me to hurry back to the computer shop as the shop owner would do the job for us.

I could not believe the document was now signed and gone. I was glad to see the back of it. Carol and I waved Alan off home and went for a well earned chip butty.

Late in the evening there was a lot of light coming from the Trog-dwelling. From around 7pm until 11pm the Trog-male was working at the top of his garden. I am suspicious of all he does at the moment as it is usually something to cause us problems. I mentioned it to Alan but he rightly pointed out that he is in his own boundaries and therefore it cannot be to do with us. I felt a little happier but was still unsure of his motives for working at the top of his garden for so many hours.

The snow and ice are beginning to thaw which means my chickens and ducks will now have water in abundance. I have placed large bins at the ends of the caravan to catch the melting snow.

15ᵀᴴ JANUARY

We still have no water at all coming into the caravan. It is a real nuisance because we have to go out regularly for water. We are trying hard to be environmentally friendly but we seem to have to go out every day! I cannot understand how a fellow human can turn off the water of less advantaged people. What gives the Trogs the right to do this? They do not even pay the water bill and have not paid for amenities since arriving on the farm in 2007. It is the old man who pays for these things.

The animals inside and outside seem to be drinking a lot of water. I find myself getting a little panicky when the water in our kitchen gets low. It seems when our water starts to diminish, the animals require even more. I get worried because the more water they drink, the less cups of tea there will be for me!

Since the snow came we have had to store rubbish outside the caravan door. Of course, it has got snowed on and this has made our rubbish heap messy and not pleasant. As the snow has melted somewhat we can get at it today so we loaded it all into the back of the Land Rover ready for a trip to the tip. I was due to meet Rob at the train station at 2.30.

We set off as the mist began to rise a little. We headed towards the rubbish tip with a boot load of stinking garbage. We had to do an errand on route which meant spending a little longer than I would have liked surrounded by the festering bags. Heading towards the rubbish dump once more, Alan pulled into the kerb as his mobile phone rang. "Oh, hi dad, are you alright?" Alan's face showed concern at hearing his father's voice. He knows only too well that his father must be desperate if he is calling upon Alan. Alan's father answered in a strained voice, "Can you take me to the hospital?"

With those words, I was elbowed out onto the ice covered pavement. I was aware that Alan, being the good son he is, had to go and help his father. I have to remind myself that Alan is still his father's son and a very good son at that.

I walked along the treacherous pavements hurrying to meet Rob at the train station. The walk was not unpleasant (in fact I rather enjoyed it). It gave me time to think about things. I was taken a little by surprise when I walked past what is known as Edinburgh Park. I suddenly burst into tears! This was the park where my first ever little dog used to run to when he escaped from the house. That was Tango, my beloved Tango, such a naughty little boy. All the locals knew my little boy. My mum had rescued him from a bad home and bought him to surprise me. What a surprise, my very own dog.

Tango was a pedigree smooth haired fox terrier. The gentlest little dog you would ever meet. It was evident he had been abused; he would cower behind the furniture when visitors called; he would shake and tremble until all the visitors were gone.

I remember getting him bathed for a fun dog show. He looked wonderful on the morning of the show. His white patches where pure white and his brown patches were shiny and soft. I opened the front door to fetch the milk from the doorstep and Tango pushed past me and ran off to his favourite haunt. This is where all his women would be, all the little bitches that adored his visits.

After chasing him all over the park and having to clean him up again we made our way to the little country show. The fun dog show had many entries and I proudly strode round the ring to show off my little dog. His proud stature made him stand out from the rest and he was awarded first prize. I was so excited and ran to my family as they all cheered. Mum told me someone in the crowd had insisted Tango was a professional show dog and should not have been entered! This made me even more proud, as he had never entered a show in his life.

All the memories came flooding back to me and I leaned on the wall looking into the park. I wiped away the tears and carried on with my walk towards the train station. Running across the train station car park, I just managed to see the train as it came in and even managed to have a coffee waiting for Rob!

January 18th

Alan had the horrendous task of meeting the Chatsworth agent down at Rufford. I did not envy him this chore but I had to let him go alone. Although everything is working out for us at the moment, I still feel strongly that what the Chatsworth House Estates did was very wrong. Therefore, I do not wish to come into contact with the agent or anyone else from that wretched place. I am sure I would say something I might regret!

Alan read the meter with the agent who had to rush upstairs as a pipe had burst. Well, that's what happens when you leave properties empty for the winter. Alan collected our mail and my old brown tea pot and he came home. And yes, the brown tea pot does fit inside my new chicken shaped tea cosy.

Missy doesn't look all that well tonight. She lives with her sister in the cattery. I hate to split them up but Missy needed to come into the caravan for some extra care. She will usually devour food before it even hits the bottom of the dish. Not tonight. She wants no food whatsoever. This sudden change concerns me.

After Missy had been inside the caravan for an hour or two, it became apparent that she must go to the vet first thing in the morning. She flopped around the caravan all evening and sat gazing at the water bowl. All her symptoms point to kidney failure. I am so worried that these are her final days.

I cannot possibly contemplate Sally being alone in the cattery; I cannot face Missy ending her days in the isolation of the cattery. Rob and I discussed the pros and cons of them living in his bedroom. Surely, we cannot fit any more in the main area of the caravan?

19ᵀᴴ January

Up bright and early ready to take Missy to the vet. Whenever I or anyone else goes to Ian Taylor's, you have to be aware that you will be there for some time. I often book myself in and then pop off and do something else like shopping or browsing round the nearby saddle shop. Today, I decided it would be a good idea to book in and then nip up the road and put my washing in at the laundrette.

After booking Missy in, I dashed up the road to put my laundry in the machines. I dashed back to the vet and, low and behold, I had missed my turn. A perfect example of the law of sod!

The vet was not over thrilled with Missy and said she was a very sick cat. He felt sure her kidneys were knackered and that there was little he could do. Luckily, I was suspicious that she could be hyperthyroid, due to her previous extremely ravenous appetite. The vet felt her neck and said that could be the case. He would do a blood test on her. I left Missy in the trusted hands of my vet and went back to the laundrette.

Upon returning home, Alan had to go and do some work for Alistair. I decided I would feed the cattery cats a little earlier so I could settle down. Took one look at my lonely little Sally and scooped her into my arms. We made a dash to the caravan where Sally stretched out on the sofa and went to sleep, as if she had always been there. Although I was worried for the health of her sister, I was a lot happier keeping Sally where I could keep an eye on her.

20TH JANUARY

Phoned the vet first thing and the news was good. Her kidneys, though stressed, were not a long term problem. Missy has hyperthyroid and an infection, so she can be treated and should respond. I was over the moon and continued to pray for her, with fingers well and truly crossed. Missy will stay at the vets, as she is not yet eating.

I went with Alan to Katie's for a shower; after all, we want to look nice for court tomorrow! Alan received a late evening phone call from the solicitor; he will be joining us in the morning at the court. It's going to be an expensive morning.

21ST JANUARY

Today is the day of reckoning. We were up bright and early to feed the stock and let the chickens out. Carol is coming to house sit for us. The enemy are aware of where we will be today and they will no doubt be expecting an empty caravan.

Luckily, I had bought some gas for my curling tongues so I made my hair look good. I squeezed the frozen toothpaste onto my brush and cleaned my now sensitive teeth! I rushed to the bathroom to apply my mascara. I had placed it on top of the fire to thaw it out. Alan was hogging the bathroom mirror but I remembered the caravan has a lovely big mirror above the dog's sleeping area. I nipped in and proceeded to apply mascara to my tired eyes. Just at the moment of application my darling Meg decided this would be a good time to give me some affection. Meg raised her regal little head and nudged playfully on the arm which had the hand that was holding the wand to my eyelashes. The mascara wand struck the centre of my eyeball, at which point tears began to flow thick and fast, leaving black streaks down my face.

Luckily, my hair remained in place; it takes a lot to mess my hair up once I have styled it. I put my best trousers on and my bright pink top and I was ready to face the worst.

I peered out of the window in time to see the sun peeping through the clouds. As I looked towards the steps, I saw Alan bent over a bucket of murky water. I was saddened to see my noble husband brushing the thick layer of mud from his best shoes. I felt angry that he has worked so hard all his life and is bent over a dirty bucket of water trying to smarten himself up. I only had so long to feel sad, as the next thing I noticed was the Prodigal Son making his way up the lane for court.

We were early and awaited the arrival of our solicitor. I looked across the crowded waiting area and noticed a man staring at me. This is not unusual and something that I have learnt to live with! I recognised the smarmy features and pointed out to Alan that it was the accountant. This man was the business accountant that has been alongside Alan's father in his attempt to do Alan over.

Next was Alan's sister, the one that has money running through her veins. This is why she needs so much and can never have enough. She scuttled into the corner and stood alongside the Prodigal Son and the accountant. Next, enter the Enforcement Officer from the council.

Our solicitor made a welcome entrance at around 10.30. I have to say, by this stage I was really feeling intimidated. As much as I tried to concentrate on the magazine I was browsing, I really would have preferred to go shopping.

By now, claimant corner was getting somewhat crowded. Alan noticed a stranger among their posse. I looked across to see a familiar figure. I could only see the stranger from the back but recognised it immediately as The Trog-male. He too had bought a fellow spectator; I suspected it was his brother-in-law. Our solicitor was adamant that they would not be allowed to give evidence. By the time we went in, the spectators had been standing for over two hours.

Prior to being called in the solicitor was advising us all about the case. He was so confident that the judge would transfer it as per his request. At the last minute, I had to sprint down to the car to replace the parking ticket. It is a good job I was on my inhalers. I flew down the stairs and pushed in front of the line of people waiting at the machine (don't worry, I did ask politely). I put my money in, pressed the button and nothing came out. I flew back up to the court house only to find the waiting room empty (another good example of the law of sod).

By this time, despite being on inhalers, I was hyperventilating. The receptionist was ready for me. "Just knock on the door; you may have to stand up."

Stand up! I thought to myself, no chance, someone will be getting off my chair.

I knocked nervously on the door and stumbled in. "Sorry to be late," I said, assertively. I did not want anyone to know that I could not breathe and I did not want to be there. I was very surprised to see a chair waiting for me. At least that shows some respect. I was only disappointed that Alan had been forced to walk into the court room with my new handbag!

I was startled to see the crowd standing at the back of the tiny room. I could not believe how pathetic they all looked. How cruel and sad that they squeezed into this little room in the hopes of seeing me and Alan turfed from the farm.

I sat trying so hard not to let anyone hear my panting for breath which had still not caught up. I sat with my head held high and watched the solicitors do their stuff. It was certainly fascinating to observe and within moments I just knew that Alan and I were going to be at Syda a while longer.

Stan of course failed to make it to court, the judge was informed, due to his just coming out of the hospital following a heart bypass. What his solicitor omitted to inform the judge was that the heart bypass was three years ago!

I held Alan's hand. Well, one finger actually. Every time the judge spoke in our favour, I squeezed Alan's finger. By the time the hearing was over, Alan's finger was blue, I had squeezed it so much. To the dismay of the packed room full of all Stan's supporters, the judge sent the case on to the High Court.

We left the court room feeling rather chuffed! Went into a small room adjacent and chatted about the affair and what would happen over the coming months. After a jubilant farewell to our solicitor, we returned to the car park to find we had been awarded a parking ticket. We made our way home to our little caravan.

After returning home, the Trog-male went up the garden to play on his digger. Odd behaviour we thought, but none of our business. It just so happens that, a couple of hours later, our water was running again. Maybe the Trogs have realised there is actually more to this saga than meets their narrow vision. Or should I say, more to this story than the old man and the Prodigal Son have let on. Who cares, we have our water back and that's fine by me. It only saddens me that there are people cold, callous and mean-spirited enough to turn it off in the first place.

JANUARY 22ND

After being awoken in the early hours by the dogs, I went out first thing to let out the chickens. I found a dead fox that had been shot in the night by the lampers that haunt this area. This explained the rumpus from the dogs at 2.30am this morning. I was sad to see this beautiful creature having been left to die. The fox was young and prior to its death would have looked in good health. I was shocked to see how close the fox was to my chicken house, but the fox had clearly been in the vicinity before and had not touched my chickens. I guess as a chicken keeper I should have been glad the fox was shot. I was not glad. I was deeply sad to see this lovely creature shot down in his prime. Holly was very cross with the dead fox and shouted at it for the rest of the morning.

Early this evening, Alan received a very sad call from our friend, Kath. Her husband Mick had passed away and funeral arrangements were being made. Mick was a mere 63 years old and a wonderful character, so full of life before cancer ravaged him. This was sad news to hear but at least he will be free from the terrible pain he has endured these last months.

I went with Rob for a long walk and actually left the farm. This is a first, as it involved taking Meg and Mimi out amidst the general public. It was Rob's idea, as I had assumed we were just taking Holly on this trek. Rob rightly felt it would be less fun with only half the family. We took lead ropes for the big girls in case we needed to contain them.

I was amazed at how well behaved they were. We walked all the way to a neighbouring farm that has a small café on it. Once reaching the café, it was rather like stepping onto the Marie Celeste. This was bad news as, since falling over a dry stone wall during the early part of our adventure, Rob was now lame. I had managed to keep him going on the promise of a coffee. The café door was open and the key was in the door. I guess we could have made our own coffee but it's not the same. Rob hobbled home to café caravan!

January 23rd

I had a wonderful day with my friend, Faith, and her family. Faith had asked me to take the lead role in a small film she was making for her school work. The filming took place in a local beauty spot and the scenery was amazing. We walked and walked and filmed as we went. I was enjoying the walk so much that I had not realised we were walking down steep hills. It became rather a shock when filming was over and we had to walk back to the start point. The return walk was most challenging as it was all up steep inclines. No wonder I enjoyed the walk into the woods as it was all downhill! Now, as I puffed and panted up the hill, I was grateful once again for my supply of inhalers.

Rob managed to accompany us all on the shoot, despite his injuries from the dry stone wall incident. It was an enjoyable excursion but I have to admit it tired me out. Sadly, I had to take Rob to the train station as it was time for him to exit the world of celluloid and return to real life in Derby.

25TH JANUARY

I fell to sleep last night with moonlight peering in through my window. I woke this morning with the sun shining in my eyes. What bliss! What joy! I feel so blessed and fortunate and thank God every day for the abundance in my life.

I took the dogs up to the top farm to feed the horses. This is always great fun and the highlight of my day. The views from the top farm are exhilarating and take my breath away. I feel sure I can never tire of the views that surround me at this present time.

The dogs have had none of their freedom taken away. This was one of my worst fears when we lost Rufford. I worried the dogs would lose the wonderful free life they have enjoyed. Their life is even richer and freer. We no longer have the fear of the main road that ran past our previous home. That road was my worst nightmare. I was sure I would die on that road at some stage. Living on it and crossing it on a regular basis made me sure the odds of getting killed were very high!

The dogs made their way with me back down to the caravan and then up to the top gate. We had gone to meet Alan who was on his way to feed the cows. I do like to have the gate open for him so that he does not have to clamber in and out of the tractor any more than necessary. I happened to notice that there was a sheep stood by the fence with its head very erect. I don't know a lot about sheep so I just thought she was looking rather strange. The dogs were intrigued as well and dashed over to investigate. The sheep never moved a muscle. I figured she must be simply outstaring the dogs. That's the best I could come up with. Poor Meg got a shock from the electric fence and let out the most piercing scream. She looked for me and came tearing over to the safety of her mummy!

I opened the gate and hurried down the field before Alan arrived. The cows followed me down to the feeders where we waited for Alan. After feeding the cows we headed back up to the lane. I got rather a shock when I saw the same sheep tangled in the electric fence. With each pulse of electric going through the fence, the poor creature jerked in time with it. I ran over, beckoning Alan as I went. I hate electric fencing and I have a big fear of it. However, the sheep had to be freed and that was that.

I kicked at the wire to release her feet and then manoeuvred the wire from around her horns. I shrieked and screamed in anticipation of getting a shock myself. After releasing the sheep, I ended up with the fencing between my legs. I let out a huge scream and jumped hysterically into the air. I was free and so was the sheep.

The sheep just lay exhausted and weary on the floor. I confess I have never touched sheep so it was wonderful to get the opportunity. We helped her to her feet. Somehow, I knew that this sheep was not right. We watched as she walked around in little circles, disorientated and confused. Alan phoned the sheep farmer straight away and informed him of the sick animal.

I sleep each night with my bedroom window open and the silence is awesome. That is of course once the generator is switched off. This sits beneath my window. Yet if I go to bed early before it is switched off, I still fall asleep rapidly. Although the generator is very noisy, the hums somehow send me to sleep.

29ᵗʰ JANUARY

After listening to rain during the night I was sad that Mick, Alan's friend, was to be buried this morning. I always think a funeral is bearable, just, for loved ones left behind if the sun shines down. I worried through the night that the morning would be miserable.

When the morning came the sun was rising well on the horizon. I was happy in the knowledge that Mick's family would be able to cope better with their ordeal. The wind blew and that was very cutting but the day was bright.

Before leaving home, we checked on the sick sheep. She was still looking confused and disorientated. She had been standing in the same area for 36 hours. We made another call to the owner to say where he would find her.

The church was full to the brim which was evidence of the popularity of Mick. That must bring some comfort to his family. I suddenly became aware that I would be lucky to fill a row at my funeral. Well, I hope that is a while off but Alan reassured me that I would possibly fill two rows.

The speakers outside the church leaked the sound of Celine Dion singing from "Titanic". Tears welled up as the crowds gathered and we stood in a long line showing respect. To see the wife and children following behind the coffin was too much. I rummaged in my pocket and pulled out a tissue.

For the moment, life looked so unfair for this family so filled with grief.

At only 63 summers old, this was no age for a man to be taken. A hard working, down to earth man that still had so much to offer the farming fraternity and, of course, his family. We have lost one of the farming community's most colourful characters and he will be missed.

We stood at the back of the church and listened to the tributes made to Mick. The attendance was such that the congregation were packed in tight. Mick's daughter of only nineteen years stood and read a poem that her father had pretended to have written many years ago. She had only recently discovered that he had in fact copied the poem.

I'm a lean dog, a keen dog, a wild dog, and lone;
I'm a rough dog, a tough dog, hunting on my own;
I'm a bad dog, a mad dog, teasing silly sheep;
I love to sit and bay the moon, to keep fat souls from sleep.

I'll never be a lap dog, licking dirty feet,
A sleek dog, a meek dog, cringing for my meat,
Not for me the fireside, the well-filled plate,
But shut the door, and sharp stone, and cuff, and kick, and hate.

Not for me the other dogs, running by my side,
Some have run a short while, but none of them would bide.
O mine is still the lone trail, the hard trail, the best,
Wide wind, and wild stars, and the hunger of the quest!

On returning home we noted the sheep had gone. She had been taken home to be tended and hopefully nursed back to health.

31ST JANUARY

I am glad to say and you can probably see that life on the farm has settled down well. This has come as a bit of a surprise to us. I am really pleased about the situation and it seems to stem from the court house on the 21st January. Yes, Alan and I do have a right to be here and let's hope that hit home.

We sleep in our cosy little bed at night leaving the front door unlocked (we don't advertise this). When we go out we leave the door unlocked. This has been necessary as the weather has been such that if we lock up when we go out, the lock freezes. If we lock up at night, we are then frozen in by morning. But who would have thought we would sleep so soundly or venture out without worry? The dogs make this even more possible. I guess without the dogs we could not contemplate such things. But even with the dogs, I never thought we would be so free and easy and feel so secure.

1ˢᵗ FEBRUARY

Up bright and early to admire the beautiful sunrise. It seems to be different every day but equally as beautiful. Carol is giving me a pamper day today for my birthday (tomorrow). She said she would pick me up really early! She arrived at 12.30 pm. Well, it suited me anyway as I did a few jobs on the farm with Alan and went on a good walk with our dogs.

First stop was the supermarket to decide what we were having for lunch, making us officially "ladies that lunch". Home to Carol's for the rest of the afternoon, where I was subjected to insurmountable torture. Carol tinted my hair, which involved an instrument fit to punish shaped rather like a hat. Carol placed the hat forcefully on my head and started to attack my head with a small but painfully sharp object! She stabbed at the hat through its little holes; through which she then tugged little shreds of my hair. Although she stood over me smiling sympathetically at my pain, I could sense that she was enjoying each prod into my head and each pull of my hair. I somehow felt that she was getting me back for all the times I had forbid her to tit bit the horses, for all the times I grumbled about her letting horses loose from their field; all the times I had said her horse riding skills were not up to standard.

Smiling with great satisfaction, Carol stood back and admired her work. By now, I was a whimpering shadow of my former self. She suggested having a go at my bushy eyebrows. I was almost too weak to refuse. However, I somehow managed to bellow out a resounding, "No!"

Off in the car for my next treat of the day, the local college for an all-over massage. Sitting in the waiting room with several other women, they were each called in one at a time. Each and every woman was called in by a female student for their massage. As I sat alone waiting to be called, a large black man put his head around the door. As he called my name, I was numb with shock. Anyone that knows me will be aware of what a ridiculous prude I am. To be called in by a large man was too ironic to be real. Had Carol done this as some sort of misguided joke? That thought left my mind as quickly as it had entered. Carol would not do this full stop, let alone on my birthday.

With my eyes wide open in shock, I felt like a rabbit caught in the headlights. My head was in turmoil as I tried to think of a way out. How could I make the scene I wanted to in this small college? How could I bring myself to humiliate this poor man just for being a man? Perhaps I should faint or feign illness.

There was only one way out of it! I lay on the bed and closed my eyes and tried to forget he was a man. Once the massage was underway, I relaxed and got into the swing of things. Every day of my life I yearn for a back massage. I was determined to enjoy Carol's treat as I cannot normally afford the time or money for a massage. My back cried desperately for a deep massage and, in the end, nothing was going to get in the way.

I closed my eyes and relaxed as much as I could. Oh, the pains of the deep, penetrating massage. The strength in his hands was amazing. I could not believe how much I began to soak up the feeling as his hands untangled my aching muscles. I gave in to it all and just allowed it to happen. By the time it was over I was putty in his hands. I have of course made a note of his name as I must have him next time!

2ND FEBRUARY

It is my birthday today which started with a call from Robbie. His happy birthday wishes were lovely. I had received a wonderful, new computer from Alan. Lynne called later, as she was free from a migraine.

When Lynne arrived we sat and had a good long chat. The dogs as usual were really pleased to see her. The animals love her and seem fully aware of her passion for animals. Lynne had bought me loads of presents including socks, knickers, bubble bath, a lovely mat with dog prints on it and a polo neck jumper. I always need polo neck jumpers in the winter months.

When we left Rufford House Farm, I had to say goodbye to some of my wonderful horses and ponies. They are still mine but are being cared for by guardians. Henry was taken to Cambridge in May last year. I only allowed him to go so far as I was in such a dilemma with the farm. However Mary, who jumped ship with her horse just before we moved, had somehow got it in her head that I had given Henry to her and her son. I could not possibly give full ownership of a rescue horse to a third party. He would be theirs until they no longer wanted him but this was not good enough for her. She wanted full ownership without any exchange of money I might add! Not that Henry is for sale.

Henry is a very arthritic horse and must never get into the wrong hands. There would be few people I would trust with full ownership of my rescue ponies and horses. They belong to Angel Wings animal sanctuary for a reason.

Henry has already had a very hard life prior to coming into the rescue. He had clearly been worked very hard over the years and had been a hunter or similar. The poor old thing upon reaching old age had 10 years deducted from his birth certificate. This makes a horse more valuable but clearly this is a terrible thing to do. Henry was then sold as a fit 9 year old hunter; he was fed pain killers to make him appear youthful and sound.

The young lady who bought him had him around a week before his severe lameness showed; once the drugs had worn off he became unmanageable. When the young lady called the dealer she was told she could have her money back but the horse would be shot. This is a terrible thing to say to a kind person who cares for horses. But this is common practice with disreputable dealers. So instead she called me and asked me to come and rescue him, which I did on Christmas Eve, four years ago. I cannot then turn round and give him away with the possibility of him ending up in the wrong hands again. It's a risk I cannot and will not take.

Mary decided to threaten me with his return if I did not hand over his passport, hence full ownership. I think she was sure I could not take him from her due to my circumstances. How little she knows me. I don't give in to blackmail. I called my reliable friend Linda and she arrived with her trailer within two hours. Henry stepped eagerly into the trailer as if he understood it was time to go back home. Mary looked on; her only concern was that we did not take his rug that she owned! I looked into the trailer and whispered to Henry, "Let's go home."

It was as if he had never been away. His friends greeted him over the wall. His special girlfriend, Bella, nuzzled him gently as she welcomed him home. This was my best birthday present and a day I shall never forget. It's a good job I am not as daft as I look!

5TH FEBRUARY

A great weekend as Rob came home to celebrate my birthday. Kate, Jodie and Tom called up and brought me some nice presents. We had a cup of tea and a slice of my home made Bakewell tart.

Rob took me out shopping so that I could pick my presents with him. We did this last year so I am hoping it will become a tradition. It is great fun to have a good look round and pick what I want. We went to Bakewell and had a good look round. I picked two sets of rosary beads and a lovely warm hat for on the farm. Not content with this, Rob took me into Chesterfield and let me run rampant around those shops too!

I ended up having a beautiful throw for the settee in the caravan and a really nice chopping board with a mare and foal on it. A pile of magazines and a computer programme followed, before he stopped spending his hard earned cash.

The evening looked set to be exciting too. We rooted round for a pizza voucher and managed to find a half price one. We picked up the food and watched a Hammer Horror Film on the TV. The pizza was delicious and I ate loads. Unfortunately the generator kept going off every half an hour. Alan was really good and just kept going out to switch it on. We managed to watch the whole of the film and then the generator went off one more time and we all turned in for bed. Watching a Hammer Horror, late a night, in a caravan hidden amidst 100 acres, is thrilling fun, by the way . . . .

FEBRUARY 8TH

Contrary to Bob Geldof, I do like Mondays, normally! However, today was the biggest test of our strength and as a couple!

The day got off to a promising start and we fed around the animals, as usual. The cats we have liberated on the farm are doing really well and generally hang by the caravan all day. Poppet is getting so very fat and she looks really cute and squidgy. My main fears when I first released them was that they would be poisoned or disappear mysteriously. That has not happened and I feel a lot more relaxed about our free cats. Pussy Woo spends hours up and down the lane hunting. My only sadness is that she hunts little field mice and shrews. I wish she was not such a good hunter.

Late morning, Alan went to town to get the generator back from the repair man. Apparently he had let the generator run for 20 minutes after he cleaned the filter. He assured us it would work fine now.

The afternoon was busy as we had to head to Sheffield hospital for Alan to see the physiotherapist regarding his drop foot. Yes, I know it sounds more like a problem the cows would have.

I always enjoy such outings as the hospital usually has a little charity shop and a coffee shop open. All these little things keep me happy. The appointment went well and Alan was fitted with a strange contraption that did actually help him walk a little better. We returned home and as usual I was too tired to live really. I was desperate for a nap in my caravan. We put the chickens away.

Mondays as you may know is my night of telly bliss. I decided, due to my extreme fatigue, I would have a little rest and wake just in time for my soaps. Alan suggested that if the generator let us down we would go and watch TV somewhere else. I pointed out to him that I had no running water and had to go out to friends for showers and it was unfair that I should now not have my TV! Besides, I had Aunt Bessie oven chips and caramelised apple crumble for tea. Nothing could get in the way of the evening I had planned. Nothing!

Alan plugged in the vacuum cleaner as soon as he put the generator on. It was over a week since I had vacuumed and the carpets were covered in dog and cat hairs. I began to clean out all the litter trays. Within minutes, the generator failed yet again. We were plummeted into darkness in the middle of the much needed housework. Patiently, Alan took a head light, strapped it around his forehead and went outside to start it up again. By now it was 6.10pm and we had little time left. Alan repeated his idea that I should go to my friend's house to watch the soaps. From this moment on I am not sure what really happened but for some reason I reverted back to being five years old!

I stomped and stropped and sulked and wailed. I wanted to rest and I wanted to settle at home. I go out for a shower and get warm in friends' houses and then I have to go out in the cold and come home. I wanted to stay at home in the warm and watch my soaps. I was so frustrated I just wanted to cry.

We remembered that Alan, a good friend, had offered us a generator some time ago. Off we went again out into the cold, freezing night. Alan and Jane were as kind as ever and we had a cup of tea and a natter. Their tortoise had come out of hibernation early and was roaming the kitchen. It has been years since I held a tortoise. I used to have one called Fred. You could buy them from the pet shop in the old days, when I was a kid in the 70s. I used to spend all my pocket money at the pet shop buying animals. Oh, thank goodness they have regulations now. You could just walk into the pet shop, pay your money and walk out with your pet. I bought my tortoise and took him home. I loved Fred and I used to paint him in oil to make him shine.

I held their lovely tortoise; you can't buy them in pet shops now! Even if you could you would have to pay around £300. I probably paid about 50 pennies. I cuddled the tortoise and remembered my own childhood. The spell was broken when he emptied his bowels on me. Jane and Alan had warned me he had not been to the toilet since waking up from hibernation! I got the lot. Thanks to a thorough wipe down with a cloth, I felt my coat was cleaner than before the tortoise pooped on me. We drank our tea and headed home with our substitute generator.

By the time we were home, I had one out of three soaps left to watch. Oh well, I still have my Aunt Bessie oven chips and caramelised apple crumble. Rushing in to put the kettle on, the caravan felt a little cold. The gas bottle was empty. I called to Alan and he swapped the bottle straight away. I sat in front of the fire to watch the last "Coronation Street" of the night. The flame was hardly visible as I huddled as close as I could. The new gas bottle was not working.

I attempted to put the oven on and a tiny flame showed itself at the back. I thought longingly of Aunt Bessie's oven chips and the caramelised crumble. Nobody said life in a caravan would be easy so I guess I just have to get on with it. Alan looked at me with his silly expression and asked if I would like a cheese sandwich. I sat shivering by a vanquished fire, ate my cheese sandwich and went to my cold bed to get some well earned sleep.

Bailey, a special cat indeed

This is little scoop relaxing in the grass

My beautiful pony Summer

Little Velvet always reminds me when I am late feeding her

FEBRUARY 10TH

We were up in reasonable time and ready to face yet another, no doubt, difficult day today. Alan delivered our two generators to a little house in Chesterfield where they will hopefully be repaired. I was dropped at the launderette where I met with Carol, who helped me with a heavy load.

Alan popped in on his way home just to see we were okay and see if we needed anything. We had a hot chocolate and a bar of chocolate, which was all we needed.

We had a big debate at the end as to whether to take home mini-fish and chips. I am so glad the debate ended with "yes" because, unbeknown to me and Carol, there would be cause for a celebration!

Upon arriving home with a boot full of clean, warm, sweet smelling laundry, Alan came to the door. It was clear he had something exciting to say. His face was a picture of contained joy but he insisted we were inside before he told us the news. He asked me if I had spoken to Robbie so I was sure by the look on his face that Rob must have had another one of his articles published. I got inside the caravan as quick as I could. The news he told me I could have shouted from the roof top (well the caravan top).

Chatsworth House Estates have seen sense and dropped the ridiculous case against us! Yes, I know, it's the best news ever! And so now we just have one fight and one court case ahead of us. We knew they could not pursue the case. I doubt any judge in the land would have said we had to pay them any money now if they could not accept our rent two years ago! We are just so lucky that Rob kindly acted for us against them. Had he not, we would have had, at least, a further £2000 solicitor's bill.

We were jubilant all afternoon and felt a massive weight had lifted from our weary shoulders. Luckily, Alan had bought a £2.00 box of misshaped biscuits, to add to the celebration.

Thank you for allowing me to share this story with you so far. I started keeping my daily diary when I first learned we were to lose our home and Volume 1 takes my account to February 2010.

Look out for **Animosity Farm Volume 2**:

Our celebrations are short lived as the intensity of the High Court case consumes us but we also start to face acts of harassment to remove us from the land unlawfully. With a detached MP and the police and local council failing to act on our behalf, but the spirit of optimism and the love of animals forever reigning supreme, Volume 2 shows how fresh animosity emerged from unexpected sources, leaving us vulnerable and exposed on our farm, without heating and electric.

17120128R00240

Printed in Great Britain
by Amazon